KING ALFRED'S COLLEGE
WINCHESTER

To be returned on or before the day marked
below :—

PLEASE ENTER ON ISSUE SLIP:

AUTHOR WARD

TITLE Land and industry

ACCESSION No. 42806

Land and Industry

LAND AND INDUSTRY

The Landed Estate and the Industrial
Revolution

a symposium edited by

J. T. WARD and R. G. WILSON

DAVID & CHARLES : NEWTON ABBOT

ISBN 0 7153 5303 9

COPYRIGHT NOTICE

Set in eleven on twelve point Imprint
and printed in Great Britain
by Latimer Trend & Company Limited Plymouth
for David & Charles (Publishers) Limited
South Devon House   Newton Abbot   Devon

Contents

Introduction

The purpose of this book is to examine the reaction of some British and Irish landowners, great and small, to the challenges and opportunities presented by the Industrial Revolution. The six contributors deal with a range of topics in different ways, writing on either particular themes or geographic areas. This variety of approaches and styles, 'case studies' and broader analyses, may more fairly indicate the extent of the fields of historical study opened up by the increasing availability of family and estate papers than would a series of uniform papers.

Knowledge of landowners' attitudes and interests has long been coloured by fictional accounts. Fielding's Mr Western is the archetype hard-hunting, rural-accented, port-sodden bucolic eighteenth-century squire; the refined gentry of Jane Austen add an early nineteenth-century snobbish tone; the strict codes of Trollope's mid-century Barsetshire illustrate the hierarchic deference of rural society; the decaying manors of Hardy's late-century Wessex represent the supposed death-knell of the squirearchy, amid the 'fall and decay of the leaf' of pastoral England.[1] A composite picture of a dissipated, 'closed', idle and grasping class often emerged from the novels, to counter the sycophantic picture painted by family hagiographers.

It is obviously dangerous to rely on the novelist for an accurate picture of an age. The clear dichotomy between land and industry often predicated by 'social' novelists, aristocratic biographers and radical opponents of the landed interest alike did not exist. But while opponents fired weapons of many calibres against entrenched 'feudalism', subservient 'retainers' invested the inheritors of ancient wealth with a venerable aura far removed from commercial and industrial life. The net result was the perpetuation of an almost pantomimic portrait.

To the Anti-Corn Law League, the most notable of the opponents, landowners were not only wicked and greedy but also stupid and reactionary. The league itself was, as John Bright frankly declared at the Covent Garden rally in December 1845, 'a movement of the commercial and industrious classes against the lords and great proprietors of the soil'.[2] The league's heirs were disappointed at the continuing social dominance of the landowners in the years after repeal of the Corn Laws. In 1857 Richard Cobden found it 'astonishing that the people at large were so tacit in their submission to the perpetuation of the feudal system in this country, as it affected the property in land, so long after it had been shattered to pieces in every other country except Russia'.[3] There were, however, some curious features in league propaganda. The support of 'the wealthiest individual of the monied interest . . . the wealthiest of the manufacturers and . . . the wealthiest of the nobility'[4] was a source of pride. But the respective individuals scarcely followed Cobdenite theory: Samuel Jones Loyd (Lord Overstone), a London and Manchester banker, was in the process of building up an estate of over 30,000 acres in eleven counties; John Marshall's Leeds flax fortune was being expended on Yorkshire and Lakeland estates; and the Marquess of Westminster was buttressing Eaton with Welsh mineral royalties and Belgravia ground rents. Nevertheless, radical attacks on the 'land monopoly', primogenture, settlement and other aspects of 'landlordism' were long continued, and local speakers often outbid national leaders in their vehemence.[5]

Much of this hostility arose simply from political partisanship. The simple contours of a 'land versus industry' struggle were easily delineated up to and beyond the repeal of the Corn Law in 1846. But basic analysis of the parliamentary votes on repeal casts doubts on facile interpretations.[6] When talk of 'feudalism', 'the politics of deference' and other vague value-judgements are put aside, the implicit core of nineteenth-century hostility to the landowners becomes clear. While brave entrepreneurs took enormous risks to create the world's workshop, effete peers languidly drew and hedonistically spent their unearned rents, brutally defended their obsolete rights and haughtily disdained the lesser breeds in trade and industry. Thus ran league legend, vociferously and financially supported by the 'liberal' creators of the new industries.

Late nineteenth-century changes in the economic desirability and social status of landownership, along with the increasing numbers of ennobled industrialists,[7] blurred the edges of many old controversies. Futile governmental inquiries did nothing to stop the agricultural depression and subsequent 'social' legislation weakened landowning power. The new radical attack of the early twentieth century was made on all forms of ownership; and gradually, though far from unanimously, owners of all types tended to coalesce in defence of property itself.

'Trade has been going ahead, but agriculture, yoked to her by legal harness, has held her back,' wrote Alexander Somerville in typical radical fashion in 1842. 'Landlords', he insisted, 'to maintain a political control over their tenants, sacrificed a large pecuniary interest.'[8] There was undoubtedly evidence to support some such accusations. Landowners did not generally share the liberal enthusiasms of Manchester, and many of them did not accept (or, at least, did not act upon) Somerville's assertion that 'an increase of wealth, a desire to possess, a desire to be something more than we are, to have something more than we have, is the very soul of all human energies'. Socially secure and usually reasonably affluent, the generality of landowners did not share the primary motivation of men making their way in the world to maximise profits.

In 1864, explaining why many proprietors preferred short agreements to long leases, the prominent Yorkshire squire H. S. Thompson wrote of 'personal ties, which . . . would be most inadequately replaced by a few shillings an acre additional rent'. He admitted that another cause of this attitude was[9]

> The repugnance of the proprietors to give up so much of the control over their estates as implied by a lease for any long term of years. They let their land below its market value, for the sake of retaining the power of resuming possession at short notice . . . the knowledge that such a power exists makes it rarely necessary to use it.

In theory, many owners thus sacrificed cash for the sake of personal power, social status and (before the coming of the ballot in 1872) political control. In practice, however, they often made very satisfactory arrangements: personal relationships and customary 'understandings' could provide as much tenant security and landlord income as any legal contract applied with Mancunian economic techniques.

The result of Victorian polemical literature has been a wide acceptance—sometimes almost subconscious—of league propaganda. Oafish, indolent aristocrats dominating Parliament for their own ends, squeezing rents from undercapitalised estates, harshly preserving their game, alternately opposing or overcharging railway promoters and in general still holding the countryside in feudal subjection form part of a picture still often painted. True virtue may be found (according to taste) in the labourers' struggles, from Loveless to Arch, or in the entrepreneurial skills of the industrialists.

The merchant marking business success by acquiring land has been a commonplace of British history since the social rise of the late medieval de la Poles, and especially since the controversial establishment of the Tudor and Stuart gentry.[10] But this social mobility was always a two-way traffic. Perusers of Victorian social registers (useful as such tomes are for many purposes) often fail to notice that a family's 'promotion' to gentility did not preclude a continuing connection with mercantile affairs, sometimes through the inheritor and more often through the activities of younger sons. Modern research shows that in many cases not only were merchant-landowners quickly accepted by county society (as is evinced by promotions to the bench and deputy-lieutenancy) but that close associations were long maintained between mercantile oligarchies and rural proprietors.[11]

Landowners' involvement in non-agricultural economic change went much further than maintaining close ties with their cousins of the established borough corporations. For some families, no doubt, the increased incomes created by industrialisation—from urban rents, mineral royalties and the like—were merely unearned accretions to estate revenues, caused by fortunate accidents of ownership and involving no risk. But many others acted sensible and often vital entrepreneurial roles. They were promoters of turnpikes,[12] river navigations,[13] canals, [14] ports and harbours,[15] banks (especially in Scotland),[16] markets[17] and urban growth. They were occasionally ruined by such involvements; for instance, a large proportion of the land in coal- and iron-rich

Ayrshire had to be sold by its old lairds after the failure of Messrs
Douglas & Heron's Ayr Bank in 1772.[18] But many concerned
themselves with mining ventures of all sorts and with Victorian
railway development. Some historians have considered that their
influence on the first group of industries was harmful and have
denied or minimised their interest and involvement in the second.
But in both cases many landowners were as important to industrial development as were purely industrial entrepreneurs.

It is impossible to categorise the types of landowners who
might support or ignore industrial opportunities. There appears
to be no obvious division between ancient dynasties and *arriviste*
squires, between Whigs and Tories or even between Protec-
tionists and Free Traders, as far as reactions to industry were
concerned. Jacobite Scottish lairds, often seen as merely 'romantic' figures, included such pioneer colliery developers as the Earl
of Mar in Fife. In the nineteenth century even such a 'Gothic'
romantic as the thirteenth Earl of Eglinton, the organiser of the
much parodied medieval 'Tournament' of 1839, maintained his
family's interest in Ayrshire mining and the harbours of Ardrossan; James Baird, the tough mining- and iron-master, had 'never
met a man with more thorough business habits, or a more lordly
manner'.[19] Business habits and lordly manners could indeed
combine in many ways undreamed of by Victorian liberals.

Some recent syntheses of studies about landownership have
suggested, though their findings are tentative, that the landowners' role in industrial development was probably of equal
significance to the part they played in the course of agricultural
change between 1700 and 1870.[20] Others would maintain that
landowners' investment in industry has been exaggerated. The
prime obstacle to precision is really one of weighting the owners'
interests. It is their complex role in society which makes an analysis of the apportionment of their resources difficult. Their economic behaviour is often only explicable in terms of the concept
of their social and political leadership. Certainly, some landowners were more concerned with the management of elections
and the intake of spa water than they were with the development
of roads and mines. Even in agriculture, the landowners' primary
sphere of economic interest, the pattern of progress is not entirely
established: the individual owner's interest in 'improvement'

varied enormously. 'Improvement' in itself was an unusual fashion, in that it was a whim subscribed to only by the diligent; the more raffish and dilettante elements in landed society allowed it largely to pass them by. For many landowners it would be dangerous to assume that any large proportion of increased agricultural incomes found their way directly into industry; in the late eighteenth century an increased rental was often swallowed up by the constant extension of the mansion, grounds and establishment which changes in contemporary taste demanded.

An analysis of landowners' attitudes to change is as important as assessing their economic effort or as reckoning the effects of their high consumer expenditure in portraits, chairs and bricks. Britain's landowners were the wealthiest in Europe and the least exclusive. But the pattern of landownership has too often been traced from the muniment rooms of Woburn, Holkham, Wentworth Woodhouse, Alnwick and their like. The great estates, however, were not typical of the pattern. The average squire kept no house in London; at best he spent a few weeks in crowded lodgings in the capital or Bath. Most of his time was taken up with life in the country, especially in all the affairs which touched upon his estate. An excellent view of the life of such a small squire is found in Nicholas Blundell's diary.[21] Admittedly Blundell was a Roman Catholic and his relationship with his Catholic tenantry was particularly close; but he moved on as easy terms with lawyers, merchants and apothecaries in Liverpool as with his Catholic gentry relatives. And he was as well informed of the problems of commerce (his brother was apprenticed to a Liverpool merchant) and domestic industry in Lancashire as he was of marling and planting. Walter Spencer-Stanhope, an MP and owner of 11,000 Yorkshire acres and a fine Grosvenor Square residence, took a keen interest in West Riding industry, which was not surprising as his father was a woollen merchant and his two uncles, from whom he inherited his estates, were lawyers and ironmasters.[22] Blundell's and Spencer-Stanhope's breadth of interest was common among the gentry. Surviving diaries and letters show that the landowner's partiality for viewing mills, mines and furnaces was as pronounced as his taste for a classical prospect or a Salvator Rosa. Sir Harbottle Grimston was most impressed with the bustle of Manchester, and the Duke of

Bridgewater's canal was the greatest tribute to its 'noble contriver' and might be reckoned one of the wonders of the world.[23]

Many landowners were never themselves directly concerned with the development of industry, even in the industrial areas, but through their investment in agriculture, their association in business, their local government administration and sometimes by marriage, they condoned the changes. It was this fusion of interest, the fact that landowners encouraged what happened in industry, that created the ideal environment for economic change. The social attitudes and economic responses of the landowners were obviously closely linked; together they played a decisive role in the pattern and timing of British industrialisation. An exhaustive analysis of the nature and extent of this role, however, both in itself and in relation to the input of the other groups concerned, awaits a more systematic plundering of the archives which have survived: estate papers, wills and inventories, land-tax reforms and the records of the county registries of deeds may reveal much further information.

The present volume explores only some of the many avenues now being opened. Its introductory chapter delineates the scope of the investigation, and other papers deal with the Ulster landowners' connection with the linen industry, the fortunes of two Yorkshire mercantile families engaged in embedding themselves in the county squirearchy, the long and varied relationships between landowners and mining industries, the particular experiences of Staffordshire estates in the industrial Midlands and the growth of a landowning merchant élite in and around Glasgow.

It is hoped that these essays may at least demonstrate the possibilities of and need for change in some historical attitudes and that they may be the precursor of further re-examinations.

J.T.W.
R.G.W.

NOTES

(Abbreviations of manuscript sources occurring in the notes at the end of each chapter are explained in the Appendix I)

1   Henry Fielding, *Tom Jones* (1749); Jane Austen, *Emma* (1816);

Anthony Trollope, *Framley Parsonage* (1861); Thomas Hardy, *The Woodlanders* (1887).

2 G. M. Trevelyan, *The Life of John Bright* (1913), 141. See Norman McCord, *The Anti-Corn Law League, 1838–1846* (1958), 59 and passim.

3 Lord Morley, *The Life of Richard Cobden* (1910 edn), 679.

4 Archibald Prentice, *History of the Anti-Corn Law League* (1853), 2, 145.

5 See *The League*, passim and O. R. McGregor's introduction to Lord Ernle, *English Farming, Past and Present* (1961 edn), passim.

6 See J. A. Thomas, 'The Repeal of the Corn Laws', *Economica*, 9 (1929); D. G. Southgate, *The Passing of the Whigs* (1962).

7 R. E. Pumphrey, 'The Introduction of Industrialists into the British Peerage', *American Historical Review*, 65 (1959).

8 Alexander Somerville, *The Whistler at the Plough* (Manchester 1852), 211, 300.

9 H. S. Thompson, 'Agricultural Progress and the Royal Agricultural Society', *Journal of the Royal Agricultural Society of England*, 25 (1864).

10 See, for instance, H. R. Trevor Roper, *The Gentry, 1540–1640*, *Econ Hist Rev*, supplement 1, nd; Lawrence Stone, *The Crisis of the Aristocracy, 1558–1641* (Oxford 1965).

11 See R. G. Wilson, 'Three Brothers: A study of the fortunes of a landed family in the mid-eighteenth century', *Bradford Textile Society Journal*, 1964–5, and 'The Fortunes of a Leeds Merchant House, 1780–1820', *Business History*, 9 (1967).

12 See, for instance, K. A. MacMahon, *Roads and Turnpike Trusts in Eastern Yorkshire* (York 1964).

13 See, for instance, B. F. Duckham, *The Yorkshire Ouse* (Newton Abbot 1967); R. W. Unwin, 'The Aire and Calder Navigation, Part I', *Bradford Antiquary*, ns 62 (1964); W. T. Jackman, *The Development of Transportation in England* (Cambridge 1916), vol 1.

14 See Frank Mullineaux, *The Duke of Bridgewater's Canal* (Eccles 1959); *An Alphabetical List of the Proprietors of the Leeds and Liverpool Canal* (Bradford 1789, 1811, 1846; Liverpool 1857).

15 D. Swann, 'The Pace and Progress of Port Investment in England, 1660–1830', *Yorkshire Bulletin of Economic and Social Research*, 12 (1960).

16 L. S. Pressnell, *Country Banking in the Industrial Revolution* (Oxford 1956); C. A. Malcolm, *The History of the British Linen Bank* (Edinburgh 1950); Neil Munro, *The History of the Royal Bank of Scotland* (Edinburgh 1928).

17 G. Scott Thompson, *The Russells in Bloomsbury, 1669–1771* (1940); Janet Blackman, 'The Food Supply of an Industrial Town: a Study of Sheffield's Public Markets, 1780–1900', *Business History*, 5 (1963).

18 Henry Hamilton, 'The Failure of the Ayr Bank', *Econ Hist Rev*,
    2S, 8 (1956); J. T. Ward, 'Ayrshire Landed Estates in the Nine-
    teenth Century', *Ayrshire Collections*, ns 8 (1969).
19 A. McGeorge, *The Bairds of Gartsherrie* (Glasgow 1875), 79.
20 See G. E. Mingay, *English Landed Society in the Eighteenth
    Century* (1963), 189; M. W. Flinn, *The Origins of the Industrial
    Revolution* (1966), 44–5.
21 M. Blundell (ed), *Blundell's Diary and Letter Book, 1702–1728*
    (Liverpool 1952).
22 Spencer-Stanhope MSS (Cartwright Hall, Bradford).
23 Historical Manuscripts Commission: Verulam, 232. F. C.
    Mather, *After the Canal Duke* (Oxford 1970), an important study
    of the administration of the Bridgewater industrial properties in
    1825–72, appeared after this book was written.

I

English Landowners and Nineteenth-Century Industrialism

DAVID SPRING

According to the new theory of developmental economics, a relative shrinkage of the agricultural sector is the inevitable consequence of economic growth. Nowhere in the world has this process gone further than in England. Yet the English landed aristocracy,* although rulers and chief beneficiaries of an agricultural society, played an important part in promoting economic growth. They were partners or associates in an enterprise that boded ill for them in the long run. This role of English landowners in nineteenth-century industrialisation and urbanisation will be the subject of this introductory essay. The treatment will be a general one. The essays which follow it will deal with particular aspects of this general account.

At first glance, it would not seem that coal and iron, towns and harbours, railways and canals have much to do with agrarian landlords. But obviously they have much to do with land and its ownership. And English aristocratic landowners, as we shall see, were singularly situated so far as the ownership and use of English land were concerned.

In the first place, although relatively small in number, they owned much of the land of England. The New Domesday Book, compiled in the 1870s, provided information from which it was estimated that 'a landed aristocracy consisting of about 2,250 persons own together nearly half the enclosed land in England

---

* I use the term 'aristocracy' throughout this paper to refer to the larger landowners, untitled as well as titled, gentry as well as peers.

and Wales'.[1] Earlier in the century the same estimate would probably have been fairly accurate. The amount of land held by the aristocracy inevitably made certain that whatever the economic enterprise launched on English land—however remote it may have been from the cultivation of wheat and barley—it touched on the affairs of the landed aristocracy.

In the second place, English landowners benefited from the law concerning the rights of ownership in mineral property. This law was not entirely clear until the late seventeenth century. The case of *Regina v Northumberland* (1568), which is sometimes taken as a watershed in the history of English mining law, still left the matter unsettled: the traditional right of the Crown to precious metals was reaffirmed, but the majority of the judges declared that if metallic ores held the slightest trace of gold or silver they too belonged to the Crown. On the basis of this decision both Elizabeth and James pressed their claims to copper; Charles I extended the Crown's rights to lead. A parliamentary statute of 1688–9 put an end to these royal raids by laying down once and for all that only mines of gold and silver belonged to the Crown, all other minerals belonging to the owner of the surface.[2] This gave English landowners a highly enviable position, perhaps unique among the aristocrats of Western Europe.[3] Being large owners of the surface, English landowners became large owners of the sub-surface minerals in an island richly endowed with mineral resources.

In the third place, English landowners were fortunate in being so disposed as to make the most of their advantages. They had always shown a proper respect for wealth. And it had not mattered much what form the wealth had taken. Admittedly it had mattered how conspicuously landowners engaged in certain enterprises. For example, as the historian of English aristocracy in the sixteenth and seventeenth centuries informs us, 'there was criticism when in the early 1560s James Lord Mountjoy set up house on the site of his alum-mine and works at Canford in Dorset and spent his time doing the daily chores of a factory manager'.[4] But to have employed a manager would have made the alum works, or the mines, or the iron foundry or the town development—all enterprises in which some of Lord Mountjoy's fellow aristocrats engaged—quite respectable. Moreover, the extent to which non-

B

agricultural enterprise was taken up by the aristocracy in the sixteenth and seventeenth centuries was considerable. For example, they gave the lead in developing the technology of the iron industry, and they left their mark on town planning in London.[5] In the eighteenth century much the same sort of story could be told: in the coalmining industry, for example, established aristocratic families provided a large part of the capital and the enterprise.[6] In short, if the nineteenth century saw a marked participation of the landed aristocracy in non-agricultural enterprise, this was by no means a new story.

The coming of the railways provides an appropriate starting point for an account of the aristocracy's role in nineteenth-century industrialism. For one thing the railway was the Industrial Revolution incarnate, generating bursts of activity in other departments of economic life, notably in the mining of coal and iron and in the growth of the city, in both of which the landed aristocracy was much concerned. For another thing, it is in connection with the railways that the notion is sometimes entertained of the aristocracy's hostility to the Industrial Revolution. To look into this at the very start of this essay would be fitting.

We might begin with two of what contemporaries called 'extended' lines, that is, trunk lines connecting populous centres: the Liverpool and Manchester, and the London and Birmingham. The Liverpool and Manchester was originally sponsored in the 1820s by Lancashire townsmen.[7] In accordance with parliamentary standing orders, prior to submitting their scheme for parliamentary approval as a private bill, railway projectors were obliged to make their plans known in detail to the public, particularly to those landowners over whose property the projected railway would run, and clearly to indicate in respective lists those who gave them support and those who did not. An impressive list of dissents would seriously prejudice the success of a bill. In the case of the Liverpool and Manchester the dissents had it on the first submission of the bill early in 1825.

The opposition to the first bill for the Liverpool and Manchester was undoubtedly in part a landowners' opposition.[8] Some small owners—the Rev John Clowe, a Mrs Atherton, and a Miss

Byrom—objected that the railway would depreciate land potentially valuable as building land. Mr Orrell and Sir William Ger-
rard complained that their coal workings would be interfered
with. And Lords Derby and Sefton, the largest owners concerned,
objected to the diminution of their privacy. Creevey, an intimate
of Sefton's, may have echoed them when he complained of 'the
loco-motive Monster, carrying eighty tons of goods, and navi-
gated by a tail of smoke and sulphur, coming thro' every man's
grounds between Manchester and Liverpool'.[9] On the other hand,
John Gladstone, one of the principal backers of the railway,
thought it no great hardship for Derby and Sefton to have the
railway crossing their land at a distance of $1\frac{1}{2}$ to 2 miles from
their mansions.[10]

Although Derby's influence was large, the opposition to the
Liverpool and Manchester probably found its greatest strength
in the canal interest—the Mersey and Irwell navigation, the
Leeds and Liverpool canal, and last but very far from least the
Bridgewater trustees.[11] The last, given their central importance
in the story of the Liverpool and Manchester, require a brief
explanation. By the will of the third Duke of Bridgewater, who
died in 1803, his canal and collieries were settled upon his
nephew, Lord Gower, later Marquess of Stafford and still later
first Duke of Sutherland; but unusual administrative authority
over the estate was placed in the hands of a superintendent of the
trust, R. H. Bradshaw.

Both parties, of course, feared for the future of the Bridgewater canal, that ducal highway which helped launch the Industrial Revolution in south-east Lancashire. It served many
purposes: bringing the Duke's coal from his Worsley mines to
Manchester; providing transportation between Liverpool and
Manchester for the use of which the Duke's agents either charged
a toll or themselves supplied carriers in the form of a fleet of
barges and boats; and stretching out to link with canal systems in
the Midlands and in Yorkshire. In 1824, the year which saw the
Liverpool and Manchester issue its first prospectus, the canal
earned its greatest annual profit in the first quarter of the nineteenth century, roughly £80,000. Although this was a most unusual year, the average annual profits since 1815 (excluding 1824)
had been about £43,000. Moreover the canal had been cleared of

the large debt which originally financed it: standing at £346,805
in 1786, it was gone by 1806.[12]

When the Liverpool and Manchester railway bill first came
before Parliament, the Bridgewater trustees petitioned against it.
Bradshaw, intransigent and reactionary, fired the opposition: on
meeting the railway surveyors engaged in a new survey on Chat
Moss, he boasted of his power to have the bill thrown out a
second and even a third time.[13] The sponsors of the Liverpool
and Manchester accordingly turned to Lord Stafford in the hope
of exerting some leverage on the Bridgewater trustees. Here their
efforts were remarkably successful within a very short time. Lord
Stafford took up a thousand shares in the railway valued at
£100,000, about one-fifth of the total subscription, thus becoming by far the largest single shareholder. Dependent on Lord
Stafford's goodwill, Bradshaw quickly capitulated, and the Liverpool and Manchester bill passed into law early in 1826.[14]

This abrupt reversal was the work of Lord Stafford's advisers
and friends, chiefly James Loch and William Huskisson. Loch, a
product of those Edinburgh circles in which rationalism, ad-
vanced economics and Whiggery flourished, balanced his loyalty
to his employer against his instinctive sympathy for the economic
innovations of Liverpool businessmen. As he was more confident
than many that the Bridgewater canal could compete with the
railway this was not too difficult a feat.[15] It was Huskisson, however, who probably decided the matter:[16] long a close friend of
Lord Stafford, MP for Liverpool, like Loch sympathetic to the
gospel of economic improvement, he counselled compromise
with the railway. Lord Stafford acquiesced: partly on the ground
that it was prudent to defer to a public opinion which had raised
the cry of aristocratic monopoly; and partly on the ground of
being guaranteed power of appointment of three directors on the
new railway's board, thereby ensuring that policies affecting the
canal remained within reach of his influence.[17] Thereafter the
Duke of Sutherland or a member of his family often sat on the
directorates of leading English railways.

As an indication of landowners' attitudes, however, the London
and Birmingham provides a more instructive example than the
Liverpool and Manchester. The former was also originally sponsored by townsmen, but without such large landowner invest-

ment as Lord Stafford's coming to their aid.[18] It was a much longer line, 112 miles, much of which crossed land more strictly agricultural than was to be found between Liverpool and Manchester. Landowners' reactions were therefore less complicated by non-agricultural interests of one sort or another.

The initial announcement of the London and Birmingham's intentions in 1830 met with a formidable opposition in the countryside. Some landowners, like Lords Clarendon and Essex, objected to the railway traversing their parks and grounds.[19] Some, like Lord John Scott, argued that the railway would destroy the coaching inns of their tenants; or, like the Marquess of Hastings, argued that it would injure their tenants' farming;[20] or, like Mr Grant, feared it would compete with canals in which they held shares.[21] Some, like Sir Charles Knightley and Sir William Wake and the Duke of Grafton in Northamptonshire, who formed a hostile committee, denounced the railway as a speculation by outsiders mischievously intent on the violation of private rights.[22] Some, like the Marquess of Camden, took to opposition, being unable to decide whether the railway was of benefit or injury to the public.[23] And some, like Lord Craven, opposed the railway simply out of loyalty to a neighbour who had strong objections: in this instance, out of loyalty to Lord John Scott. Craven confessed to his private belief that the railway would benefit the national interest; he had recently travelled on the Liverpool and Manchester 'with which he was much delighted'.[24]

The London and Birmingham's directors at once took steps to cope with this opposition. The original survey of the line, admitted by the Secretary of the London Board as having made free with gentlemen's parks, was rendered less offensive: the line was altered, tunnels were projected. Company officials attended meetings of hostile landowners held along the line, and spoke where they could to remove prejudices. Above all, they sought to gain the ear of 'the influential landlords in each locality'; thus, for example, Captain Moorsom of the Birmingham Board visited Lord Craven, accompanied by Mr Carter of Coventry, a local businessman.[25] There was delay in Parliament owing to the distractions of the first Reform bill; but in June 1832 the London and Birmingham bill was read for the third time in the Commons. On going to the Lords in July, however, the House Committee found a preponderance of dissenting landowners and the bill was rejected.

Nothing daunted, the directors shortly afterwards held a public meeting at the Thatched House Tavern to allow the peers and commoners interested in the success of the London and Birmingham 'to put their sentiments on record'.[26] Lord Wharncliffe was in the chair, having also just chaired the House of Lords Committee on the bill. His speech on this occasion added to his reputation as a mediator. He confessed that at the start he had listened indifferently to the railway's purported virtues, but with the unfolding of the evidence he had changed his mind. He was now sure that the railway was no mere speculation but of 'vital importance' to the trader and manufacturer. He was also sure that the railway would increase both the landowner's convenience and his rental. Still he urged that landowners who might yet differ with him be treated sympathetically; they were faced by an omnipotent Parliament ready to violate the rights of private property and their resentment was understandable. Accordingly he counselled that landowners should not be 'hurried and forced, but rather wooed and won'.[27]

The directors of the London and Birmingham acted at once upon this advice. In October 1832 a short list of influential landowners was drawn up: Lords Essex and Clarendon, Mr Estcourt, Lord Brownlow acting for the Countess of Bridgewater, Mr Pulsford, Mr Grant, Lady Lovatt, Sir W. Wake, the Duke of Grafton, Sir Charles Knightley, Mr Thornton, Lord John Scott, the Marquess of Hastings and Lord Digby. It was resolved that with these landowners 'a system of negotiation for obtaining their assents should be adopted as soon as possible'.[28] Success was quick. By January 1833 it was found that instead of going to Parliament with 70 miles of dissents and 40 miles of assents, as in the previous year, the situation was now reversed. In May Parliament approved of the bill for the London and Birmingham railway.

The financial provisions of the new 'system of negotiation', although by no means fully revealed in the records of the London and Birmingham, doubtless account for the sudden reversal. It seems clear that some, if not all, of the landowners on the short list obtained special arrangements. The Marquess of Hastings,

for example, received £2,800 for 20 acres of land, and, in addition, £5,500 as 'compensation for severance, general incon-
venience and loss'. So the transaction was described in the Minute
Books of the London and Birmingham.[29] But the Marquess's
agent, Edward Mammatt, explained that the first sum more than
covered what he took to be the value of the land, and that the
second sum was '*pour la poche*'.[30] Possibly the Bridgewater trustees
made a similar bargain: £5,623 for 43 acres of land, and £2,178
'on account of expenses incurred in the opposition of the last
Session and attending the Surveys etc, in reference to the contract with the trustees'.[31]

Significantly, perhaps, the negotiations for a part of Lord
Southampton's London estate—Lord Southampton not being on
the list of influential owners—suggest a less lavish payment.
Lord Southampton's property comprised 13 acres on ninety-nine-
year building leases returning £287 annually; about 10 acres of
pasture and other land returning £100 a year; and two cottages
with gardens on ninety-nine-year lease returning £30 annually.
Lord Southampton's agent valued the whole of this land at
£30,000. The railway's agent, Philip Hardwicke, valued it at
£25,635: the land on ground rent, at thirty years' purchase, being
worth £12,510; the remainder, being good building land, worth
£50 an acre at twenty-five years' purchase, ie £13,125. Hardwicke was authorised to offer Lord Southampton £25,000, one-
fifth of which was to be paid in railway shares. Lord Southampton's agent asked for £30,000, with £5,000 in advance. They
settled on £30,000, of which £7,500 was to be paid in cash as
soon as the bill became law.[32]

Contemporaries and railway historians underlined the financial
consequences of these negotiations with landowners. Robert
Stephenson, in referring to the experience of the Liverpool and
Manchester as a guide to what might be expected by the London
and Birmingham directors, declared that 'the charge for land was
greatly augmented by the enormous and unreasonable compensation required by some proprietors beyond the correct value of
the land'.[33] In the same vein, after the completion of the London
and Birmingham, the story was soon commonly told that the
original parliamentary estimate of expenditure on land had in
fact been increased threefold—a statement that was repeated by

historians in this century.[34] The sober Jackman, in discussing the costs of railway building generally, followed suit: 'vast sums of money were required at first under plea of "compensation", to buy off the opposition of property holders'.[35]

There is a touch of melodrama here. In the case of the London and Birmingham, the parliamentary estimate of £250,000 was only one of several estimates which Robert Stephenson drew up for the directors. His first estimate had been £413,000, arrived at by assuming a need for 1,377 acres at an average cost of £300 an acre, which he warned might rise to £481,000 if the Liverpool and Manchester's experience was taken strictly as the standard of railway expenditure on land. This estimate was revised downward a year later to £250,000, a figure based on 1,250 acres at an average cost of £200 per acre.[36] As it turned out, even on the basis of this later figure, the cost of land by the time of the railway's completion was £506,500, not three times but twice the parliamentary estimate, and not so very different from Stephenson's original figure.[37]

This is not to deny that railways paid liberally for their land. Generally, as was only to be expected, they paid a non-agricultural price for agricultural land. What in these special circumstances, however, was excessive only a theorist of the just price could determine. Influential owners had their own scale of payment which sometimes reached unusual heights in a few instances (as in the notorious Petre case) because the company was irresponsible.[38] It would seem that landowners without marked influence received for agricultural land something like sixty years' purchase, arrived at—according to surveyors connected with the building of the Great Western, the Grand Junction and the South-Eastern Counties in the 1830s—by calculating a full rent of thirty to thirty-five years' purchase and adding to that 25 per cent for compulsory sale and a further 50 per cent for severance.[39] From another point of view, an economic historian of the early railways has concluded that 'only seven [companies] spent more than 16 per cent of their total expenditure on land, fourteen spent between 11 per cent and 15 per cent and six below 11 per cent'.[40]

There is no mistaking, however, the effect of the railways' liberality. Herbert Spencer, who was trained as a railway surveyor, took the landowners' experience with the London and

Birmingham as a turning point.[41] Thereafter even those who were agricultural in outlook and interest were more and more likely to find the railways beneficial both from a private and a public point of view. 'Ten years' teaching', according to Spencer in 1845, 'had changed their ideas, and made them anxious to profit by the raised value of land which railway proximity gave.'[42] In the same year the Duke of Bedford informed his chief agent, Christopher Haedy, that 'railways are now becoming so great a national object that I am inclined to think it right that landowners should take shares on their respective lines'.[43] And also in this year a leading railway engineer on a visit to the Duke of Devonshire at Chatsworth described the gathering of guests as 'quite a railway party! —Lord Morpeth who talked to me about Irish railways; Lord Jocelyn, about Indian railways; Mr Lascelles, MP about the North Kent; and Mr Talbot, the parliamentary agent, about railways in general. The Duke spoke chiefly about the Derbyshire lines.'[44]

A certain kind of landowner usually needed no teaching at all that railways were good for him. This was the owner of mineral lands. After all the railway itself had been in its beginnings, as Sir John Clapham put it, 'a coal pit accessory'.[45] Whatever the mineral, coal or tin, or ironstone, and in whatever part of England it lay, its owner was likely at one time or another in the nineteenth century to be actively initiating short lines of railway. Lord de Dunstanville was a moving spirit in early Cornish railways, Lord Lowther and Sir Wilfrid Lawson and the Senhouse family in the Maryport and Carlisle, the Earl of Burlington (later the seventh Duke of Devonshire) and the Duke of Buccleuch in the Furness railway, Earl Fitzwilliam in the South Yorkshire, the Duke of Norfolk in the Manchester and Sheffield, Thomas Assheton Smith the great foxhunter in a Welsh railway, and many others.[46] When such a landowner opposed a railway line it was often because of its favouring a neighbour's mineral land to the prejudice of his own. A Staffordshire landowner, Ralph Sneyd, once observed: 'contiguous collieries must by the force of circumstances be rivals and enemies'.[47] Hence the opposition of Lord Durham and his agent, Henry Morton, to the South Durham railway which would open Teesside collieries in competition with his Wear collieries,[48] or the opposition of Lord Francis Egerton to the projected line of the Bolton, Wigan and Liverpool because among other things it would help in the sale of Lord Balcarres's coal.[49]

Landowners' investment in mineral lines in the thirties and forties was almost certainly more significant than their investment in trunk lines. Lord Stafford's investment in the Liverpool and Manchester seems to have been a unique instance, whereas the investment of the Duke of Devonshire and the Duke of Buccleuch in the Furness mineral line seems to have been far from unique. Their initial investment was not especially large, amounting to £15,000 a piece.[50] Two decades later the Duke of Devonshire told W. E. Gladstone that the *yearly* return on his railway investment amounted to £12,000.[51] This was no longer a modest affair, the Duke having in the interval embarked on a variety of large-scale enterprises at Barrow-in-Furness. In all likelihood the aggregate investment of landowners in railways had grown appreciably. It was a sign of the times when a House of Lord's Committee in 1863 recommended that tenants for life have the power to borrow on the security of family estates in order to invest in local railways.[52]

Obviously, from the very first the opposition of landowners to the coming of the railways was a very mixed affair. Although some took the ground, like Lord Derby in the case of the Liverpool and Manchester[53] and like the Northamptonshire landowners in the case of the London and Birmingham, that railways were townsmen's speculations bringing no benefit to the countryside, some, like Lord Stafford, bowed to the railway on the ground of national interest and enlightened public opinion. Although some feared (and often with good reason) for their privacy or for the undisturbed pursuit of foxes, some like Sir James Graham of Netherby saw the coming of the railway as an unmixed benefit to their estates, in Sir James's case an agricultural estate: 'it is the interest of any Proprietor', he wrote as early as 1825, 'to open up his Estate by every possible means'.[54] Owners of mineral lands usually agreed with him, unless the building of a railway adversely affected the exploitation and sale of their minerals.[55] For those who learned slowly what Graham understood from the start—that railways like canals were good for agricultural rentals —there was the spur of generous monetary compensation.

Owners in mineral and urban districts must have done especially well from the sale of land.[56] Even less fortunately located ones came to agree with Disraeli's Lord Marney that 'railroads are very good things with high compensation'.[57]

J. E. Denison, a Nottinghamshire squire, wrote to William Huskisson in 1830:

> I have just been in Durham travelling on one railroad, and inspecting the progress of another which passes through Coal property of mine there—I have been astonished at the fruits which spring from planting these iron rails on the ground— Liverpool is not a greater lesson of the results of free Trade than the Darlington railroad is, of the effects of free and cheap communication.[58]

'The fruits which spring from planting these iron rails', as we shall see, were not confined to the mining of coal, although coal in sheer volume outran iron, copper and lead. In 1858, 95,000 tons of lead were mined in England and Wales as compared with 226,000 tons of copper, 8 million tons of iron ore and 65 million tons of coal.

The ancient industry of mining tin and copper in Cornwall, with its idiosyncratic customs and language and its peculiar and precarious modes of working, was further complicated by the marked subdivision and intermixture of Cornish landownership. The estate of the Robartes family, for example, comprised twenty-four manors in eighty-two parishes, from the extreme west and south of the county as far as Tintagel in the north.[59] These small intermixed parcels of land often made for several Cornish landowners—known as 'lords'—sharing the returns of a single mine. The proceeds of the Biscovey mine in 1824 were shared in the following fashion: the Rashleigh family 35/60ths, Mrs Agar 10/60ths, Mrs Rogers 8/60ths, and the Carlyons 7/60ths. It was justly said that 'the Cornish certainly have need to possess more than common powers of calculation'.[60] Not surprisingly, they were much given to litigation in mineral matters.

Probably the most important of the Cornish lords were the Duchy of Cornwall, Lord de Dunstanville, the Duke of Bed-

ford,[61] Lord Mount-Edgecumbe, Lord Falmouth, Sir Richard
Vyvyan, and the Robartes and Buller families. Of these the first
three were the greatest; and it is perhaps significant that two of
them were not properly West Country families, their preponderance thus acting as a drain on West Country wealth (the Duchy
produced about one-sixth of the tin raised in the 1830s and about
one-eighth of the copper),[62] and thus helping to account no doubt
for the lack of great families and great houses in the West
Country.

The mineral returns of Cornish landowners were almost entirely rent. Apart from the activities of a few landowners like
Lord Falmouth who worked Wheal Falmouth in the thirties or
Lord de Dunstanville who took a sixth-share in the company
working his Dolcoath mine,[63] Cornish mines were let to mining
operators who were ready to face the numerous hazards of
Cornish mining and who paid the landowner a portion of the
value of the ore raised, generally from a fifteenth to a twenty-
fourth part. In the fifties the Duchy took one-fifteenth on the
value of the ore raised; the Duke of Bedford in the forties and
fifties increased his dues from one-fifteenth to one-twelfth when
the profits exceeded £20,000.[64]

Cornish mining found its most prosperous decades during the
thirty years after 1826, reaching a peak in the 1850s. The mining
of copper outran the mining of tin: in 1856 the value of copper
ore extracted in Cornwall was almost £1,300,000, that of tin
£663,850.[65] It was these years which saw on the Duke of Bedford's estate the spectacular rise of Devon Great Consols, at the
time one of the largest copper mines in the world. In the first
twelve years of its existence it brought the Duke of Bedford
£102,453 in dues, about 70 per cent of his total mining receipts
in the West Country.[66] At about the same time the Duchy of
Cornwall's mineral dues were said to be £6–10,000 a year. After
the fifties the mining of copper ore fell sharply, and although the
mining of tin briefly made up for this, by the seventies the
Cornish mining industry was in serious difficulty owing to world
competition, and the dues of Cornish landowners fell off markedly;
by 1889 gross royalties from copper and tin were estimated at
£39,129. Even Devon Great Consols produced no royalties after
1884.[67]

Lead was chiefly produced in the northern counties, and the landowners most concerned with its production were the Bishop of Durham, the Dukes of Devonshire and Cleveland, and the Bowes and Beaumont families. Most landowners, like those of the West Country, let their mines in return for a proportion of the ore raised, usually a sixth or an eighth. But at least two land-owners, the Duke of Devonshire and the Beaumonts, worked their mines, or some part of them.

The Duke of Devonshire had two lead-mining properties, the first in Derbyshire which he held of the Duchy of Lancaster and leased to others, and the second in Yorkshire, the Grassington mines, which he worked himself at different times in the nineteenth century.[68] John Taylor, a leading mining engineer, reported in 1831 that the Duke's agents had 'laid out the most systematic plan of ore-dressing that I know of'.[69] The Beaumonts had been working lead mines since the early eighteenth century— those in their own possession in Northumberland, together with those in Cumberland which they leased from the Bishop of Durham. They also operated smelting mills—two in Allandale and one in Weardale.[70]

Apart from some fluctuations, lead mining also had its boom period in the years 1827–57. The Duke of Devonshire was making a profit of £12–15,000 a year in the 1850s.[71] The Beaumont mines had languished in the forties, but in the two decades after 1845, under the management of Thomas Sopwith and with the encouragement of a new owner, Wentworth Blackett Beaumont, the mines and works were transformed. 'The most extensive lead mines in the world', Sopwith described them in 1856; 2,000 persons were employed, and during the twenty years 1845–65 lead ore was produced to the average value of £500 a day.[72] After 1865 lead mining like that of copper and tin underwent a severe decline and for the same reason; by 1889 the gross royalties from English lead (and zinc) were estimated at £31,861. The Beaumont mines were shut down in 1890, the Duke of Devonshire's in 1896.[73]

In a century in which it could be written that 'it would be superfluous, even if it were possible, to trace the gradual metamorphosis which is going on around us of familiar objects into iron',[74] the owners of iron ore were bound to do well. It was found in many places; west Cumberland, the North and West Ridings of Yorkshire, the Furness peninsula and the Black Country were perhaps the chief ones. Among leading owners were Lord Lonsdale in Cumberland; Lord Normanby, the Marquess of Zetland and the Marquess of Ailesbury in the North Riding; Earl Fitzwilliam and Lord Wharncliffe in the West Riding; the Duke of Buccleuch, Lord Muncaster and the Duke of Devonshire in the Furness peninsula; and Lord Granville, Ralph Sneyd, Lord Dudley, the Dukes of Cleveland and Sutherland and the Duchy of Lancaster in the Black Country. Most landowners let their mines, often to ironmasters, at a rent proportioned to the output of ore or to the size of the working. A few landowners, however, both mined their own iron and were themselves ironmasters.

It would seem that this latter group diminished in size during the course of the nineteenth century. Earl Fitzwilliam gradually detached himself from such business, and so did Ralph Sneyd, who was unfitted for any business, let alone one so complicated. But the Earls Granville, to mention a notable example, persisted. The first Earl had taken over a lease of mineral lands in north Staffordshire from the Duchy of Lancaster, previously held by the Marquess of Stafford. In 1813 it was first proposed that iron ore be got for smelting, but no action was taken until 1832, after which year the ore was got 'on an extensive scale'. During the last ten years of the first Earl's life, that is, from 1835 to 1845, his affairs touched their nadir as profits vanished. His son experienced similar troubles and there was anxious interchange of opinion in the late forties with his fellow ironmaster, Ralph Sneyd. Finally in the fifties, after a large expenditure in mines and works, Lord Granville began to make a profit. The Shelton Coal and Iron Works, as his property was called, then employed 1,400–1,500 men and boys, worked eight blast furnaces, and raised about 80,000 tons of ore a year.[75]

It was said that between 1840 and 1860 'the make of iron trebled'.[76] These years saw a vast expansion of the mining of iron ore, particularly of haematite ore, which was found in great quantity in north-west Lancashire, west Cumberland, and the North Riding, and which became even more valuable with the invention of the Bessemer process in 1856. The haematite field in the Cleveland hills of the North Riding began to be exploited in 1850 and by 1862 was said to be the greatest of the iron-ore areas. The field of the Furness peninsula had long been known but new discoveries and the Furness railway helped much to bring it along. Park Mine, the largest mine, leased from the Duke of Devonshire, produced 10,000 tons in 1850, 150,000 in 1857, and the Duke was in receipt of £8,000 a year.[77] The rapid development of the fifties in the mining of iron ore, unlike that of lead, copper and tin, underwent no serious reversal in the next three decades.

Of all the fruits of the soil which the building of railways nourished, none was so plentiful as coal. It was roughly estimated that 10 million tons of coal were mined in 1800 and something like 16 million in 1816. By 1854, when coal-trade statistics were reliable, production had leapt to 54 million tons, fifteen years later to 107 million, and by 1885 to 160 million.[78] This revolutionary growth brought coalmining close to the centre of the Industrial Revolution. Sober observers pointed to England's heavy dependence on coal: 'it stands not beside but entirely above all other commodities. It is the material source of the energy of the country—the universal aid—the factor in everything we do.'[79] Rhapsodists sang the praises of coal: 'More powerful than destiny itself, it annihilates both time and space. Mastering the winds of heaven it enables Britannia, without a metaphor, to Rule the Waves.'[80]

Inevitably the mining of coal often touched on the affairs of landed estates. It seemed to be everywhere: in the Forest of Dean and north-west Somersetshire, in the Midlands, in Yorkshire, Lancashire, and Cumberland, and above all in the great northern field of Northumberland and Durham which supplied in 1840 not only those counties but the North Riding and the Scottish Border and 'the whole eastern and southern coasts of England as far as Cornwall, including the metropolis itself'.[81] If landowners lacked coal, their agents hopefully searched for it, anxious to carve out what a French traveller on Tyneside described as 'farms under ground'.[82] If they had coal, they sometimes worked it beneath the very foundations of their mansion houses, as did the Lambtons in county Durham. Lord Londonderry fondly referred to his collieries as 'our Black Diamond trade'.[83]

A comprehensive list of colliery owners in the landed society would be unwieldy here. Perhaps the following adequately lists the most conspicuous, excluding for the moment those in Northumberland and Durham: in the Midland field Lords Dudley and Hatherton, the Earl of Dartmouth, the Dukes of Portland, Rutland and Cleveland and the Marquess of Hastings; in Lancashire the Earls of Ellesmere, Derby, Sefton and Crawford, the Heskeths, Leighs and Blundells; in Cumberland the Earl of Lonsdale, the Senhouses and the Curwens; in the Yorkshire–Derbyshire field the Dukes of Norfolk and Devonshire, Earls Fitzwilliam and Manvers and the Earls of Wharncliffe, Cardigan and Mexborough.

As for Northumberland and Durham, a complete list of the colliery owners there would also run to many pages, being very nearly a handbook of the nobility and gentry of those counties.[84] As the most productive of English coalfields for much of the nineteenth century, the northern field showed a heavy concentration of great owners. Overtopping them all stood the Bishop of Durham and the Dean and Chapter of Durham, letting their coal to mining operators and to landed families who in turn might let it to sub-lessees or work it themselves or simply allow it to lie dormant. For the first half of the century at least, the letting of the Bishop's and Chapter's coal was on a distinctive footing: 'I question', said a North Country lawyer with a mixture of pride and annoyance,[85]

> whether any general principle that could be applied to land would apply to that particular species of property . . . it is a difficult species of property to understand; and nobody does understand it but gentlemen from the county of Durham who have been brought up professionally to it.

However, it was not so obscure as to forbid a brief definition. According to the Episcopal and Capitular Revenues Committee of 1851,[86]

> the tenure of such property generally is by lease, either for three lives, renewable at the dropping of any one life; for 21 years, renewable at the expiration of every seven; for 30 years, renewable every 10, or for 40 years renewable every 14: and in such leases a rent usually little more than nominal, is reserved, and a fine varying in different cases (being in fact the principal source of emolument to the lessor) is payable at each period of renewal.

It was the Bishop who had gone in for leases on lives, of which about ten still existed at the end of the century, when it was estimated that the Church coal, now administered by the Ecclesiastical Commissioners, brought in about £200,000 annually in county Durham.[87]

After the clerical came the great lay owners. They fell into several classes: those whose mines were near the Tyne, or the Wear, or (as the century wore on) the Tees, and those who mined their own coal or let it to others. The historians of the eighteenth-century coal industry have written that 'most of the proprietors worked their minerals directly or through salaried agents'.[88] By 1829, according to John Buddle, the leading colliery engineer of the day, this was no longer the case in the Northern field: on Tyneside only five of forty-one owners worked their colliery, and on the Wear three of eighteen did likewise.[89] Perhaps the greatest of the owner-lessors was the Duke of Northumberland, and among the owner-operators the greatest were Lord Londonderry, the Earl of Durham and Lord Ravensworth and Partners (Lord Wharncliffe and the Bowes family), the last sometimes known as the Grand Allies. These owner-operators were the grandees of the trade; it was said that their investments about 1840 were of the order of half a million pounds each; and together they sought with varying success to regulate the output and sale of coal from the Tyne and Wear.[90] When landowners let their own property they usually required what was known in the North as a 'certain' rent, that is, a fixed sum paid for a term of years (usually twenty-one) whether the coal was worked or not, and a royalty or 'tentale' rent (again northern usage) to be paid for each 'ten' of coal (roughly 40 tons) mined in excess of the minimum covered by the certain rent.[91] This arrangement was not too different from colliery leases elsewhere in the country.

Those landowners who were content to let their coal were sometimes drawn into their lessees' operations. At least so this appears in the Duke of Northumberland's case.[92] In Walbottle colliery, for example, first let in 1792, the Duke continued to own part of the working stock until at least the 1860s. In the Percy Main colliery, although leased in 1827 for twenty-one years at specified certain and tentale rents, the Duke revised the terms of the lease when the lessees met with setbacks: as in 1837 when a

C

large proportion of inferior coal was produced, or as in the next year when serious flooding took place. In this latter emergency the lessees installed a new and expensive pumping engine, and the Duke substantially reduced both certain and tentale rents, eventually contributing a lump sum to meet the cost of pumping the mine. The reduction of the tentale rent was part of a general policy begun in 1833, applicable to all collieries on the estate, whereby a sliding scale of tentale rents came into effect when coal prices fell.[93]

Such risk-sharing, however, did not expose the Duke to severe fluctuations in his rental returns. He maintained a fairly even keel, sailing smoothly through periods of depression in the coal trade in which some of his more enterprising brethren were severely battered. In 1790 his colliery rental amounted to £2,255, in 1813 to £13,215. In the mid-1820s it began to climb again, reaching £23,400 in 1831. Although the sliding scale on tentale rents went into effect in 1833, the Duke's annual colliery returns fell below £19,000 in only six years during the next two decades: in 1834 when they fell to £14,700; in 1835, £16,200; in 1844, £16,300; in 1845, £15,400; in 1849, £18,500; and in 1853, £15,500. The sixties and seventies showed an even better record until the very last two years of the seventies.[94]

These colliery returns, it should be noted, included a special charge from wayleave rents which rose from £2,677 in 1835 to £8,786 in 1852. Wayleave rents were charges levied by the Duke on mining operators who carried their coal over (and sometimes under) his land. The Duke was lord of the manor of Tynemouth, a property so situated that his lessees had to cross it to bring their coal to Tyneside. This valuable interest, it would seem, was in some measure responsible for the Duke's promotion of the Tyne Docks in the fifties; these would attract fresh coal across his land, and keep coal coming across it which might be drawn elsewhere, perhaps to newly-improved ports like Blythe. Wayleaves also helped make the Duke an opponent of parliamentary railways. In order to stave off the threat of such lines, the Duke progressively lowered his wayleave charges from 12s a ton in 1832 to 8s in 1851.[95]

The colliery affairs of the Earl of Durham, in contrast with those of the Duke of Northumberland, were bustling, complicated, and sometimes precarious. Lord Durham—the first Earl was once referred to as 'His Carbonic Majesty'[96]—operated six working collieries in the 1830s while keeping four more in a dormant state, hired and housed hundreds of pit workers, and ran a private railway to Sunderland whence his coal was shipped (later in the century in his own ships) to the London market. John Buddle in 1835 valued the working collieries at £384,331, and the colliery stock (including the railway line) at £156,364. Henry Morton, the Earl's chief agent, estimated that the mineral property alone, working and dormant collieries, was worth about half a million pounds. Its output, according to the arrangements fixed on by the leading collieries of the Tyne and Wear in 1828, ranked first: 162,000 chaldrons, a chaldron containing 53cwt.[97]

Troubles and apprehensions, however, were not unknown on the Lambton estate. The first crisis for which there is evidence came in the 1820s. Colliery profits jumped from £15,344 in 1819 to £29,537 in 1820 and then fell to £16,514 in 1824 and to £6,405 in 1826. At this point, through the auspices of 'Bear' Ellice, a London barrister by the name of Henry Stephenson was brought in to investigate the condition of the Lambton collieries and finances. He found indebtedness rapidly growing—'there is little or nothing left upon which a further mortgage can be placed'— and colliery expenditure, unchecked by proper book-keeping, was mounting with equal speed.[98] Stephenson overhauled the estate administration and when in the thirties profits recovered— by 1834 the Lambton agents were counting on a minimum annual profit of £30,000—there was some thought of selling out. Presumably this was behind John Buddle's valuation of the collieries in 1835. A possible purchaser appeared, but somehow nothing came of it. Meanwhile the colliery profits rose to new heights: about £70,000 in 1837, and nearly £60,000 in 1838. According to Henry Morton, these were profits 'beyond the fair and reasonable remuneration for Capital at present in the coal trade'.[99]

A new time of troubles came in the forties. The first Earl died in 1841, and his heir was a minor who distressed his father's executors by exhibiting signs of youthful exuberance. More seriously, the colliery profits fell again: from £29,995 in 1842 to £19,767 in 1845 and £14,590 in 1848.[100] Coalmining in the 1840s suffered from a glut with a consequent fall in price. In

Lancashire Lord Francis Egerton reported that his colliery income had fallen off by two-thirds, owing 'to the opening of sources of supply by new railroads'.[101] In county Durham Lord Londonderry complained, with characteristic excitability and melodrama, that[102]

> with the great prospect of Competition by Proprietors and Directors of Railways becoming Coal owners, and buying up the collieries in Derbyshire and Staffordshire and carrying Coals at a farthing per Ton . . . and making the Passengers pay for this Tonnage and Merchandise of their own article, it is very probable our Seaborne Coal will be driven out of the London markets.

The Lambton agents and advisers were also gloomy but less sure of disaster. 'Whether the coal trade is to recover or not from its present state of depression', the young Earl was informed, 'is a matter of opinion. Mr Morton is sanguine in his expectation that the best Collieries, of which yours is one, will yield a fair profit—but even he allows that we can never again expect the profits that were formerly realised.'[103]

As the depression in the coal trade deepened, reaching its nadir in 1851, the Lambton agents—chiefly Henry Morton—sought strenuously to cut costs. In September 1851 Morton proposed the following economies: reduction in the pitmen's wages; a saving on railway and port charges at Sunderland; a different mode of working the mines, practised in Derbyshire and Leicestershire collieries, by which a better grade of coal would be obtained; and finally a reduction in the cost of carrying coal to London and of selling it once it got there. The last items were the most important. Morton estimated the cost of carriage per ton in the past year had been 7s 3d—'a most important feature in the cost of production, amounting to 17s 2d per chaldron, nearly as much as the coal is sold for at Sunderland'. It had occurred to him that iron, screw-propelled vessels, operated by the Lambtons, might carry their coal more cheaply, perhaps at 5s per ton, at which price, he said, 'I should not fear competition from the Great Northern Railway.' Furthermore he proposed that instead of employing coal factors to sell the coal in London on the Coal Exchange, they employ an agent of their own, whose salary would save them about £3,000 on coal factor commissions.[104]

Hugh Taylor, the Duke of Northumberland's colliery agent, predicted in 1853 that the depression would lift:[105]

A want of coal is felt both in this Country and on the Continent . . . Our own consumption has gone on increasing until it amounts to a present estimated quantity of 39½ Millions of Tons yearly: which it may fairly be assumed will progressively augment, considering the extension of steam navigation, Railways, Manufacture, Gas and House Consumption.

At the same time Henry Morton reported that the trials of the first new vessel, the *Lady Alice Durham*, had proved successful: 'with the aid of these we shall drive the Yorkshire coals out of the London market'—or, less exuberantly—'at least check the increase'. Only a few years later, in 1856, the profits of the Lambton collieries were £84,207: 'the most profitable year ever known'. Less spectacular were the returns of the sixties, but in the early seventies they were: £80,163 in 1871, £122,658 in 1872, £380,000 in 1873, £71,648 in 1874.[106] This was a pitch of prosperity far beyond Morton's expectations.

Not all landowners who mined their coal in the Northern coalfield did so well as the Lambtons. A Tyneside landowner, R. W. Brandling, who was part owner of three collieries and principal owner of two, ended his long career in the 1830s with an indebtedness reputedly amounting to half a million pounds and his affairs in the hands of trustees, who pensioned him off at £2,000 a year.[107] In the 1850s Lord Ravensworth and Partners ended an even longer career as Tyneside coalminers. The last phase of the partnership began in 1825 with Lord Ravensworth, Lord Wharncliffe and the Countess of Strathmore each having a one-third share in the undertaking and with a capital stock valued at £121,000. By 1852 their debts—'continually increasing'—had reached £110,000. Lord Wharncliffe could no longer carry his share of the losses and all three partners were anxious to sell. As they put it, since 1825[108]

a large and constantly increasing amount of Capital had been employed in the Coal Trade in the North of England, and that in very many instances such Capital was employed by Persons well acquainted with the Business of winning and vending Coal, who directed their Time and Attention to the Superintendence and

Management of the Works . . . [and] that none of the Persons then interested in the said Copartnership Collieries . . . were willing to devote their attention to the Business of winning and vending coal.

In short Lord Ravensworth and Partners had lost their entrepreneurial nerve. So did the Lambtons, but under happier circumstances and much later, in the 1890s, when they invested the large proceeds of the sale of their mines in stocks and bonds.

It may seem like a curious choice of witness to turn to Lord Palmerston—commonly regarded as a child of the *Ancien Régime*—for evidence of what the coming of the railways meant for the growth of towns. But Palmerston, among other things, was a dealer in Welsh slates, with a keen eye for the impact of the Industrial Revolution on landowners' finances. Welsh slates, as he explained, were closely connected with housebuilding: they provided the best roofing material. Thus his remark: 'The rage for railways is in our favour, because railways create stationhouses, and station-houses beget villages, and little towns are springing up everywhere upon the lines of railways.'[109] Palmerston would have appreciated the jingle that appeared some decades later in Tarbuck's *Handbook of House Property*:[110]

> The richest crop for any field
> Is a crop of bricks for it to yield
> The richest crop that it can grow
> Is a crop of houses in a row.

The great increase in the number of Englishmen in the nineteenth century was largely an increase in urban Englishmen. As population had grown from 10·6 million in 1801 to 33·1 million in 1891, something like 80 per cent of the population lived in towns and cities at the latter date. London, with a population of roughly 865,000 in 1801, had grown to 4·25 million in 1891; Sheffield in the same years grew eightfold, from 50,000 to 400,000. In 1801 there was one city, London, with a population of 100,000; in 1891 there were twenty-three. In 1801 there were fourteen towns with a population of between 20,000 and 100,000; in 1891 there were 161.[111] This vast urbanisation was, to quote

Sir John Clapham, 'a situation which had probably not existed before, in a great country, at any time in the world's history'.[112]

Contemporaries marvelled at the unprecedented building. In London in 1829 General Dyott was astonished 'on observing the extraordinary extent of the new squares, streets, places, etc. on the back of Grosvenor Place, which I recollect wet, low swampy meadows'. Coke of Norfolk in 1833 told the artist, Benjamin Haydon, that 'he remembered a fox killed in Cavendish Square, and that where Berkeley Square now stands was an excellent place for snipes'. In the provinces Charles Greville took a day off from horseracing in 1845 to view the wonders of Birkenhead: 'Not many years ago the ground was an unprofitable marsh . . . The present population is 16,000 . . . they are building in every direction.'[113] And on the coasts Lewis Carroll's Alice had to conclude 'that wherever you go to on the English coast, you find a number of bathing-machines in the sea, some children digging in the sand with wooden spades, then a row of lodging houses, and behind them a railway station'.

It was said in 1859 that 'the zone around London is far more valuable than that round any town in the world'. In Birkenhead a parcel of land, it was reported, rose in value in a few years in the 1840s from roughly £6,000 to roughly £30,000. What was once agricultural land in and around Blackpool, selling for several pounds an acre, fetched £60 an acre in the 1860s.[114] In many places in England, especially 'in the neighbourhood of great towns', land was rapidly 'passing from one condition to another', from agricultural land to accommodation land, 'then perhaps nursery ground, from nursery ground to building and so on'.[115] It has been estimated that urban land values in the United Kingdom rose from £3 million in 1845 to £8·6 million in 1857, to £16·6 million in 1867 and to £30·1 million in 1882.[116]

English landed families who benefitted from London property alone constituted a formidable list. A beginning might be made with those families who helped create the quiet grace of Georgian London: the Dukes of Bedford and Portland, the Marquess (later Duke) of Westminster, and Lords Berkeley and Portman. Second, there were landed families owning adjacent properties, still in central London but where the mark of taste was less discernible: Lord Southampton, the Marquess of Salisbury, the

Duke of Norfolk and Lord Northampton.[117] Third, beyond the core of London, out to the nineteenth-century suburbs, north and south of the Thames, there were the properties of landed families like Cadogan (Chelsea), de Crespigny (Camberwell and Peckham), Evelyn (Deptford), Ladbrooke (Kensington), and Fox (Kensington).[118] Most, if not all of the above-named families held their land in freehold. Some families like the Claytons and Thistlethwaytes leased land from corporate owners, the one from the Duchy of Cornwall, the other from the Bishop of London.[119]

The Russells held one of the greatest as well as one of the oldest of London estates. By the middle of the nineteenth century it comprised roughly 119 acres in the centre of London, of which the following were the main districts: Bloomsbury, 80 acres; Bedford New Town, 20 acres; Covent Garden, 16 acres; Covent Garden Market, 1 acre.[120] The Covent Garden property was acquired in the sixteenth century and rebuilt by the Russells in the seventeenth. In Bloomsbury, the Bedford Square area had been completed by 1786; the Woburn Square–Bloomsbury Square area by 1822, building having begun about 1800; and in 1824 Cubitt took over what remained of unbuilt-on land south of Euston Road, such as parts of Tavistock Square. Finally, between 1843 and 1856 Bedford New Town—north of and separate from the Bloomsbury estate—was built. In 1851 the Duke of Bedford's agent observed that some seventy houses remained to be built: these done, 'all the building land on your Grace's London Estate will have been built upon; and then, as a House Estate, it may be said to be completed'.[121] This came nine years later with the building of the east side of Gordon Square.

In the 1840s about half of the houses on the Duke of Bedford's estate—those built most recently—were let on ground rent. The ground rent was paid by the builder of the dwelling, who, like Thomas Cubitt, contracted to pay a certain sum to the Duke of Bedford for an area of building land on which he agreed to build a certain number of houses, the ground rent on each house not exceeding a certain proportion of the rack rental—or full commercial value—of the house. In short, the capital of the Duke of Bedford and that of Thomas Cubitt were joined together, the Duke taking a small fixed sum as his share of the profits, although

acquiring an increasing interest in the joint capital as the lease
approached its end. It was common on the great London estates,
in the eighteenth and during most of the nineteenth centuries,
for building leases to run ninety-nine years. In the building of
Bedford New Town, as on some other parts of his estate, the
Duke made substantial advances to his builders, thereby encouraging them to build more quickly and in a style more befitting the Duke of Bedford's estate: without advances, Christopher
Haedy observed, the builders 'would have made of Figs Mead a
second Somers Town'.[122]

The other half of the houses on the Bedford estate in the forties
was on rack rents. Earlier building leases had fallen in and the
houses had become the Duke's property, on which occasion he
stepped into the builder's place, dealing directly with the occu-
piers, renewing their leases, usually for shorter terms and at rack
rents or at such equivalents as took account of the tenants' repairs. In the course of time houses required complete rebuilding,
and then rents resumed their original state of ground rents. Thus
the Duke of Bedford's estate, having been built on at different
times, was partly on ground rent, partly on rack: a state of affairs
which the Duke's agent found most agreeable, for it allowed the
falling rents of one part of the estate to be offset by the rising
rents of another:[123]

> The old parts of the Estate [he wrote] sink into ground rents, thro'
> the houses upon them requiring to be rebuilt, the new parts will
> rise by the falling in of the building leases, from ground-rents to
> house-rents, and this process will always be going on as the new
> parts of the Estate become old and the old parts new: and thus
> kept up, the Rental . . . may be said to be as permanent as if it
> were the Rental of a Landed Estate.

The Duke's rental of his London estate was both permanent
and impressive: from 1830 to 1870 it stayed within the range of
£70,000 to £80,000 gross; in 1871 it was £80,131.[124] Owing to
the falling-in of the Bedford Square leases, the seventies wit-
nessed a surge ahead and by 1880 the Duke's gross rental from
London was £104,880. Under the old leases the Bedford Square
rental had been £2,191; under the new it was £18,848. Similar
leaps ahead were bound to come on other parts of the estate after

the turn of the century. They seem to have been little affected by sales of land which statutory powers forced on the Duke: land for the British Museum, for the London and Birmingham railway, for New Oxford Street, all of which in the regime of the seventh Duke brought £225,024.[125]

Not all of the Duke's London rental came from land and houses. King Charles II had granted the Russells the right to hold markets in Covent Garden—a right which grew in value as London grew into a metropolis, and as Covent Garden became 'the principal Sale place for London and the standard for quotations throughout the country'. By 1830 permanent market buildings had been constructed, the first of their sort, it was said, in which any effort at arranging displays of produce was attempted.[126] A staff of about a dozen men managed the market—letting stalls, collecting tolls levied on produce sold, and keeping the peace. In 1832 the net return from Covent Garden market was £4,825; in 1880 it was £15,537. Market rights were commonly held by landed families, but few if any held one so valuable as that held by the Russells.[127]

In turning to provincial England, it soon becomes apparent that many sizeable towns had one or more landed families receiving income from ground and houses. In the South there was the Duke of Devonshire at Eastbourne and Lord Radnor at Folkestone; in the South-West, the Marquess of Ailesbury at Marlborough, the Duke of Cleveland at Bath, Lord St Levans at Devonport, the Palks at Torquay and Lord Clinton at Redruth. In the Midlands and the North, there were Lords Calthorpe, Dartmouth and Hertford in Birmingham, the Duke of Cleveland in Wolverhampton, the Marquess of Westminster in Chester, the Earl of Wilton in Manchester, and in Liverpool Lord Stanley of Alderley, the Marquess of Salisbury and the Earls of Sefton and Derby; the last, it may be noted, also held property in Macclesfield, Bury and Preston. In the North-East there were the Duke of Northumberland on Tyneside, the Earl of Durham at Sunderland, the Marquess of Londonderry at Seaham, and the Ridleys at Blyth. In Yorkshire there were the Ramsdens at Huddersfield, Lord Howard of Effingham at Rotherham, Lord Rosse in Bradford, and Earl Fitzwilliam and the Duke of Norfolk in Sheffield. Finally, in Lincolnshire and its neighbourhood, there were the

Earl of Yarborough and the Heneage family at Grimsby, Lord Burleigh at Stamford, Earl Fitzwilliam at Peterborough, and the Duke of Newcastle in Nottingham.[128]

In this short list, the Duke of Norfolk's estate in Sheffield was among the most impressive. It was said to be 20,000 acres in size, of which, although 8,000 acres was unproductive moorland, 12,000 acres comprised the northern and eastern parts of the city, particularly the industrial district of Brightside. At the beginning of the nineteenth century, under the eleventh Duke, the potentialities of building land in Sheffield were overlooked and parts of the property were actually sold in order to raise money for the Duke's estate in Sussex. Under the twelfth Duke, however, and his agent, Michael Ellison (1819–61), the property was developed on ninety-nine-year leases,[129] and in the city's centre public improvements were made at the Duke's expense: a bridge over the River Don, a new post office and exchange rooms, and alterations in the market buildings which were in the Duke's management. By 1860 his income from Sheffield ground rents had more than doubled, and two decades later the net return of his markets alone amounted to £10,000 a year.[130]

The Sheffields of nineteenth-century England unfortunately (for the bulk of their inhabitants) made necessary a new sort of town, the seaside resort. The railway and the cheap excursion train helped turn obscure fishing villages into large towns, and not a few landed families both promoted and benefitted from this unexpected consequence of the Industrial Revolution. Eastbourne and the Duke of Devonshire, Torquay and the Palks, Folkestone and Lord Radnor, already noted above, were three such places and three such families. There was also the Scarisbrick family at Southport, the Duke of Northumberland at Alnmouth, Sir William Tapps-Gervis at Bournemouth, Lord Cornwallis at Hastings, the Earl de La Warr at Bexhill, and the Cliftons at Blackpool.

In 1849 the Duke of Devonshire wrote in his diary: 'I had a good deal of talk with Wm. Simpson today about building plans here—but I hesitate—the railway has certainly improved the prospects of the place considerably.'[131] William Simpson was the Duke's agent on the Compton Place estate in Sussex, a property of 12,000 acres which took in a good deal of the seashore and

contained several detached villages. It was not long before the
Duke began to act on Simpson's advice. He put in roads and a
drainage system, built a sea wall costing £300,000 and turned the
house-building over to contractors on ninety-year leases.[132] By
1864 the *Saturday Review* was congratulating the Duke for
making 'as charming a seaside snuggery as the man weary of
share-lists and blue-books could desire'.[133] By 1888 over 2,000
houses had been built, covering an area of 600 acres, all done
with an eye to future growth 'so that there would be', explained
an agent, 'the extension of good large houses in one direction and
there would be the extension of smaller houses in another direction; they are not all mixed up. We have what we call our artizan
town, and we have the high-class villa town, and we have our
terrace houses; and they are all quite separate.'[134] Evidence is
lacking as to the growth of the Duke's rental at Eastbourne. But
some indication may be gathered from Lord Radnor's rental at
Folkestone: £838 in 1851; £8,222 in 1886.[135]

Land beside the sea or along a river's edge close to the sea was
fit for purposes other than holidaymaking. For one thing it might
accommodate lighthouses; and some landed families—a mere
handful, it is true—found a profitable trade in lighthouse-
keeping in the early decades of the nineteenth century. Lord
Braybrooke of Audley End and Coke of Holkham both operated
lighthouses, the one at Wintertoness and Orfordness, and the
other at Dungeness, holding them on lease from the Crown, and
collecting tolls from passing vessels at the chief ports. Lord
Braybrooke's net annual proceeds for the years 1823–5 were
£12,359, £13,479 and £14,345 respectively, in return for which
he paid the Crown £120 a year. After 1826 his lease was renewed on condition that it lapse in 1849 and that the net annual
proceeds until then be shared equally with the Crown. A somewhat similar arrangement was made by Coke in 1828; in that
year, the last of the old lease, the revenue from his lighthouse
amounted to £5,861.[136]

For another thing, land on the water's edge might accommodate docks which grew with the growth of commerce and industry: as the third Duke of Northumberland himself observed
in 1845, 'since the introduction of Steam Navigation, I am well
aware of the value which ground may now have acquired in the

Vicinity of a Harbour'.[137] In the fifties his successor lent £10,000 to the commissioners of the Northumberland Docks. Prior to the building of the docks it was said that the Duke's land along the Tyne accommodated fourteen shipping places for coal, 'constituting in fact the most important shipping places on the Tyne, about 900,000 Tons of coals being shipped here annually', the Duke's annual rental being about £1,900 a year.[138] The Earl of Yarborough was interested in the Grimsby Docks. Still other landowners, usually owners of mineral land built their own: the Marquess of Bute at Cardiff; Lord Londonderry at Seaham; and the Dukes of Devonshire and Buccleuch at Barrow-in-Furness.[139]

In putting land to these various uses so far described—railways and docks, mines and towns—landowners fell into two classes: the first and by far the larger class, the rent receiver; the second, the entrepreneur, who mined his coal, or made iron, or planned and built railways and harbours, or did all of these things together. It might profit us to take a closer look at two examples of the entrepreneurial class: the seventh Duke of Devonshire and the third Marquess of Londonderry.

The Duke of Devonshire's estates and enterprises were more varied and farflung than were Londonderry's. As Earl of Burlington he had owned estates in Lancashire and Sussex; on his accession to the dukedom in 1858 he acquired estates in Derbyshire, Yorkshire and Ireland. He had more houses, he once confessed, than he knew what to do with: Compton Place, Chatsworth, Hardwick Hall, Bolton Abbey, Holker, Lismore Castle, and Devonshire House in London. Apart from farms he had on his estates a bathing resort at Eastbourne and a spa at Buxton; collieries and lead mines in Derbyshire; lead mines in Yorkshire; slate quarries, iron mines, railways and other enterprises in Lancashire.[140] The most spectacular development, however, was at Barrow in Lancashire's Furness peninsula. Barrow has had its historians who have amply and admirably chronicled its growth.[141] A few paragraphs here will suffice to indicate its main outlines. It was the scene of the Duke's most active entrepreneurship.

Before the building of the Furness railway, Barrow was a 'quiet little sea-side village' comprising a handful of fishermen's cottages, some farm houses and buildings, a couple of public houses, and jetties to which slates and iron ore were brought for shipment; [142] lying along the narrow channel which separated the Furness peninsula from the island of Walney, Barrow had the makings of a good harbour, the island serving as a natural break-water. In 1842 the Duke noted in his diary that he had an iron pit in the vicinity as well as slate quarries, and that he was looking about for 'space for wharf etc. if a railway is carried there from the iron and slate works'.[143] The advantages of Barrow as a har-bour had long been apparent to Furness merchants and ore-dealers, as had the conveniences of a mineral railway; and the coming of the Furness railway in 1846 was very much to be ex-pected. A director from the beginning, the Duke of Devonshire became chairman in 1848 as well as a member of the newly estab-lished Barrow Harbour Commission.[144]

In the next dozen years or so Barrow came to national promi-nence. On the Duke's property in 1850 the Park Mine was dis-covered, 'the second greatest haematite ore deposit in British history'. Impressive as it was, the working of this mine would not have been of such consequence to Barrow if it had not been for the radical new departures undertaken by the mine's lessees, Messrs Schneider and Hannay, who erected four blast-furnaces in 1859, adding three more in 1862 and a further three in 1866. At the same time it was decided to establish a steel works, em-ploying the new Bessemer process, for which the Park Mine ore was ideally suited. As late as 1862 Furness was still largely a supplier of raw material for iron and steel production elsewhere. But in 1866 the formation of the Barrow Haematite Steel Co, 'the second largest firm of its type in Britain', second to John Browns in Sheffield, ended this subordination. According to Barrow's historian, the Haematite Steel Co was 'a Furness Railway-Cavendish organism', with the Duke of Devonshire and his family taking a leading place among its directors and investors, along with Messrs Schneider and Hannay and others.[145]

The growth of Barrow in the seventies had a feverish quality. When the Iron and Steel Institute met there in 1874, *The Times* remarked editorially that the growth of the town was not unlike that of Chicago.[146] Its population almost doubled in the first five years of the decade. The construction of docks in the late sixties

—the first appropriately named the Duke of Devonshire Dock—
had helped make Barrow a considerable port. The iron and steel
works had become the largest Bessemer works in the country.
New industries came into the town during the seventies—a jute
and flax works, as well industries to make machinery, railway
rolling stock, and even ships. In 1880 the largest iron ship,
second only to the *Great Eastern*, was being laid down in Barrow.
In most of these enterprises the Duke of Devonshire took a
leading part.[147]

In his diary for 1869 the Duke entered the following account
of 'a very busy day, of almost constant occupation':[148]

> I attended the monthly meeting of the Royal Agricultural Society
> which lasted nearly three hours though there was no business of
> much importance. I then went to Currey's [his lawyers] where
> we had meetings of the Furness Gas and Water Co, and of the
> Furness Railway Directors and of the Barrow Steel Directors. At
> the Furness meeting we had a good deal of discussion about the
> Belfast steamer and the question of improving the present paddle
> wheel boats or substituting screw steamers. . . At the Steel meet-
> ing we sanctioned outlay of various kinds which including a new
> furnace will amount to £37,000, the furnace alone costing
> £10,000. . . I afterwards saw Mr Purdon with reference to the
> Fernway and Lismore line.

What did such activity signify? It fitted very well what we
know of the Duke. He was an Evangelical—an admirer of Wilber-
force—and moral purpose, austerity, industry and simplicity sat
close to his inner nature, in spite of the outward trappings of
great wealth. He never missed a meeting of the Ulverston Board
of Guardians, of which he was chairman, as he never missed a
meeting of the Furness railway directors. Moreover, he was an
intellectual, first Smith's Prizeman at Cambridge and Chancellor
of the University of London at the age of twenty-eight. Perhaps
the pyramiding of industrial enterprises provided that intellectual excitement which, according to *The Times*, may have been at
the bottom of his success as a shorthorn breeder.[149] At the same
time, although he was much more assiduous than his fellow
nobleman and investor, the Duke of Buccleuch, in keeping his
eye on Barrow affairs, he was himself dependent to no small degree on his advisers, agents and associates. It would seem, for

example, that the enthusiasm of his lawyer and auditor, Benjamin Currey, carried him into the Furness railway enterprise at the very start—an enterprise to which he was not markedly attached for some years.[150] Nor can we conceive him undertaking the establishment of the Barrow Haematite Co without the cooperation of Messrs Schneider and Hannay. In short, Barrow was neither the singlehanded creation of the Duke of Devonshire nor the working-out of a vision entertained by him from the 1840s onwards. If there was vision, it grew only gradually, strengthened probably by the need to establish the Cavendish family fortunes more securely, a need which he came to understand better when he took over the bulk of the estates in 1858 and which called up inner resources such as few noblemen in his day could muster.[151]

Seaham was by contrast a singlehanded effort, in the sense that Lord Londonderry had no associates like Devonshire's fellow investors in the various Barrow enterprises. Lord Charles Stewart, brother of Castlereagh, and later third Marquess of Londonderry, married the heiress Frances Anne Vane Tempest in 1819, she aged nineteen and he forty. The lady brought to her marriage ancestral properties in county Durham to which were attached valuable collieries on the River Wear. Two years later the Londonderrys purchased the Seaham estate in the same county from the father-in-law of the poet Byron, Sir Ralph Milbanke.[152]

Byron described Seaham as 'this dreary coast [upon which] we have nothing but county meetings and shipwrecks'.[153] But both his father-in-law and Lord Londonderry saw something else there, namely the opportunity it afforded to provide a seaport for coal shipments. The Londonderry coal at Rainton and Pittington was carried to staithes at Penshaw on the Wear, then to Sunderland where it was reloaded on to seagoing colliers. Londonderry—or his agent—estimated that shipment via the Wear and Sunderland cost him £10,000 a year. At Seaham, however, as he explained to his brother,[154]

> there is a fair prospect hereafter of making a better harbour of our own than Sunderland for a large export of our coals, bringing them by railway of four miles from our freehold collieries to the port, and supplying all this coast free of port duty of Sunderland

with our own coals, giving us thus an increased channel for our supply without the tax of six shillings a chaldron, which we pay now at Sunderland for port duties.

Whether through financial stringency or the distraction of other pursuits—Londonderry was an ambassador and politician —the plans for Seaham gathered dust until the late 1820s, when the construction of a harbour finally began. The original plan, drawn up for Sir Ralph Millbanke, had been to extend 'certain of the inlets in the high lands on the coast . . . and [to shelter] them by piers on the rocks without'. Londonderry asked his engineers to design something bigger, and an inner and outer harbour were constructed, the former being completed in July 1831. With a colliery railway in operation, and over a hundred houses erected for a new town, the first vessel was loaded 'amidst the cheers of an immense concourse of spectators'.[155] It was said that no private harbour of such size had been built with such speed; and probably Seaham had no match until the Marquess of Bute built his docks at Cardiff.[156] Londonderry's spirits were high in November 1831 when he wrote to his friend, Lord Burghersh, that 'Seaham Harbour promises well'.[157] Two years later he was utterly despondent: 'Our Commercial distress in this Mining District', he wrote to Peel, 'becomes so great, that it has determined me to part with my Corregios and my collection of pictures.'[158]

But the Corregios remained on Lord Londonderry's walls. A report on his finances two years later revealed no serious cause for gloom. Londonderry's agricultural rents amounted to £18,047 and colliery returns were estimated at £40,000. Indebtedness was £106,900, and it was proposed to purchase the North Pittington colliery, thus adding a further £92,500 to the debt. By the Londonderry marriage settlements, which had been written in the Court of Chancery, a portion of the debt was redeemed annually.[159] Although Londonderry, as we have seen, complained to Peel in the forties that he was threatened with ruin by the railways' opening the inland coalfields, he was also gleefully assuring Peel that, having set aside the monopoly arrangements among the great collieries, he was underselling the Lambton coal. 'I am trying all I can to get a living', he reported in 1845, 'by double Quantities and greatly reduced prices.'[160] Two years

D

later, 'the Coal Trade never better', he exulted.[161] Although one might still gather in 1849 from a further letter to Peel that his enterprises hung in the balance,[162] shortly before he died in 1853 even Londonderry publicly intimated that Seaham had been a sound investment. In the 1840s enlarged accommodations at Seaham brought an annual profit of £5,000 from port tolls.[163] Under his wife's management after his death, four blast-furnaces were built and the remaining debt on the estate was paid off. One must conclude that Lord Londonderry's venture in the coal trade had done very well.[164]

What are we to make of Lord Londonderry the colliery entrepreneur? Plainly he was a very different man from the Duke of Devonshire. Londonderry had been bred a soldier from the early age of fifteen and had gained a well-earned reputation for gallantry. But his bravery was matched by conceit and silliness which earned him a different reputation in political life: according to the *Spectator* he was 'the Sibthorpe of the Upper House'.[165] Devonshire had been neither a soldier nor an eccentric in politics. Moreover, where Devonshire strenuously avoided the life of the royal court and preferred private retirement, Londonderry relished gold sticks, gorgeous uniforms, a duel or two, and the Asiatic glories of tsarist palaces.[166] Neither Devonshire's moral austerity nor his intellectuality touched Londonderry. He thus seems something of an incongruous figure to have presided over one of the great colliery estates of the nineteenth century. Yet as Henry Morton once conceded—and Morton wasted little time in commending his noble competitor—Londonderry was indefatigable. Like most great landowners he never lost sight of the need to maintain if not enhance the social eminence of his family. Perhaps it appealed to his soldier's instinct to contest the leadership of the coal trade with his Whig neighbours, the Lambtons. Moreover, he had the advice of John Buddle—of which there was no better in the North. It was Buddle who urged him to take up the Seaham project in the beginning.[167] And finally there was Frances Anne who, it may be, had more flair for business than her husband. So Henry Morton thought. She had shown an unusual interest in her collieries at the age of sixteen; in her widowhood she brought her husband's projects to a successful completion.

In this brief conclusion, it might be profitable to note certain general consequences for the landed society of the growth of industrialism and the city. Whatever the qualities of the landed entrepreneur in the nineteenth century, and however remarkable his achievements, his numbers in the course of the century became fewer. In the direct administration of non-agricultural enterprise, as in politics, the landed society retreated. Its economic position became increasingly that of a rentier. This waning has been noted in the coal trade of the North. It was not unknown in other coalfields. And a parallel decline has also been found in the making of iron and steel.[168] However much the landed society appreciated its wealth, however prudent and sensible the management of its affairs, it would seem to have lost an earlier confidence in and a taste for direct managerial effort involving competition and innovation. Perhaps these had never been very great by modern standards, as the historian of management in the Industrial Revolution has argued,[169] but they cannot be dismissed altogether.

This decline of landed entrepreneurship, however, did not prevent a great increase in the wealth of the landed society. In 1876 *The Times* in remarking on land values—which it described as 'our many composite forms of half-agricultural, half-manufacturing value'—observed that 'we think it would be impossible to find a single acre not worth more today than before the introduction of railways'.[170] Sir James Caird also remarked on the general increase in land values in the sixties and seventies owing to the growth of towns and industry, estimating it as 'three hundred and thirty one millions sterling in these twenty years, at a cost [to the landed interest] which probably has not exceeded sixty millions'.[171]

In particular cases one is struck by the increase in gross incomes and the reduction of debt. Of those estates which in the first forty years or so of the nineteenth century acquired or inherited debts, it seems to have been the case that those estates with non-agricultural sources of wealth were more likely to reduce indebtedness without selling large blocks of land than were purely agricultural estates. Sir James Graham's debt at Netherby, an agricultural estate, went unchanged in the nineteenth century. So did the Fitzwilliam indebtedness on their Milton estate, also

an agricultural estate, which went to a younger son in 1857. On
the other hand, the Fitzwilliams's West Riding estate with its
collieries did far better. Or there was the case of the Russells who
removed a sizeable debt in about fifteen years, providing at the
same time for a large expenditure on agricultural improvements.
This was done partly by careful management, partly by fresh
sources of income from West Country copper mines and partly
from forced sales of land in London to the London & Birmingham
Railway and to the Government.[172]

How large a proportion of the wealth of the English landed
society eventually came from non-agricultural sources it is impossible to say with any precision. It is unlikely, however, that
more than a handful of estates in the first half of the nineteenth
century derived a half or more of their gross incomes from such
sources. A few of the great London landlords like the Russells
and the Cavendish-Bentincks did. So did that great canal-owner,
the Duke of Bridgewater, and his successors. And the grandees
of the northern coal trade like the Lambtons were outrunning
their agricultural rents in years of good colliery returns as early as
the 1820s. Otherwise in the period 1815–46, when the Corn
Laws were being debated, the economic interest of English
landowners was very largely rooted in agriculture. In the second
half of the century this handful undoubtedly · increased in
number, with the development of the inland coal and iron-ore
fields and with the growth of provincial towns and suburban
London. Many estates acquired a non-agricultural income which
if not half their gross income was in all likelihood a very useful
addition especially in the agricultural depression of the late
nineteenth century. Such vague general statements will have to
satisfy us until further research is done in estate account books.

More information is also needed on the extent to which the
landed society invested in stocks and bonds in the nineteenth
century. It would seem that for the greater part of that time this
was not much done. But from the 1860s onwards there is evidence
on some estates, for example, the second Earl of Leicester's, for
significant stock-market investments. It is not altogether clear in
this case where the money came from—possibly from a tapering-
off of investment in farming and land purchase. But whatever
its origin, the Earl's investment in stocks was sizeable enough by

1890 to compensate him for the drastic decline in his agricultural rents.[173] It was a favourite theme of conservative critics of the landed society in the late nineteenth century, for example, the historian Lecky, that the landed aristocracy was being converted into a rootless and restless plutocracy. But this social criticism still waits for statistical verification.

One point remains: the price which the landed society paid for the growth of its wealth through non-agricultural means. Obviously a severe price was paid in the long run, in the sense that a society came into being in which the political ascendancy of landowners was extinguished and their social ascendancy diminished. Walter Bagehot in the 1860s described this process in general terms as a loss of aristocratic visibility. A successful aristocracy, he explained, imposed on the popular imagination.[174] In the 1860s however, this was becoming increasingly difficult:[175]

> Every day our companies, our railways, our debentures, our shares, tend more and more to multiply these *surroundings* of the aristocracy, and in time they will hide it. And while this undergrowth has come up, the aristocracy have come down. They have less means of standing out than they used to have. Their power is in their theatrical exhibition, in their state. But society is every day becoming less stately.

Yet even when Bagehot was writing these words, the political power of the landed society seemed as impressive as ever, its finances sounder than ever. The process of aristocratic decline was one of slow, at times almost imperceptible erosion, and although the Industrial Revolution contributed to it, this took a long time in showing itself plainly. That only a few landowners viewed the coming of the railways as the work of the devil is therefore not surprising.[176]

NOTES

1 G. Broderick, *English Land and English Landlords* (1881), 165.
2 The legal history is put straight by L. Stone, *The Crisis of the Aristocracy, 1558–1641* (Oxford 1965), 338–9.
3 T. S. Ashton and J. Sykes, *The Coal Industry of the Eighteenth Century* (Manchester 1929), 1.

4   Stone, *Crisis of Aristocracy*, 336.
5   Ibid, 348, 363.
6   Ashton and Sykes, *Coal Industry of the Eighteenth Century*, 2.
7   H. Pollins, 'The Finances of the Liverpool and Manchester Railway', *Econ Hist Rev*, 2S, 5 (1952).
8   *Proceedings of the Committee of the House of Commons on the Liverpool and Manchester Railroad Bill* (1826), passim; G. S. Veitch, *The Struggle for the Liverpool and Manchester Railway* (Liverpool 1930), passim.
9   Sir H. Maxwell, *The Creevey Papers* (1903), vol 2, 86–7. Creevey was also a member of the parliamentary committee on the Liverpool & Manchester.
10   British Museum, Add MSS, 38746, f 51, J. Gladstone to W. Huskisson, 14 Nov 1824.
11   A valuable account of the part played by the Bridgewater trustees is to be found in F. C. Mather, 'The Duke of Bridgewater's Trustees and the Coming of the Railways', *Transactions of the Royal Historical Society*, 5S, 14 (1964).
12   Ellesmere Brackley MSS (NRO), volume entitled 'General State of His Grace the Duke of Bridgewater's Navigation Colliery Lime and Farm Concerns in Lancashire and Cheshire 1759–1835'.
13   Sir J. Rennie, *Autobiography* (1875), 237.
14   Mather, 'Duke of Bridgewater's Trustees'.
15   For Loch's opinions on canals see D. Spring, *The English Landed Estate in the Nineteenth Century: Its Administration* (Baltimore 1963), 93–4.
16   Mather confirms Veitch's shrewd guess about Huskisson's role; see Veitch, *Struggle for the Liverpool and Manchester Railway*, 51.
17   Mather, 'Duke of Bridgewater's Trustees'.
18   For the financing of the London & Birmingham, see Parliamentary Papers (hereafter PP), 13 (1839), *Minutes of Evidence before the Committee on the London and Birmingham Railway Bill*, appendix 32.
19   London & Birmingham MSS, Minutes of the London Board, 18 Feb 1831. I consulted these papers before they were transferred to the British Transport Commission Archives.
20   Ibid, Minutes of Birmingham Board, 28 Jan 1831; 5 May 1832.
21   Ibid, Minutes of London Board, 2 Dec 1831.
22   J. Wake, *Northampton Vindicated* (Northampton 1935), 9–10; see also London & Birmingham Railway Collection, Goldsmiths' Library, University of London.
23   London & Birmingham MSS, Minutes of the London Board, 9 May 1832.
24   Ibid, Minutes of Birmingham Board, 28 Jan 1831.
25   Ibid, Minutes of the London Board, 13 May 1831; 11 Dec 1830.
26   Ibid, Minutes of London Board, 18 July 1832.

27 Printed Reports of the London & Birmingham Railway, July 1832.

28 London & Birmingham MSS, Minutes of the London Board, 10 Oct 1832.

29 Ibid, Minutes of Birmingham Board, 8 May 1833.

30 Hastings MSS (Huntington Library, California) Box 150, E. Mammatt to Lord Hastings, 25 Oct 1832.

31 London & Birmingham MSS, Minutes of the Birmingham Board, 8 May 1833.

32 Ibid, Minutes of the Committee of Management, 7 Dec 1832; 9 Mar 1833.

33 Ibid, Minutes of London Board, 21 Feb 1831.

34 J. Francis, *A History of the English Railway: its Social Relations and Revelations 1820–1845* (1851), vol 1, 189; 'Railway Morals and Railway Policy', *Edinburgh Review* (Oct 1854); H. G. Lewin, *Early British Railways* (1925), 22.

35 W. T. Jackman, *The Development of Transportation in Modern England* (1916), vol 2, 499.

36 London and Birmingham MSS, Minutes of London Board, 21 Feb 1831; 19 Jan 1832.

37 Printed Reports, 31 Dec 1836.

38 Champions of the railways usually made much of the Petre case. For the details see Francis, vol 1, 256–8; also decision in Vice-Chancellor's court, 1838. The MSS Minutes of the Eastern Counties Railway throw little new light on what Francis described as a case 'almost unparalleled in the history of railway adventure'.

39 PP, 18 (1845) *Report from the Select Committee (H. of L.) on the Practicability and Expediency of establishing some Principles of Compensation to be made to the Owners of Real Property*, evidence of E. Driver (for the Great Western), of J. Clutton (for the South-Eastern), and of J. Swift (for the Grand Junction).

40 H. Pollins, 'A Note on Railway Constructional Costs 1825–1850', *Economica*, 19 (1952). John R. Kellett's valuable study, *The Impact of Railways on Victorian Cities* (London & Toronto 1969), appeared after this paper was written. Kellet has concluded that Pollins's article, although 'a valuable corrective to the wilder stories of "blackmail" land prices, leans in the direction of understating the quantities of investment capital consumed in land purchase'. He has also concluded that small landowners were likely to be more rapacious in their claims than large landowners, and that lawyers were not immune from making a good thing out of railway business. See Kellett, *Impact of Railways*, 427, 158, 270.

41 See Jersey MSS (MRO) 510/259, Mr Trumper to Lord Jersey, 26 Sept 1834. It is plain from this letter that London & Birmingham negotiations served as a guide.

42   H. Spencer, *An Autobiography* (New York 1904), 325.
43   Bedford MSS (Bedford Estate Office, Bloomsbury, London), Duke of Bedford to C. Haedy, 8 Nov 1845.
44   O. J. Vignoles, *Life of C. B. Vignoles* (1889), 269.
45   Sir J. Clapham, *An Economic History of Modern Britain* (Cambridge 1926), vol 1, 86.
46   A. K. Hamilton Jenkin, *News from Cornwall* (1951), W. Jenkin to Hon C. B. Agar, 23 May 1806; J. Simmons, *The Maryport and Carlisle Railway* (1947), passim; Maryport & Carlisle Railway MSS, Minutes of Committee, 2 Nov 1837; W. Mc G. Gradon, *Furness Railway: its Rise and Development* (1946), 7; Furness Railway MSS, Minutes of Committee, 19 Jan 1857; Wentworth Woodhouse Muniments (SCL); *Railway Times*, 17 Aug 1839; Sir J. E. Eardley-Wilmot, *Reminiscences of the Late Thomas Assheton Smith* (1902), passim.
47   Sneyd MSS (ULK), R. Sneyd to Mr Peake, 24 Oct 1840.
48   Lambton MSS (Lambton Estate Office, Co Durham).
49   Sefton MSS (LRO), correspondence of C. P. Grenfell with Lord Sefton, 1844–5.
50   J. D. Marshall, *Furness and the Industrial Revolution* (Barrow-in-Furness, 1958), 177. See also S. Pollard and J. D. Marshall, 'The Furness Railway and the Growth of Barrow', *Journal of Transport History*, 1 (1953), where the Earl of Lonsdale is referred to as an original investor.
51   Chatsworth MSS (Chatsworth House, Derbyshire), Duke of Devonshire to W. E. Gladstone, 20 Feb 1865.
52   F. M. L. Thompson, *English Landed Society in the Nineteenth Century* (1963), 257.
53   Lord Derby continued to oppose the railway even after the Liverpool & Manchester surveyors altered the line to avoid his estate.
54   Netherby MSS (on microfilm, reel one, Johns Hopkins University Library), Sir J. Graham to J. Yule, 6 June 1825.
55   See J. T. Ward, 'West Riding Landowners and the Railways', *Journ Trans Hist*, 4 (1960).
56   It is instructive to scan the catalogue of the deeds of sale (with sale prices) in the Derby MSS in the Lancashire Record Office.
57   B. Disraeli, *Sybil* (World's Classics edn), 127. For numerous other examples of landowners profiting from railways, and in general for a valuable account of landowners and railways, see Thompson, *English Landed Society*, 256–63.
58   British Museum, Add MSS, 38758, f 232, J. E. Denison to W. Huskisson, 10 Sept 1830.
59   Jenkin, *News from Cornwall*, 7.
60   'The Recollections of Loveday Sarah Gregor', typescript MSS (CCRO), 131.

61 The Duke's mines were on the Devon side of the Tamar, but were considered Cornish.

62 PP, 16 (1856), *Report from the Select Committee on Rating of Mines*, 131.

63 T. Spargo, *Mines of Cornwall and Devon* (1865), 50; PP, 41 (1890–1), *Second Report of Royal Commission on Mining Royalties*, 155–6.

64 PP, 16 (1856), 66, 112, 132; Spargo, *Mines of Cornwall and Devon*, 158; Bedford MSS, Report for 1845.

65 J. Rowe, *Cornwall in the Age of the Industrial Revolution* (Liverpool 1953), 324. These figures do not adequately reflect the subsidiary nature of Cornish tin to copper before the 1850s, nor do they indicate that large fortunes were made chiefly from copper. See D. B. Darton, *A History of Tin Mining and Smelting in Cornwall* (Truro 1967), passim.

66 PP, 16 (1856), 29–30; Bedford MSS, Report for 1864.

67 PP, 16 (1856), 141; PP, 41 (1893–4), *Final Report of Royal Commission on Mining Royalties*, 12; D. B. Darton, *A History of Copper Mining in Cornwall and Devon* (Truro 1968), ch 4.

68 The Duke leased his Derbyshire property at a royalty of one-thirteenth; see PP, 16 (1856), 187–8. His Yorkshire property is described in PP, 11 (1857), *Report of Select Committee on Rating of Mines*, 115ff.

69 A. Raistrick and B. Jennings, *A History of Lead Mining in the Pennines* (1965), 219.

70 PP, 11 (1857), 1–17.

71 Ibid, 115ff; see also A. Raistrick, 'The Lead Mines of Upper Wharfedale', *Yorkshire Bulletin of Economic and Social Research*, 5 (1953).

72 PP, 11 (1857), 1–17; B. W. Richardson, *Thomas Sopwith* (1891), 296–308.

73 PP, 41 (1893–4), 12; see also A. Raistrick, *Two Centuries of Industrial Welfare: The London (Quaker) Lead Company 1692–1905* (1938), 123.

74 'Iron—Its Uses and Manufacture', *Edinburgh Review* (July 1862).

75 English Law Reports, Paddock v Forrester, 133 (1842); Sneyd MSS, Lord Granville to R. Sneyd, 15 Aug 1848; PP, 12 (1857), *Report of Select Committee on Duchy of Lancaster* (Bertollacci's Petition), evidence of Lord Granville; PP, 11 (1857), 205–10.

76 'Iron—Its Uses and Manufacture', *Edinburgh Review* (July 1862).

77 PP, 11 (1857), 122–7, 132.

78 PP, 18 (1871), iii, *Report of the Royal Commission on the Coal Trade*, ii; S. G. Checkland, *The Rise of Industrial Society in England 1815–1885* (1964), 157.

79   Quoted in Earl of Crawford and Balcarres, 'Haigh Cannel' (Manchester Statistical Society 1933).

80   W. Fordyce, *A History of Coal, Coke, Coal Fields* (1860), 5.

81   PP, 15 (1842), *First Report of the Children's Employment Commission*, 6ff.

82   L. Simond, *Journal of a Tour and Residence in Great Britain* (New York 1815), vol 2, 75.

83   British Museum, Add MSS, 40599, f 112, Lord Londonderry to Sir R. Peel, 31 July 1847.

84   A useful list of colliery owners is to be found in J. Kirsopp, *The Northumberland and Durham Coal Field* (Newcastle-upon-Tyne 1908); for a list of owners in 1800, see T. V. Simpson, 'Old Mining Records and Plans', *Transactions of the Institution of Mining Engineers*, 81 (1930–1).

85   PP, 9 (1838), *Report from Select Committee on Church Leases*, 95.

86   PP, 20 (1850), *First Report from the Episcopal and Capitular Revenues Commissioners*, 1.

87   PP, 36 (1890), *Report on Mining Royalties*, 5–7.

88   Ashton and Sykes, *Coal Industry of the Eighteenth Century*, 2–3.

89   PP, 8 (1830), *Report of Select Committee on Coal Trade*, 31.

90   Ibid, 57; also P. M. Sweezy, *Monopoly and Competition in the English Coal Trade 1550–1850* (Cambridge, Mass 1938), 22–31.

91   PP, 8 (1830), 270–1.

92   R. W. Brandling, a Tyneside owner, considered this sort of association between lessor and lessee rare; see PP, 8 (1830), 264.

93   Alnwick Castle MSS, Alnwick Castle, Northumberland, Business Minutes, 28 May 1861, 24 July 1848.

94   Ibid, Accounts and Business Minutes.

95   Ibid, Business Minutes, 20 Sept 1852, 3 Nov 1851, 27 Dec 1851. See also Spring, *English Landed Estate*, 125–6.

96   Countess of Airlie, *Lady Palmerston and Her Times* (1922), 126.

97   D. Spring, 'The Earls of Durham and the Great Northern Coal Field, 1830–1880', *Canadian Historical Review*, 33 (1952); PP, 8 (1830), 57.

98   D. Spring, 'Agents to the Earls of Durham in the Nineteenth Century', *Durham University Journal*, 54 (1962). Since this article was published, I have learned that more Stephenson letters have been found.

99   Lambton MSS, H. Morton to Lord Lambton, 4 May 1834, 10 July 1839, 16 June 1838.

100 Lambton MSS, 'Comparative Account of the Profits of the Collieries 1842–8'. In my article, 'The Earls of Durham and the Great Northern Coal Field, 1830–80', the figure for colliery profits for 1847 is incorrect: £19,034, not £11,695.

101 British Museum Add MSS, 40543, f 171, Lord F. Egerton to Sir R. Peel, 25 April 1844.

102 Ibid, 40568, f 378, Lord Londonderry to Sir R. Peel, 9 June 1845.

103 Lambton MSS, 'Comparative Account of the Profits of the Collieries, 1842–8'.

104 Ibid, Henry Morton to Lord Durham, 25 Sept 1851.

105 Alnwick Castle MSS, Business Minutes, 5 Nov 1853.

106 Lambton MSS, Henry Morton to Lord Durham, 8 April 1853; Spring, 'The Earls of Durham'.

107 PP, 8 (1830), 251; Lambton MSS, H. Morton to Lord Durham, 21 Nov 1835.

108 *Private Acts*, 13 & 14 Vict c 18. For other examples of land-owners who lost their entrepreneurial nerve, see Thompson, *English Landed Society* 264–6.

109 E. Ashley, *Life and Correspondence of Henry John Temple, Viscount Palmerston* (1879), vol 1, 488, Lord Palmerston to his brother, 16 March 1845.

110 Quoted in H. J. Dyos, *Victorian Suburb: A Study of the Growth of Camberwell* (Leicester 1961), 87.

111 A. F. Weber, *The Growth of Cities in the Nineteenth Century* (New York 1899), 40–57.

112 Clapham, *Economic History*, vol 1, 536.

113 R. W. Jeffery (ed), *Dyott's Diary* (1907), vol 2, 53; *The Autobiography and Memoirs of Benjamin Robert Haydon*, ed Tom Taylor (New York 1926), vol 2, 557; L. Strachey and R. Fulford (eds), *The Greville Memoirs* (1938), vol 5, 218.

114 Lord Stanmore, *Sidney Herbert, Lord Herbert of Lea* (1906), vol 2, 292; English Law Reports, 67, Dale v Hamilton; Clifton MSS (LRO) DDC1 1235, Mr Fair to Colonel Clifton, 19 March 1869.

115 PP, 20 (1850), 258.

116 H. W. Singer, 'An Index of Urban Land Rents and House Rents in England and Wales 1845–1913', *Econometrica*, 9 (1941). Singer notes that his figures represent 'a "functional income" of urban land which does not necessarily coincide with the income of the legal owners of urban land'; none the less such figures do serve to indicate orders of magnitude. See also Kellett, *Impact of Railways*, 392, where the author usefully distinguishes land values in the central city from those in the 'more favoured streets' and from those in the suburbs.

117 See F. Banfield, *The Great Landlords of London* (1888); and D. J. Olsen, *Town Planning in London: the Eighteenth and Nineteenth Centuries* (New Haven 1964).

118 Some account of the Fox (Lord Holland) property in Kensington is to be found in Earl of Ilchester, *Chronicles of Holland House 1820–1900* (New York 1938); of the de Crespigny property in PRO, C38/1464, *de Crespigny v Windsor*, and Dyos, *Victorian Suburb*; of the Evelyn property in PRO, C38/1465,

Evelyn v Evelyn. There is, of course, a vast amount of information about London landowners generally in PP (1886–91), *Reports from the Select Committees on Town Holdings.*

119   Sir William Clayton gave up his lease of the Duchy of Cornwall's Kensington estate in 1839; see *English Law Reports*, 132, *Simpson v Sir W. Clayton*, and Panshanger MSS (HRO), Box no 83, private papers of Lord Melbourne, 1838–9. For leases of land from the Bishop of London, see PP, 30 (1850), 1.

120   Bedford MSS, Report for 1873.

121   Ibid, Report for 1851. See also Spring, *English Landed Estate*, 41–3, and Olsen, *Town Planning*, ch 2.

122   Bedford MSS, Report for 1851. Figs Mead was the original name of Bedford New Town; Somers Town was the adjoining —and socially inferior—estate of Lord Southampton.

123   Ibid.

124   Ibid, Middlesex Rental Books.

125   Ibid, Reports for 1877 and 1861.

126   Ibid, Report for 1859.

127   Ibid, Report for 1880; see also PP, 66 (1886), *Return of Markets in England and Wales.*

128   See Thompson, *English Landed Society*, 268, for an estimate of provincial towns where the owners of ground rent were aristocratic. Kellett, *Impact of Railways*, passim, is also valuable for its running down of ground rent owners in London and provincial towns.

129   Building in the provincial towns and cities was often done on 999 year leases, as in parts of Lancashire, or on leases for three lives, as in the West Country. But there were also provincial towns—Liverpool, Birmingham, Sheffield, Oxford, Great Grimbsy, Yarmouth—where the shorter lease prevailed.

130   Much of this information is derived from an anonymous pamphlet, *The Retirement and Death of Michael Ellison, Esq, Steward of the Sheffield Estate of the Duke of Norfolk* (Sheffield 1861), reprinted from *The Sheffield and Rotherham Independent.* Information about Sheffield improvements is found in *Priv Acts*, 26 & 27 Vict c 7. Information about the Sheffield markets is found in PP, 22 (1888), *Report from Select Committee on Town Holdings*, 339; and PP, 53 (1888), *First Report of Royal Commission on Market Rights and Tolls*, 213ff.

131   Chatsworth MSS, Diary of 7th Duke of Devonshire, 15 June 1849.

132   M. A. Lower, *A Compenious History of Sussex:* 1 (1870), 148–9; PP, 22 (1888), 118.

133   *Saturday Review*, 23 July 1864.

134   PP, 22 (1888), 122.

135   Radnor MSS (KRO), Folkstone Estate Accounts.

136   PP, 33 (1833), *Lighthouses in the United Kingdom in the Hands of*

the Crown. The Cokes gave up their lease in the 1840s before it fell in, settling for a monetary compensation; see Holkham MSS, Agent's Letter Book, W. Baker to Sir W. Foster, 26 Feb 1844.

137 Alnwick Castle MSS, 3rd Duke of Northumberland to Master-General of Ordinance, 11 Feb 1845.

138 Ibid, Business Minutes, 3 July 1854, 27 Aug 1849.

139 The Dukes of Devonshire and Buccleuch were not sole owners of the Barrow Docks, but large investors in them.

140 See D. Spring, 'English Landed Estate in the Age of Coal and Iron', *Journal of Economic History*, 11 (1951).

141 J. D. Marshall and S. Pollard, 'The Furness Railway'.

142 F. Leach, *Barrow-in-Furness* (Barrow 1872), 16.

143 Chatsworth MSS, Diary of Duke of Devonshire, 10 Sept 1842.

144 Marshall, *Furness and the Industrial Revolution*, 94; Furness Railway MSS, Minutes of Committee, 12 Dec 1848.

145 Marshall, *Furness and the Industrial Revolution*, 203, 251-2.

146 *The Times*, 4 Sept 1874.

147 S. Pollard, 'Barrow-in-Furness and the Seventh Duke of Devonshire', *Econ Hist Rev*, 2S, 8 (1955).

148 Chatsworth MSS, Diary of Duke of Devonshire, 8 Dec 1869.

149 *The Times*, 21 Sept 1878.

150 Marshall, *Furness and the Industrial Revolution*, 177, 190. The Duke was ready to lease the line in 1849.

151 See his correspondence on the subject in Spring, 'English Landed Estate in the Age of Coal and Iron'.

152 Edith, Marchioness of Londonderry, *Frances Anne* (1958), 31-58, 69-70.

153 Quoted in Sir T. Eden, *Durham* (1952), vol 2, 416-17.

154 Marchioness of Londonderry, *Frances Anne*, 70.

155 E. Mackenzie and M. Ross, *An Historical, Topographical and Descriptive View of the County Palatine of Durham* (Newcastle-upon-Tyne 1834), vol 1, 374-80.

156 T. Y. Hall, *A Treatise on the Extent and Probable Duration of the Northern Coal Field* (Newcastle-upon-Tyne 1854), 15-16.

157 R. Weigall (ed), *Correspondence of Lord Burghersh* (1912), 270.

158 British Museum, Add MSS, 40403, f 301, Lord Londonderry to Sir R. Peel, 27 Dec 1833.

159 PRO C38/1624, *Marquess of Londonderry v Beckett*, 1835; *The Times*, 20 June 1818.

160 British Museum, Add MSS, 40572, f 417, Lord Londonderry to Sir R. Peel, 23 Aug 1845.

161 Ibid, 40599, f 410, Lord Londonderry to Sir R. Peel, 29 Nov 1847.

162 Ibid, 40609, f 351, Lord Londonderry to Sir R. Peel, 11 May 1849.

163 Marchioness of Londonderry, *Francis Anne*, 253, 228.

164   Ibid, ch 9; Sir A. Alison, *Some Account of my Life and Writings* (Edinburgh 1883), vol 2, 25.

165   *Spectator*, 14 Sept 1839.

166   Marchioness of Londonderry, *Frances Anne*, passim.

167   Ibid, 157.

168   C. Erickson, *British Industrialists: Steel and History* (Cambridge 1959), 17.

169   S. Pollard, *The Genesis of Modern Management: A Study of the Industrial Revolution in Great Britain* (1965), 25–30.

170   *The Times*, 8 Feb 1876.

171   Sir J. Caird, *The Landed Interest and Supply of Food* (1877), 98.

172   Professor J. D. Chambers in *Eng Hist Rev*, 80 (1965) in a review of my book *The English Landed Estate in the Nineteenth Century: Its Administration* rightly criticised my explanation of the removal of the Russell debt. My statement (p 39) that 'careful management and living under his income did for the duke of Bedford what sales of land or enhanced incomes did for other landowners' is incorrect.

173   Holkham MSS, Estate Accounts.

174   W. Bagehot, *The English Constitution* (World's Classics edn), 79.

175   Ibid, 83. What Bagehot does not explain—and is perhaps not explained even by Professor Thompson's brilliant study of English landed society—is the process by which the political *élan* of the landed aristocracy was enfeebled and ultimately extinguished by the growth of an alien society.

176   I am indebted to Mr W. Corbett and the Bedford Estate Office, His Grace the Duke of Northumberland, Sir Fergus Graham, Bt, Lord Lambton, MP, Earl Fitzwilliam and the Trustees of the Wentworth Woodhouse Estate, His Grace the Duke of Devonshire and the Earl of Leicester for permission to use their muniments.

2

Landowners and Mining

J. T. WARD

For centuries landowners have had a natural interest in the extraction of the minerals beneath their property. Monastic communities, medieval noblemen and *arriviste* Tudor gentry passed on a long tradition to Whig magnates, country squires and venturesome entrepreneurs in the eighteenth and nineteenth centuries.[1] In the early years of most mining districts both established and 'new' landed families exploited their minerals; but as the scale of operations grew most squires gradually abdicated their managerial roles, although a considerable number continued to run family concerns. Even the majority who contracted out of personal involvement nevertheless often retained close connections with the mining companies. Mineral receipts formed an important part of many estate incomes. But owners were affected by more than considerations of immediate profit. Life-tenants of entailed property were often subject to stringent legal obligations to their successors. Social, sporting, agricultural and personal factors variously affected decisions and attitudes and might provoke hostility to prospectors' proposals. Opposition was rare, however, and many owners remained vitally concerned with nineteenth-century mining undertakings.

Until the twentieth century British minerals, apart from gold and silver, belonged to the surface owner, who often initiated early winnings. Most pioneering ventures were inevitably small, but from 1726 the 'Grand Alliance' of George Bowes, Sir Henry Liddell and Edward Wortley started to dominate the great Durham coal royalties, setting a precedent for further efforts at regulation.[2] The sinking of deeper pits led to an extension of larger-scale concerns in the dominant North-Eastern coalfield, and the negotiation of mineral leases became an increasingly common task for landowners, agents and viewers.

Early leases often provided for payment in minerals, the amount generally depending upon the field's extent and quality and the state of the market. In Cornwall, where Stannary law and custom allowed wide freedom in working tin or unenclosed 'wastrel', the tinners' 'bounding' rights were heritable and the 'dish' (ranging from one-sixth in the eighteenth century to one-thirtysecond in the 1890s) was shared between 'bounders' and 'lords' until the nineteenth century.[3] Lead-mining districts also developed local traditions. Generally, the richer fields were charged at one-fifth, and owners insisted on regular working by specified labour forces. Such large proprietors as the Dukes of Devonshire and Earls of Pomfret undertook many expensive initial operations and encouraged lessees to develop lower beds by reducing charges or sharing risks. While major companies could organise every stage of production, small operators were obliged to use the owner's smelting mills and to sell their lead to his agent. Where small ventures were general, as in Derbyshire, the powerful smelting firms were merchant-dominated.[4]

Collieries also were for long leased for a proportion of the product, but by the eighteenth century money rents were general, although free coals for the owner were often demanded. Initial leases might stipulate only an annual 'fixed', 'certain' or 'dead' rent, the filling-up of disused pits, removal of waste and reparation for damage. As owners learned lessees' ways and their own power, they turned to charging on amounts mined (by royalties, lordships or tentale rents), and in the nineteenth century simple rents were rare, most being merged with royalties.[5] Ironstone leases required either annual or tonnage payments, and often proved extremely lucrative. Other minerals were treated similarly and sometimes paid well, if carefully sold. The second Earl of Breadalbane, for instance, joined a marble and slate partnership in 1746; twenty years later the third Earl let Easdale quarries for thirty-five years at £400 a year; and by 1842 the second Marquess was drawing £13,961 from his Perthshire lessees. But quarries were unpredictable: Joseph Pocklington-Senhouse of Netherhall in Cumberland received £18 in 1841, £627 in 1844 and £23 in 1846.[6]

Coal rents were usually determined in relation to probable output and development potentialities. In 1893 the Royal Commission on Mining Royalties reported that rents averaged £1-2 per surface acre, exceptionally rising to £5. Royalties were computed on tonnage raised, acreage worked or selling prices and amounts sold. Tonnage charges, varying with local custom, coal types, seams, values, costs and colliery allowances, were general in the North-East, Cumberland, South Wales and Scotland (where many leases took account of price-changes). Lancashire, Yorkshire and Midlands royalties were usually charged on acreage (standard or Cheshire) and often by foot thickness per acre.[7] The owner's natural concern was to secure maximum working with minimum disturbance. Consequently, increasingly complicated and sophisticated Victorian leases provided that lessees should pay for damage, restore agricultural land, repair buildings, fill or enclose disused pits, pay fixed rents for stated tonnages (whether mined or not, but with opportunities of recouping early under-production) and royalties on extra production, submit to lessors' inspection, accept liability for mismanagement and leave collieries in good order. In 1890 royalty rates ranged from 7d per ton in West Scotland to 3d in the Forest of Dean (where custom restricted the Crown's grant of 'gales' to 'free miners' of the hundred of St Briavels). Yorkshire, the North-West, South Staffordshire, the West, South Wales and East Scotland averaged 6d, North Staffordshire 5½d, Durham 5d, Nottinghamshire 4¾d and North Wales and Northumberland 4d. Earlier charges on smaller production had been considerably greater.

Further sums sometimes accrued to owners for transport and other facilities. The operator's 'liberty to make advance or to use . . . a road or way' was often costly. Underground wayleaves (as outstroke rents or tonnage or acreage payments) on the carriage of coals under the owners' land might be followed by shaft rents and surface wayleaves. Although some mining companies bought surface road-land, most paid rent or tonnage wayleave, with higher rates on 'foreign' minerals. Occasionally water-leave and airleave charges were exacted for drainage and ventilation. But

E

wayleaves of any sort affected comparatively few areas: in the
1890s about a third of the coal in the North-East and South
Wales and a quarter in Yorkshire was subject to such charges.

Legal difficulties often limited owners' granting powers: many
settled estates were restricted to twenty-one-year leases. But
from 1856 legislation allowed English, Welsh and Irish life-
tenants greater discretion. A series of Settled Estates [or Land]
Acts extended the principle in 1858, 1877, 1882 and 1890, eventually permitting sixty-year leases (while protecting beneficiaries
of settlements by providing for the capitalisation of some of the
mineral income). Although entail provisions were less onerous in
Scotland leases there were usually restricted to between twenty-
one and thirty years. Both legal systems retained some troublesome points, however. As R. W. Cooper pointed out, in the
1890s an English life-tenant stood to gain most by granting short
leases without further obligations. In any case, granting powers
remained rather doubtful.[8] Scots law was no easier. In 1845 the
tutors of Horatio Murray-Stewart of Broughton and Cally raised
a peculiar case. The previous laird had granted a six-month preliminary licence at Broughton for lordships of one-twelfth on
copper and one-seventh on lead, promising a twenty-one-year
lease. This option had fallen to the Kirkcudbrightshire Mining
Company, which claimed the lease and alleged that the charge
had been reduced to one-fourteenth. One advocate warned the
trustees against a grant, while another held that if the licence had
been used the agreement was binding.[9] In the event, from 1849
the estate's commissioner made several agreements.

The general liberalising of restrictions benefitted both owners
and tenants. And increasing numbers of seemingly rural mansions,
castles and palaces came to rest at least partially on coal. Sometimes they (literally) rested uneasily: in 1854 the Earl of Durham
had to spend £20,000 on filling the workings under Lambton
Castle, and further sums on major repairs; and mining under the
Lowther baronets' Yorkshire estate eventually caused the subsi-
dence of Swillington House.[10]

Undoubtedly, the magnificence of several nineteenth-century
landed families depended upon mineral incomes. In 1889 coal,

ironstone, iron ore and other metal royalties were estimated at
£4,665,043, with £216,000 for various wayleaves.[11] During the
coal booms of the late nineteenth and early twentieth centuries
some large owners received vast sums. The greatest of all, the
Ecclesiastical Commissioners, drew about £300,000 in 1888 and
£370,000 in 1917, with £41,000 from benefices where wayleaves
belonged to incumbents. Lord Durham received £58,911 from
royalties, wayleaves and railway rents in 1913 and £40,522, with
free coals, in 1918. Between 1916 and 1918 Lord Dynevor
charged an average of £7,543 royalty and £1,778 wayleave; in
1918 Lord Dunraven had £58,854 royalty and £5,516 wayleave;
the Duke of Hamilton's coal lordships produced an average of
£113,793 in 1908–17; the Duke of Northumberland had a gross
mineral income of £82,450 in 1918; and Lord Tredegar had
£74,397 (with £9,430 for wayleaves) per annum between 1912
and 1918, when the Marquess of Bute had £109,277 and
£6,495.[12] Such receipts were very rare; indeed, their recipients had
been selected for the often banal cross-examination of the Sankey
Commission. But the publicity at least revealed what was possible.

Negotiations over leases were often protracted by cautious
fencing. 'A friend and myself wish to take a lease of the iron ore
or ironstone belonging to the Lords of Swaledale, I mean your
employers', George Allison told James Littlefair, Sir George
Denys's mineral agent, in 1836,

> and to work and manufacture the same into iron. To do this, the
> most important article wanted is a good coalfield, and as the coal,
> such as it is, belongs to Lord Smith, it is highly prudent not to
> divulge this to any but your confidential friends.

Littlefair asked for a proposal and the partners' names. Allison
then offered no rent for the first year, £100 in the second, £200
in the third and £300 annually through the rest of a twenty-one-
year lease. When asked about duties he evasively preferred rents,
and on learning that leases were conditional on royalties he asked
what was wanted. A second duel began with Littlefair's insistence
on a positive proposal, which prompted Allison to request an
interview and eventually to suggest a twenty-one-year lease to his
four-member group with a tonnage royalty of 6d.[13] Denys pro-
longed the affair by demanding 5s.

Coalowners dealing with metallurgical firms often had a strong negotiating position. In 1826 the second Marquess of Bute's Cardiff man of business, G. P. Richards, was assailed by John Guest, the Dowlais ironmaster—who was 'in . . . a fury (for it was beyond rage)'. Political and economic controversy continued, but in 1847 John Clayton of Newcastle visited Cardiff and Merthyr and pointed out that Bute held the upper hand:

> Looking at the immense capitals [Guest and Alderman Thompson] have embarked in plant and machinery, the value of which is entirely dependent on the possession of your Lordship's mines, it may be safely assumed that, however decisively they may express themselves during the treaty and whatever manoeuvres of diplomacy they may adopt, they must ultimately come to an agreement with your Lordship on fair terms.

Clayton considered the rent policy reasonable: the coal was costly but good, while the iron was cheap—and as ore could be imported 'the sound policy . . . was to charge the *heavier* rent on the coal, which could not be dispensed with, and the lighter rent on the ironstone'.[14] With property in eight counties (116,668 acres paid £151,135 to the third Marquess in the seventies), the Butes were experienced owners. From 1830 to 1887 they spent huge sums on Cardiff docks; in Durham, with Miss Simpson of Bradley, they won and managed three collieries in the early nineteenth century; from the fifties the third Lord's trustees mined upper Rhondda coal, opening a new colliery in 1877, though the family took little interest in the district, apart from providing good housing; and on the great Ayrshire estate minerals were let to the Baird family and the Dalmellington Iron Company for £3,000 and £2,500 respectively in 1867. By 1918 the fourth Marquess was letting nearly 49,000 proved mineral acres to twenty-five undertakings.[15]

Such magnates as the Butes inevitably operated through a hierarchy of agents. But even small owners might enforce special terms. For example, in 1878 Sir Andrew Orr insisted that the Clackmannan Coal Company should prevent its colliers from keeping dogs and dismiss convicted poachers.[16] Nevertheless, even canny Scottish lairds could make mistakes. 'Carnbroe coal was let hurriedly by Mr Meiklam . . . in 1833, when the price of coals was very low, at a permanent lordship of 4d per cart of 13cwt, which was about one-eighth at that period, but the error was that one-eighth was not taken on the amount of sales, which would have given [him] his share of the advantage of a rise in price . . .'[17] The lesson was not lost on other Scottish landowners.

Troubles with under-paying lessees were gradually mastered, but owners only gradually and painfully learned how to avoid under-capitalised ventures. Furthermore, it was fatally easy for rural squires to treat new mineral receipts like farm rents. But 'a lease of coal', as B. P. Broomhead, an experienced businessman, asserted, 'was in effect not a lease at all, but a sale of part of the hereditament'.[18] Consequently, family lawyers warned young squires against the rash expenditure of non-recurrent mineral receipts. Thus in 1875 John Clark, QC, told twenty-three-year-old Sir George Clerk, eighth baronet of Penicuik, that 'the minerals which are now being raised at Loanhead, especially the iron, are not likely to last for a great number of years . . . There is a great quantity of good coal . . . but . . . the iron ore ought not to be looked upon as a source of *permanent income.*' The royalties might total £75,000 for iron and £25,000 for coal:

> during the working of the iron a very large increase of income would come to [Clerk], but it would not be permanent. Even if he received £5,000 a year in royalties it *would* or *might* then become exhausted. . . It would be right and prudent to consider the whole of the royalties . . . as so much capital.

Sir George's income from the Shotts Iron Company was in fact used on capital items, paying-off encumbrances and investments 'in good 4% securities'.[19] Such a strategy was fair to subsequent life-tenants and also avoided the hazards of undue reliance on an income which might fluctuate fantastically. The second Earl of Durham, an owner and lessor with an agricultural income of £27,000 and coal profits (excluding lessees' payments) of £52,000 in 1867, was one of several owners who faced rapid changes of fortune. Profits of £380,000 in 1873 were followed by a loss of £65,000 in 1876. The Lambton family sold out in 1896, by which time such aristocratic industrialists were already rare.[20]

Some prominent families were closely connected with mining and allied industries. 'Colliers we are and colliers we must ever remain', the sixth Earl of Balcarres told his grandson.[21] The extent of the family's dependence on minerals, and particularly on the Haigh cannel, was obvious: by 1879 only £7,152 were received from 10,549 acres in Aberdeenshire, Caermarthen and Westmorland, while 1931 Lancashire acres at Haigh Hall near Wigan yielded £31,763. The accident (through the sixth Earl's marriage to Elizabeth Dalrymple, the heiress of the Bradshaigh baronets, in 1780) of owning a small mineral property created a handsome income worthy of the double earldom of Crawford and Balcarres. But the 'accident' was carefully cultivated. After notable development of their cannel in the sixteenth and seventeenth centuries, the Bradshaighs latterly allowed their estate to run down, but the first Balcarres owner devoted all his energy to further exploitation of minerals, even extending his coal ownership at the expense of surface acres. From 1788 to 1835 the Earls ran the Haigh ironworks with less success; and they maintained a fleet of thirty-five boats and barges. But coal remained the 'root, basis and stamina' of their fortune; 'the trade of Coalmaster', as the energetic sixth Earl wrote, 'was their vocation'.[22]

In South Yorkshire the scientifically inclined second Marquess of Rockingham developed an eighteenth-century industrial empire of collieries, ironstone mines and blast-furnaces around his palace of Wentworth Woodhouse. From 1782 these ventures were continued and expanded by the Earls Fitzwilliam; the second (fourth Irish) Earl spent some £122,000 on nine small collieries between 1807 and 1820. The returns, from both estate-operated and tenanted concerns, were vast by any standard. Even in 1801 coal and ironstone receipts amounted to £4,214, and the Fitzwilliams' mineral income subsequently varied between £2,576 in 1831 and £87,743 in 1901. Gradually, however, the estate's immediate involvement was reduced. The ironworks were disposed of in 1849, and by the end of the century the fourth Earl's own collieries paid only £13,701.[23]

The scientific experiments of all aristocrats did not lead to such happy results. For instance, the ninth Earl of Dundonald, like Rockingham, tried to develop coal tar manufacture on his Perthshire estate at Culross Abbey. He subsequently suggested other chemical schemes but, dogged by heavy encumbrances and often rejected or cheated by possible allies, he made no fortune.[24] His son, another scientist, is more famous as a liberal admiral in the Royal and South American navies. Dundonald's failure largely resulted from lack of capital. Fitzwilliam's neighbours, the Dukes of Norfolk, suffered no such restraint. They were smaller owners than the fourth Earl, whose 115,743 acres in nine counties paid £138,801 (excluding mineral receipts of over £37,000) in the seventies. But the fifteenth Duke's 49,866 acres in eight counties then paid £75,596, of which 19,440 acres in and around Sheffield produced £39,897. The Yorkshire land had long been valuable: the rental was £16,873 in 1799 and £30,759 in 1866 (when markets and fairs added £7,682). The Dukes were also substantial coalowners, who operated some collieries and let other coal and iron during the eighteenth century. Some ventures jointly controlled by the eleventh Duke and his Sheffield business manager, Vincent Eyre, were let in 1805 to a partnership headed by Eyre. But the owners still cherished a lucrative source of income. The twelfth Duke sought to protect local collieries by opposing the Sheffield and Rotherham railway bill in 1835–6, and in the eighties the fifteenth Duke had a good reputation for aiding hard-pressed lessees. By 1866 the mineral income totalled £14,286, and from 1865 ducal agents were again involved in colliery winning (on which they had spent £54,184 by August 1868).[25] Thus the Arundel estate in rural Sussex was buttressed by the coalmines and steelworks of Sheffield.

Prominent landowners often continued to explore their land. 'Boreholes to prove unexploited [West Riding] areas have been put down in all directions', declared C. E. Rhodes, a mining engineer, in 1919. 'Earl Fitzwilliam bored to the coal . . . of Doncaster, and that coalfield is now being developed. Many other boreholes have also been put down by royalty owners themselves and by prospective lessees.' T. H. Bailey instanced the work of A. L. Vernon, Sir Francis Newdigate and Lords Dartmouth, Calthorpe, Hatherton and Crewe in the Midlands; C. E. Forrestier-Walker maintained that 'the development of the South Wales Coalfield had been greatly due to the enterprise and expenditure of the owners of the minerals'; and J. D. McLauchlan mentioned Sir R. M. Ferguson, Charles Balfour, the Duke of Portland and

Lord Howard de Walden as recent examples of Scottish owners
proving their coal.[26] Nevertheless, most landowners had ceased
to operate their own concerns during the nineteenth century.
Even in the North-East such magnates as the Dukes of Northumberland, the Ridley baronets and the successors of the
'Grand Allies' (Lords Ravensworth, Strathmore and Wharncliffe)
gradually withdrew from active management. Indeed, as early as
1830 local collieries 'were usually won by adventurers' and only
eight owners operated mines on the Tyne and Wear, according to
the celebrated mining viewer John Buddle. By the nineties mines
were run 'exceptionally by proprietors', and 'the greater number
of proprietors working their own mines were . . . also lessees'.[27]

There were many reasons for landowners' withdrawal. The
immensity of the capital involved (Lord Ravensworth and his
partners and the Marquess of Londonderry and the Earl of
Durham were all supposed to have invested half a million, as
'grandees of the trade' by 1843)[28] and the enormity of some risks
doubtless influenced many decisions. The comparative tranquil-
lity (sometimes more apparent than real) of a *rentier* status had
obvious attractions. And the complexity of mining techniques
doubtless dismayed other owners and agents. A new race of
viewers, managers and mineral agents, with technical and legal
knowledge, took over the management of mines on great estates
and groups of smaller properties, operating mines or, more often,
negotiating leases and inspecting workings. Some, like Northumberland's Hugh and Thomas Taylor, Norfolk's John Curr, Fitzwilliam's Joshua and Benjamin Biram, the Lowthers' Carlisle
and James Spedding, Lord Mar's Alexander and Robert Bald and
Bute's W. S. Clark and W. T. Lewis (first Lord Merthyr), de-
servedly achieved fame. For instance, the Speddings created
Whitehaven's great undersea pits; Curr developed railroads,
conductors and ropes; and Benjamin Biram patented rotary
ventilators, including his celebrated anemometer.[29] At the top of
this new hierarchy were the pioneer industrial consultants, often
themselves mineowners around Newcastle and as ubiquitous as
their lease-searching neighbours: the Buddles would supervise
north-eastern developments while advising Norfolk at Sheffield,
the Tennysons in Lincolnshire and the Lowthers and Curwens
in Cumberland.

The expense of employing such experts probably deterred some small squires. Furthermore, mineral agents and owners sometimes disagreed. Curr, though undoubtedly able, was scarcely satisfactory as a manager. His first railroad provoked riots; irregular seams and flooding were unforeseen; and from 1793 Sheffield benefit clubs ran a successful rival concern. Yet, after twenty years' service, he was shocked at his dismissal in 1801. 'It is publicly known that I have rendered services in my professional line of business rather in an extraordinary way to the country at large as well as my employers', he told Norfolk in a curious letter. He hinted at the value of his knowledge of ducal secrets, listed his inventions, blamed flooding for the collieries' troubles and insisted that

> bad as the collieries have lately proved, they would have been much worse if I had not made the improvements . . . Seldom a year has passed but some idea of improvement has struck me, which alone was in these works of much more importance than the whole of my salary; and who will venture to say my inventive genius is now exhausted?

Norfolk did not care to discuss the point. He disclaimed any 'personal dislike' and continued to buy Curr's goods, but reasonably insisted that 'the want of success in concerns so important to himself and the trade of Sheffield appeared to him a sufficient reason for placing the management of them in other hands'.[30]

Similar experiences led the Earls of Mar to give up mining ventures initiated by medieval monks in Fife and Clackmannan. In 1709 the sixth (or, by different counts, eleventh or twenty-fourth) Earl sent his colliery manager 'to inspect the machinery of [the Newcastle] district and learn the mode of conducting colliery operations in every department', and he later invited George Sorocould, the Derbyshire engineer, to inspect his pits. This entrepreneurial peer lost his lands as a Jacobite, but his Alloa property was retained by the Erskine family, who regained the title in 1824. From the late eighteenth century the Erskines' collieries served the local iron industry. New machinery was quickly adopted, a harbour tramroad was constructed and the Balds were sensibly employed. The ninth Earl, who was also eleventh Earl of Kellie, was a sizeable industrialist, a mechanical enthusiast and the owner of both mines and barges. But eventually he disagreed with Robert Bald's unpopular puritanical paternalism and in 1835 he retired from the industry. Bald then unsuccessfully leased several pits which he had previously managed, while larger coal and ironstone areas were let to the prosperous Alloa Coal Company, which also worked the estates of Lords Mansfield, Elgin and Balfour of Burleigh and in 1915 bought Sir Hugh Shaw-Stewart's Carnock property. In 1872 the thirteenth Kellie's Clackmannan coal paid £1,260 and by 1879 (as tenth Earl of Mar) he received £5,320 from mines and feu duties.[31]

Some great landowners, against the general tide, long retained their collieries. From the early seventeenth century the Lowthers had expensively developed the town, harbour and collieries (the kingdom's deepest in the eighteenth century) of Whitehaven. The profits of a near-monopoly of the Dublin coal trade helped them to build a territorial and political empire in Cumberland and Westmorland. Income from iron, sulphur and lead augmented the fortune. There were fluctuations in the success story. According to John Peile, a nineteenth-century mineral agent, the first Earl of Lonsdale 'nearly brought the collieries to a standstill; he would not allow any new works to be undertaken without his sanction, and that could never be obtained'. But his successor (for whom the earldom was re-created in 1807) increased investment to about £5,000 a year. Between 1812 and 1841 he spent almost £145,000 beyond normal working costs, opened fourteen new pits and received (in 1812–43) colliery profits of £1,146,313. In 1834 four collieries paid £24,005 net, but by 1887 the profit had fallen to £4,094, though harbour receipts still totalled £14,302 in 1898. The fifth Earl finally let the long-established Whitehaven collieries in 1888. Consequently, by 1890 only Lord Leconfield, the Carron Company, J. H. Dalzell and Myles Postlethwaite were working their own coal in west Cumberland.[32]

In north-eastern England several noble proprietors survived. The Lambtons owned ten collieries in 1835 and 1853, twelve in 1871 and fourteen (with nineteen steamships) in 1896, when their enterprise was sold to Sir James Joicey. Their political rivals, the Vane-Stewarts, were equally involved, with eleven collieries in 1853, seven in 1871 and three (still employing 7,000 men and boys) in 1919. This long-continued involvement owed much to

the third Marquess of Londonderry and his able wife, who promoted both coal and iron industries and risked even their large
fortune on creating Seaham Harbour in 1828-31. The gamble
paid well; during the first World War the seventh Marquess
received an average mineral income of £15,334. Lesser owners in
1871 included Sir C. F. Maclean with two collieries and Northumberland, Bute, Lord Dunsany and Lady Waterford with
one each.[33]

By the seventies few landowners still operated their own mining concerns in other areas. The largest of such undertakers were
the Bridgewater Trustees, controlling the Earl of Ellesmere's
nineteen Lancashire collieries. The enterprising third Duke of
Bridgewater had largely determined future developments by
heavy eighteenth-century investments in Worsley mines and his
celebrated coal canal to Manchester. His successors, the Marquess of Stafford and four Lords Ellesmere, regularly enlarged
the workings. In all, between 1759 and 1918 the owners spent
£3,583,089 on their mines; and from 1912 to 1919 mineral profits
averaged £16,788 and lessees' payments £26,709.[34] Other Lancashire colliery owners included the Earl of Bradford with three
and Lord Skelmersdale with one. In South Yorkshire Fitzwilliam
and Sir John Lister-Kaye of Denby Grange each owned three
mines in the seventies, while Charles Winn ran a 'home colliery'
at Nostell Priory. The first Ellesmere's cousin, the second Earl
Granville, owned three North Staffordshire collieries and eight
blast-furnaces. As a politician, he found the management of his
ironworks 'a necessary but tiresome occupation'; and the
notorious Countess Waldegrave doubtless devoted little of her
time to her two Somerset mines. But the Earls of Dartmouth, in
addition to being considerable lessors in West Yorkshire from the
early eighteenth century, took great care over their two West
Bromwich collieries. The fourth Earl tried to compose differences
during the 1842 strike-wave in Staffordshire, and his successor
proved Sandwell coal in the fifties. The Earls of Shrewsbury also
had two Staffordshire collieries (with one in Monmouth) and Sir
Horace St Paul owned two with a blast-furnace.

Proprietors of single collieries in 1869 included the Earl of
Chesterfield and Colonel Francis Newdigate of Byrkley in
Derbyshire, C. N. Newdegate of Arbury in Warwickshire, Lord

Maynard in Leicestershire, Lord Vernon in Cheshire, H. H. Vivian (Lord Swansea) in Glamorgan and Lords Hatherton and Lichfield, Sir Stephen Glynne and Sir Edward Blount in the South Staffordshire and Worcestershire area. The extent of interest and involvement varied, but some such families remained active industrialists. The Lister-Kayes, for example, were energetic mineowners on their own and other estates; Newdegate's successors spent £190,000 on proving and mining Arbury coal; Hatherton proved the Teddesley coal in 1897; Glynne and Lichfield both owned blast-furnaces. Not all such ventures were successful. The Glynne enterprise severely harmed the family fortunes, being (thought W. E. Gladstone) 'a most wild and extravagant and . . . immoral speculation, namely, conducting an ironworks without either the knowledge or the means for doing this with safety'.[35] The financial foundation of several other landowners' concerns would, no doubt, have appeared equally strange to the prim mercantile code of the young Gladstone.

The largest Midlands owner-operated concern would meet the criteria of the best-established Liverpool businessman. The 19,428 Worcester and Stafford acres of the Lords Dudley and Ward provided £117,005 of the first Earl of Dudley's income of £123,176 (from 25,554 acres) in the seventies. The interests of that controversial seventeenth-century experimenter with coal and iron, Nat Dudley, were long maintained by his family. By the 1840s the trustees of 'Dud's' successors had let 52 furnaces and 13 collieries to the British Iron Company and themselves controlled 6 blast-furnaces, about 27 pits and several mining villages in various conditions. Dudley owned a large undertaking in 1869, with 12 collieries, 9 blast-furnaces, 96 puddling furnaces, 10 rolling mills and 50 miles of railway. This enterprise was well maintained and even extended: 'up to the present time', declared John Tyron, a trustee and director of the family businesses, in 1919, 'the whole of the profits (including royalties) of the [Baggeridge] colliery have been expended in developments', Lord Dudley having provided or borrowed some £400,000. The Earl then owned a colliery company, blast-furnaces, iron and aluminium casting foundries, brickworks, limestone, engineering and iron and steel manufacturing concerns, a railway and a canal;

and he also let collieries.[36] His was the greatest example of aristocratic industrialism to survive into the twentieth century.

Withdrawal from actual control of mineral concerns did not
absolve landowners from all responsibility and interest. Many
squires took the trouble of learning something of the complexities
of pillar systems, with posts and stalls of very different sizes for
advancing and retreating, and longwall working with stone or
wooden props. Accounts of the Durham 'bord and pillar' technique, geological survey reports and evaluations of different
seams mingled with heavy packets of railway literature on many
Victorian landowners' desks. As increasing numbers of owners
developed mines and 'services' in the hope of attracting lessees,
country house muniment rooms came to contain voluminous
mineral information, scientific, technological and financial. The
start of some ventures was hastened by reports from unexpected
sources. 'Sir', wrote 'Thomas goulding miner Worsborough' to
William Aldam of Frickley Hall near Doncaster, in 1850,[37]

> You will Excuse my freedom for the following in veiwing the
> Country and outbreaks of the minerals I am of this opinion that
> there is in your Estate two Coal Mines which Might bee [opened?]
> at a trifling Expence . . . [which] if serveed and found of Good
> Quality would bee very valuable.

More normally, Adam Fyfe was asked to report on Thornton
coal to James Kyd, factor to the seventh Earl of Leven and Melville's creditors, in 1812. 'I went to the Bridge of Orr', he wrote,[38]

> and Looked at the Coall that is presently working and finds that
> is close by Lord Leven's march and according to the Stretch of
> the Coall the Grater part by far is on Lord Leven's Property and
> it is my opinion that if my Lord were to sink a pitt on the East
> Side of the turnpick rod it maight be wroght to Great Advantage
> . . . and it is my opinion that Lord Leven should look that Earl of
> Rothes should not carry his workings too near the water of Orr
> nor the working from the Present pitt upon my Lord's Property
> as the stretch of Coall Layes that way. Dear Sir I am very happy
> to see such a valabl subject on Balgonei Esteat.

By one means or other, nineteenth-century owners soon learned
of their mineral property.

Energetic developers often took a lead in transport developments. The Morgans of Tredegar Park, for instance, played a
notable role in the promotion of Monmouthshire undertakings:
Sir Charles, first baronet, was a pioneer of colliery tramways at
Sirhowy in 1804; Sir Charles, second baronet, was a leader of the
Monmouthshire railway of 1852; and the first Baron and first
Viscount Tredegar invested over £1,000,000 in the Alexandra
docks at Newport. Their Welsh neighbours were often closely
associated with mineral ventures. Until the mid-eighteenth century the Lords Mansel worked their own coal and iron near
Swansea, and their successors, the Talbots of Penrice and Mar-
gam, continued the tradition as mine leaders and builders of
Port Talbot. In Pembrokeshire such squires as the Owen baronets
of Orielton had been active mineowners. Other South Wales
owners included the Duke of Beaufort (a major lessor in Monmouth and Glamorgan), Lord Plymouth (who was heavily involved in the Penarth and Barry docks), Lord Dynevor (whose
family had worked their Caermarthen and Glamorgan mines
from 1541 to 1793) and Lord Dunraven (a lessor in Glamorgan).[39]
North Wales lead, iron, coal, copper and stone provided potential profits for owners like the Grosvenors in Flint and Denbigh.
Various mineral ventures were developed by the ninth Lord
Paget (first Earl of Uxbridge) and helped to produce an average
income of £76,200 for his son, the one-legged soldier Marquess
of Anglesey, between 1819 and 1835. Improvements in Caer-
narvon slate quarrying made a fortune for the first Lord Penrhyn,
and Lord Newborough, Assheton Smith of Dinorwic and other
owners sought to emulate this example.[40] Although few Welsh
proprietors maintained their own workings in the nineteenth
century, many helped their lessees by continuing traditional
connections with industry.

Scottish coalfields provided very varied lordship payments for
a large number of proprietors. Great magnates, like the Dukes of
Buccleuch and Hamilton, and hosts of smaller lairds shared in
the prosperity created by coal and iron. The fifth Buccleuch,
second largest landowner in Britain in the 1870s, drew £216,473
from 459,108 acres in fourteen counties, together with £10,601
from Granton harbour (expensively built in 1835–45) and £4,091
from collieries and quarries. He owned coal in Dumfries, Mid-

lothian and Furness and still maintained two Scottish collieries in 1869.[41] The twelfth Hamilton was a smaller owner, with 157,386 acres in six counties and a rent-roll of £73,636 in the seventies; but he already had a mineral rent of £67,007. In 1891 Hamilton's mineral factor, James Barrowman, revealed the increasing Scottish royalties and eighteen wayleave rights (six of which were rented). And in 1919 the estate solicitor, Timothy Warren, explained that the Hamilton Estate Trust had let 20,500 acres of coal on its 56,000-acre property, receiving lordships of £1,137,931 in 1908–17, along with limestone, ganister, fireclay, brick, stone and sand payments of £15,568 and wayleave charges of £16,393.[42] Such an income was unique; and even families long and closely connected with collieries often faced great hazards. At Wemyss Castle in Fife, for example, Ralph Wemyss ran his own mine in the sixties and drew £12,314 from 6,925 acres and £8,492 from his coal in the seventies. But the construction of a tramway and good miners' cottages, along with the abandonment of leases, caused the family serious financial troubles. By 1918, according to Lord Strafford (an estate trustee), the mineral income had fallen to about £1,564.[43]

In 1857 other Scottish landed colliery owners included Sir John Maxwell, Lord Belhaven, Charles and James Balfour, Sir John Wauchope, the Earls of Moray, Elgin and Hopetoun, Sir Archibald Edmonstone and R. B. Wardlaw-Ramsay, all of whom were missing from the 1869 list. The last owners were the Countess of Stair, the Hon T. F. Kennedy, Buccleuch, the Earl of Rosslyn, Sir George Suttie, Sir George Clerk, the Marquess of Lothian and Captain G. R. Beresford. Many of these lairds had managed their own ventures for many years. The Elgins, for instance, had continued and expanded monastic mines at Culross and established a great limeworks near Rosyth in 1777.[44] At Edmonstone in Midlothian the Wauchopes were enterprising eighteenth-century colliery owners and early users of Newcomen engines.[45] The Lothians had worked coal at Newbattle Abbey since the last abbot brought the estate to the family.[46] And the Clerks of Penicuik had a long history of involvement in mining; in 1724 Sir John, the distinguished second baronet, had visited and examined northern English collieries, subsequently adopting their practices.[47] In general, such enterprise was eventually well rewarded:

in 1874, although the Wauchopes received only about £300, the Balfours' successors £573 and £530 and Kennedy £900, minerals gave Sir George Clerk £2,421, Lord Stair £1,122, Rosslyn £1,224, Suttie £1,195, Lothian £6,296, Sir William Stirling-Maxwell £4,389, Belhaven £19,621, Moray £2,350, Elgin £3,710, Hopetoun £3,974, Sir William Edmonstone £8,451 and Wardlaw-Ramsay £2,312.

At least forty-four other Scottish landowners, great and small, anciently genteel and *nouveau-riche*, drew over £1,000 a year from minerals in the seventies, when the Scottish 'Domesday' return reported on both land and sub-surface receipts. They were headed by James Houldsworth, laird and ironmaster of Coltness, with £21,239, D. C. Carrick-Buchanan of Drumpellier (£16,424), the Duke of Portland (£16,199), W. H. Gillespie of Torbanehill (£13,125, as against £776 from 706 surface acres) and J. C. C. Hamilton of Dalzell (£10,779). The fourteenth Earl of Eglinton received £9,520 from Ayrshire minerals and £4,525 from the harbour at Ardrossan, on which his ancestors had spent enormous sums. The Hon Mrs Jean Cathcart had £8,734 and the Earl of Zetland £7,723. Ten proprietors receiving between £4,000 and £7,000 included the Earls of Glasgow, Home and Dunmore, William Forbes of Callendar and Robert Dundas of Arniston. The Duke of Abercorn, Lords Cardross, Ruthven, Minto, Rosebery, Loudoun, Wemyss, Oranmore, Elphinstone and Mansfield and sixteen other owners were in the £1,000 to £4,000 range.[48] The mines and collieries of Fife, Linlithgow, Midlothian, Haddington, Stirling, Ayr, Dumbarton, Dumfries, Renfrew and, above all, Lanark, considerably altered the balance of Scottish landowning society by their lordship payments.

Almost inevitably, the Irish story was different. Collieries regularly made losses—according to English experts, partly because of the proclivities of the native labour force to drunkenness, idleness and theft. Certainly by 1869 the picture was gloomy. The Wandesfords' sizeable Castlecomer undertaking was running down: three collieries were closed, two partially working and four still operating. Lord Ormond's Kilkenny colliery, Sir Thomas Butler's Carlow colliery, Sir J. H. Walsh's two Queen's County mines and the Munster ventures of Lords Devon, Clare and Monteagle and the Knight of Glin were all closed.[49]

Many descendants of mineral developers had cause for grati-
tude. The expenses of proving, winning and sometimes initially
operating or subsidising colliery ventures often proved to be
superb investments. 'There is no disguising the fact that you are
living a good deal beyond your income . . .', the second Earl of
Wharncliffe (with an income of £18,850 and expenditure of
£21,657) was told by his trustees in 1900. The warning was
familiar to young aristocrats with *fin du siècle* tastes, inherited
obligations and growing taxation problems. Coal helped the
situation: the Wortley mineral estate had provided £6,628 for
six months in 1891 and £6,038 in 1898 (when arrears totalled
£9,859) for the first Earl. The new peer, succeeding in 1899, was,
however, no rash young man but an experienced naval officer.
His misfortune was that he received only about half of the gross
mineral payments, though this amounted to roughly a third of
his income.[50] He nevertheless owed much to the Wortleys' long
involvement with West Riding coal and iron undertakings.

The nineteenth-century Vernon-Wentworths of Wentworth
Castle similarly benefitted from their ancestors' participation in
industrial developments. Their Worsborough pits had been let
by the Earl of Strafford in 1663, and coal and iron ventures provided an increasing proportion of the estate's income. By 1814
the colliery rent was £1,023, with additional payments for coal
mined above 15,000 tons, brick royalties and colliers' rents.[51]
But descendants of squires who failed to seize early opportunities
rarely received a second chance. For instance, in 1786 Walter
Spencer-Stanhope of Cannon Hall near Barnsley, a descendant
of ironmasters and woollen merchants, turned down the possibility of buying the potentially lucrative Low Moor; and his
family, rapidly dropping their mercantile background, never
made much money even from Silkstone coal. The entrepreneurial virtues which had originally established the Spencers'
and Stanhopes' fortunes were assumed by their steward, John
Hardy, who gained a fortune by joining a partnership to work
Low Moor's famous iron and coal. Hardy's son and three
grandsons all became considerable landowners.[52]

One major hazard for the mineral owner was the failure of a
lessee. In order to safeguard his rights and property after an
operator's collapse, an owner would often manage his mine until

F

another tenant was found. In Northumberland, for example, Earl Grey ran the Broomhill colliery between leases. And in Wales Bute's Merthyr Associated Colliery, started in 1850, was let in 1857, surrendered in 1859 and re-let in 1861 under the supervision of the estate mineral office.[53] Relations between landowners and lessees were, indeed, not invariably happy. One 'case study' may suffice to illustrate this point. In 1800 the seventh Lord Leven was forced by financial difficulties to put his Nairn and Fife estates in trust for his creditors. Marital alliances doubtless provided some relief: the Earl and four of his children married into the Thornton and Smith banking families. More important, however, was the advice of the trustee, William Keith. 'It would be of very great consequence to establish a foundry and ironworks upon your estate', he told Leven's heir, Lord Balgonie, in 1800, 'provided a respectable company with a sufficient capital would undertake it.' Balgonie thereupon advertised his minerals, though not without some misgivings. 'I observe you are apprehensive that the proposed establishment of ironworks could hurt Balgonie as a place', wrote Keith. 'Perhaps they may in some degree have that effect'—but they would also provide 'a certain rent for his Lordship's coal and ironstone'.[54]

The Levens had experienced mixed blessings from mining ventures since the seventeenth century. In 1731 expenditure of £1,836 produced six months' income of £1,492; from the 1730s there were recurrent difficulties with the principal tackmen, the Landale family; and in the 1790s the mineral income ranged between £833 in 1792 and £335 in 1797. But after these vicissitudes the future appeared to be bright. In 1801 Alexander Anderson reported on coal 'of an exceeding fine quality' at Markinch, and in the following year Balgonie coal and ironstone was let to the Leven Iron Company for thirty-eight years at £1,300 a year with free coal for Melville and Balgonie castles.[55] But great expectations soon yielded to hard times. Within a year the company was in debt for rent and wages. Leven lent cash for the latter item and obtained an act of sequestration, himself receiving most of the property.

A further chapter opened when Robert Puncheon reported, in 1804, that he 'must upon the whole say that the [Balgonie] workings in general, as far as he had seen them, were in an unexceptionable good order and condition'. The area was consequently let in 1805 to George Losh, a former partner, for £500 rising to £1,000 a year, with £700 for each additional furnace. But by 1808 Losh was failing and borrowed £5,000 to regain the works. The eighth Earl could only deplore the firm's 'hopeless state' and press Losh's brother James for his rents. Losh's final effort, the New Balgonie Iron Company of 1810, collapsed within two years. Encouraged by rent remissions, another singularly brave partner, Thomas Lewis, took over the decrepit concern; but, defeated by accidents, floods, fires and thefts, he yielded his lease in 1815.

Although James Kyd naturally fostered further opportunities, in 1817 Robert Bald pessimistically reported that

> as to value of [the Balgonie] mineral field, no correct estimate can at present be formed, as the colliery has almost gone to ruin. From what I know of the iron trade in general, and its depressed state at present in particular, I have no hope of the Balgonie iron-works being revived, for if it would not work at a profit formerly it cannot possibly do so now, and it is well known that immense sums have been lost at this ironworks since it commenced. There is [however] a very considerable demand for coal in the district, and by good management Balgonie colliery may soon command a fair proportion of the sale.

Bald considered an ironstone tonnage royalty of 1s reasonable, but doubted rumours that a Newcastle enterprise would pay it: 'the Carron Company could afford to give more than any other iron company, [but] he much questioned if they would give the above royalty, [though] a trial might be made'. He maintained that 'the only way to establish [the field's] value was to push a sale and then an annual rental'. In the event, the expert was wrong: Bulmer's Tyne Ironworks operated the mines from 1817 to 1822, producing surpluses at Balgonie and Thornton collieries of £712, £872 and £714 in 1821, 1822 and 1823, along with many free loads for Melville. But, not unnaturally, the earls had had their fill of mining companies. In 1823 Balgonie was sold to James Balfour of Whittingehame, a younger son of the coal-owning lairds of Balbirnie, for £104,000. Balfour continued the mining interest, and his successors developed Thornton coal.[56]

Other financially-embarrassed owners sought to expand and

exploit mineral opportunities. For instance, George Lane-Fox of Bramham Park in Yorkshire, the owner of an estate starved of capital by heavy family commitments, let his famous Allerton Bywater coal and Rimmington lead, bought interests in colliery undertakings, served on the committee of the Aire & Calder Navigation and had his own parkland surveyed by mining experts. His coal rents rose from £750 to £1,156 between 1846 and 1852, but the estate was saved by other means.[57] Sir James Graham, Peel's Home Secretary in the 1840s, similarly hoped to repair his inherited financial difficulties by finding coal on his Netherby estate in north Cumberland. He discovered nothing, but he also preserved his inheritance.[58] George Tennyson of Bayons Manor, a Lincolnshire squire, hopefully employed John Buddle to survey his property in 1801. Thanking him for a copy of the 'valuable report', the local magnate, Lord Yarborough, wrote that[59]

> how far it may be thought proper by any Gentlemen in the Neighbourhood of Tealby and Willingham to make any further trial and experiment on account of the inflammable *shale* as an object of fuel for the burning of Lime, Bricks &c. may be a matter worthy of consideration ... With respect to *Coal*, nothing can be clearer than the opinion Mr Buddle has given as to the futility of any of us making *any* future attempts to find that valuable article in this part of the World.

The only importance of such examples is the evidence which they provide of landowners' hopes, so often dashed. And though few were subjected to such classic misfortunes as those endured by the Levens, several owners disagreed with lessees. From 1824 to 1828, for example, the lords of Silkstone Common, headed by John Spencer-Stanhope, argued with Jonas and Robert Couldwell Clarke over both charges and tonnages worked. This controversy was eventually arbitrated upon by Joshua Biram.[60]

The landowner's role in the mining industries did not end with surveying, winning and letting. He was expected to support local societies: the initial patrons of the pioneer North of England Institute of Mining Engineers in 1852 were the Duke of Northumberland, Lords Londonderry, Lonsdale, Grey, Durham, Wharncliffe and Ravensworth, the Bishop and Dean of Durham, the Warden of Durham University and W. B. Beaumont of

Bywell Hall. He was expected to subscribe to local ventures: when Northumberland became patron of a proposed Newcastle mining college in 1856 he almost inevitably offered to add his third to any subscription. The owner was at least invited to remit rents and sometimes to make loans to temporarily embarrassed lessees; these aids were given by such owners as Norfolk, Vernon-Wentworth, the Marquess of Crewe and Bute.[61] Some owners participated in, or presided over, joint-stock mining companies. The Earl of Tyrconnel and John Bowes, for instance, were honorary directors of the Durham Coal Company of 1836–52 and Sir John Heron Maxwell of Springkell was a director of the Garpel Company (an Ayrshire ironstone venture) in 1859. Others initially held aloof from such undertakings. 'I shall be much obliged to you to see Mr Roy and ask him to explain the grounds upon which he expressed his hope that I should encourage a Joint Stock Company for the Dowlais Minerals', the second Marquess of Bute told his lawyer in 1847. 'When Lady Bute and I have conversed with Mr Geddes on these questions, we always arrived at our opinion against having to do with a Joint Stock Company.'[62] Traditional agricultural views on leases often left their mark on mineral negotiations. Yet later in the century several landowners were as glad to join boards of directors as the companies were to welcome them.

Such a great enterprise as the Carron Company, requiring large amounts of iron and coal and consequently working on many properties, developed powerful negotiating techniques. In its early years the company had difficulties with legalistic lairds like James Bruce of Kinnaird and Thomas Dundas of Fingask. But it sought ironstone as far afield as Lord Egremont's Cumbrian lands and later evaded disputes by buying both surface and minerals, thus becoming a considerable landowner. Lairds and factors exchanged information on the policies of such a major power. When, in 1836, Robert Speir of Burnbrae solicited advice about sending his ironstone to the Broomielaw or Carron Iron-works, John Miller of Cumbernauld told him that 'it was almost impossible to tell him the value of any ironstone at Carron—[the Company] were such monopolists all around their neighbour-hood that they just gave what they pleased'. Miller himself then received 10d per 25cwt of ball ironstone, but noted that the Company 'had to pay handsomely [for the Monkland blackband ironstone], having to compete there with other works'. If Speir had blackband, along with his coal and limestone, 'it would be of immense value'—and letting further acres 'would be a better speculation . . . [for Speir's brother] than the best factorship on the carrots'. Speir profited from the advice: in 1874 his grandson Robert supplemented the £5,879 rental of 3,194 Perth and Renfrew acres with a mineral income of £2,735.[63]

Partly to maintain their own monopolistic position, many owners continued ancient practices on renewal fines by raising demands on the extension or re-negotiation of leases. After many initial errors, they generally employed negotiators as well equipped as the lessees' agents to cost, measure and estimate the extent, value and potentialities of mineral fields. But lessees complained most bitterly of the problems caused by divided ownership, when minerals belonged to various squires or the surface and mineral property were separate, and of trustees' limited powers. And many lessees professed themselves satisfied with their situation. The Duke of Portland's declaration at a colliery opening that while 'he had no particular wish to see even a model colliery so near to Welbeck, as an owner of minerals he felt he had no right to lock up the mainspring of England's wealth and prosperity' was approvingly quoted in 1890 by B. P. Broomhead, chairman of Thomas Firth & Sons. 'As long as the great landowners in England behaved in this spirit with regard to their minerals [lessees] did not want any interference with them . . . [or] to introduce the State; they were better off as they were.' It was held in the nineties that royalties were far from being curbs on development, and the reluctance of some owners (like the Duke of Leeds at Wakefield) to work their coal was ascribed to legal difficulties. Even Sheffield businessmen were scarcely given to sycophantic adulation of noblemen; but, according to J. D. Ellis, chairman of the South Yorkshire Coal Owners' Association and of John Brown & Company Ltd, they had found such owners as Norfolk, Fitzwilliam, the Earl of Effingham and F. J. S. Foljambe of Osberton and Adwarke 'most liberal, honourable landlords'. Their villains were 'cantankerous small owners'.[64]

The small proprietor demanding (sometimes excessive) wayleaves was inevitably annoying to large mining firms; the Earl of

Westmorland, as surface owner, held up the Sharlston collieries for a year. On the other hand, minor landowners often faced difficult problems in relationships with plausible 'sharks'. Captain William Blair of Blair, for instance, learned vital lessons by bitter experience on his 7,200 acre Ayrshire estate. In September 1845 he recorded that, despite his financial concessions, Messrs Jollie 'never explored or laid open the mineral field . . . [which was] in the hands of a Mr Thompson, who was as much fit to be manager as he was fit to be Pope of Rome'. Blair then 'put his iron affairs in the hands of William Patrick', on whose advice he reduced his lordships of 6d for lime and 1s 3d for clayband to 4d and 9d, only to discover that the charges were uniquely low. Yet the old naval officer eventually benefitted. In 1851 the Ayrshire Iron Company (which was taken over by the the great Baird enterprises in 1852) paid him £2,513, including £1,000 rent and coal and ironstone royalties of £1,058. His net mineral income fluctuated between £3,966 in 1860 and £1,868 in 1863, and the 'mine rent' still amounted to 'at least £2,000' in the seventies (when his agricultural rents were £5,828).[65]

For such owners as Blair, lacking the advice of a network of agents, the best aid was often consultation with their kind. A prominent consultant might be brought from Newcastle to advise on initial decisions, but later tactics depended upon local knowledge. In 1865 Colonel Claud Alexander of Ballochmyle solicited Blair's views on 'the propriety or otherwise of extending [Messrs Bairds'] lease, there being at present an unexpired period of 17 years . . ., whether he should allow [them] power free of charge to work, calcine and carry away by means of pits on his property minerals of the adjoining properties' and whether to consult an engineer and to accept an offer of cash instead of ground restoration. Blair thought the extension fair as an incentive to further work. He had himself allowed free wayleaves, while insisting on heavy damage payments. The matter was 'one of *very* great moment, [and] he would recommend the advice of a mining engineer, but those gentlemen all played into the hands of the great iron company'. Alexander took a fixed rent of £1,500 and 2s per 22½cwt ton of calcined ironstone. 'He was paid last year £3,500 for ironstone alone: they have not got his coal', Blair enviously noted. 'He still has about 1,000 acres to work out, which, if fortunate, will give him a very large sum, say at 3,000 tons per acre.' But Alexander was not entirely satisfied. 'Perhaps I am wrong, but I cannot help thinking that I should have tried to make the Bairds give me more than 2s per ton', he told Blair. '. . . I am told that Mr Campbell of Blythswood has been offered 4s.' In the event, he did well; by 1879 his rental of £4,359 from 4,339 acres (excluding feus) was supplemented by a 'fluctuating mineral rent of over £6,000'. Campbell then had £1,906.[66]

Lead mining provided varied opportunities for many land-owners. In Derbyshire, for example, the Duke of Rutland had ore royalties in six High Peak liberties, the Duke of Devonshire in four and Lord Scarsdale in one. Such Scottish magnates as the Earl of Hopetoun (at Leadhills) and the Duke of Buccleuch (at Wanlockhead, which was let to Bute in the early nineteenth century) owned notable lead-mining areas 'in the midst of the wild and elevated moorlands which separate the southern part of Lanarkshire from Dumfriesshire'. And in Wales Sir Thomas Bonsall and Lords Bute and Cawdor helped to expand the eighteenth-century industry.[67] For many years the colossus of the ('Quaker') London Lead Company towered over the industry, but other groups gradually entered it.

In the lonely areas at the head of the Yorkshire dales several landowners financed mines and mills, generally letting the former to miners' gangs and later to more substantial partner-ships. They also provided roads, water courses and smelting centres. The Earls of Burlington and Dukes of Devonshire, for example, for long promoted and controlled the old lead areas on Grassington Moor, investing considerable capital on estates where the seventh Duke had 31,366 acres in 1875. Several com-panies were attracted to the district, and during the second quarter of the nineteenth century rents, wayleaves, royalties and other charges produced about £30,000 a year for the sixth Duke; indeed, the mines almost trebled his West Riding revenue. But after 1869 the once-booming industry declined, and the income fell to the £16,750 arising from agricultural rents in the seventies. Ducal energy and capital were by then being lavished on the creation of Barrow-in-Furness. Lesser dalesland squires, however, faced a serious loss of income with the gradual death of lead mining. John Yorke of Bewerley Hall was typical. He owned lead at Appletreewick and in Nidderdale, where he built a mill in 1855. Between 1811 and 1883 the family's income rose from £5,081 to £11,000, subsequently falling with mining's decline.[68]

Other dales-head proprietors shared the profits of lead. In Arkengarthdale the Bathursts developed and then let the C[harles] B[athurst] mines. Lord Ribblesdale owned Malham Moor lead in Airedale, and in Wensleydale Lord Bolton was a large royalty owner and builder of two mills. The London Lead Company leased eighteenth-century Wensleydale mines from Edward Wortley Montague and the successors of the Duke of Wharton. Swaledale also was largely owned by the Whartons, who developed the Old Gang and Lownathwaite mines. The Wharton property passed to the second Countess of Pomfret, and the third Earl and his brother-in-law, Peter Denys, built up the Swaledale industry, establishing the celebrated Old Gang mill in the 1790s.[69] In the early nineteenth century the income from a growing number of mines was divided between Denys's widow (Lady Charlotte), her son (Sir George) and General Thomas Fermor, the future fourth Earl. By the seventies Sir George, second baronet, had a half share, while quarters fell to the last Lady Pomfret and Sir George Shuckburgh, ninth baronet (a grandson of Peter Denys).

The Old Gang mines were let in 1811 for £2,163 and one-fifth of the production. There were bad periods: in 1817 Lady Charlotte's agent, John Davies (who was apparently both inefficient and dishonest and who curiously combined the posts of Pomfret-Denys Steward and Old Gang manager for the lessees, the Alderson family) reported an income of £723 and expenditure of £1,219. The Denys family and their London solicitor, Ottiwell Robinson, were, however, astute businessmen, determined to avoid the Pomfrets' leasing errors and shrewdly assessing both their property and their lessees. Sir George, first baronet, was a member of the Arkengarthdale and Derwent Mining Company of 1819, and his son was managing director of the AD mines from 1873. Decline set in during the reign of the third baronet, Sir Francis, in the eighties.

Until Sir Francis sold them to Lord Leconfield in 1894, the

Denys dynasty also owned Cumbrian lead mines near Caldbeck.[70] Their North Riding neighbours, the Chaloners of Guisborough, had also been Cumbrian proprietors as lords of the manor of St Bees, but sold their property (largely to the Lowthers) in the seventeenth century. Robert Chaloner owned 8,569 acres on his settled estate in 1825, together with sundry rights. But in that year the Wentworth, Chaloner and Rishworth Bank collapsed. One partner, Godfrey Wentworth of Woolley Hall, was compelled to sell his West Riding property at Hickleton, Darton and Kexborough, thus losing valuable coal-land to Sir Francis Wood (father of the first Viscount Halifax) and T. W. Beaumont of Bretton Hall.[71] And Chaloner personally discharged many creditors, selling his personal property, putting the entailed estate under his brothers-in-law, George and Sir Robert Dundas (brothers of the first Earl of Zetland) and for many years earning his living as Irish agent for his relation, Earl Fitzwilliam, at Coollattin.

From the mid-nineteenth century the Chaloners started to resume the status of landed gentry. In 1879 Admiral Thomas Chaloner drew almost £6,000 from some 3,500 acres. His successor, R. G. W. Long (who assumed the family name and was created Lord Gisborough in 1917) had £6,412 from 4,038 acres in the early twentieth century, together with moors and a waterworks. Lead, Cleveland ironstone and other minerals greatly increased his income: receipts in 1904 totalled £13,477 (including fixed rents of £3,624) and, augmented by such sums as £902 from the waterworks, made the total income from 8,730 acres £20,791 19s 1d.[72]

In Allendale the Blacketts had worked their lead since 1694 and from 1696 had also leased the Bishop of Durham's Weardale rights, eventually creating a prominent business. Their property passed to Sir Thomas Wentworth, fifth baronet, and, through his illegitimate daughter's marriage, to Colonel T. R. Beaumont, who thus became a large early nineteenth-century owner. Until 1883 Colonel Beaumont, his son Thomas and his grandson Wentworth Blackett (created Lord Allendale in 1906) owned a major group of pits and mills on the Durham and Northumberland estate around Bywell Hall. Such prominent mineral agents as James Dickinson, the Westgarth Forsters (father and son) and

Thomas Sopwith were engaged to improve and extend these lead enterprises.[73] And on their Bretton estate in Yorkshire the Beaumonts possessed valuable coal near Wakefield. From £1,470 in 1829 the colliery payments rose to £1,800 in 1844, £6,727 in 1866 and £9,280 in 1874, thereafter falling to £3,505 in 1894.[74] Coal receipts thus declined simultaneously with lead profits and agricultural rents. Such were the obvious hazards of mineral ventures. Mining helped to restore the Chaloners and made W. B. Blackett 'one of the wealthiest commoners in the country' in the sixties.[75] But it was subject to more changeable factors than even agriculture.

One such factor, the confident 'front' paraded by undercapitalised prospective lessees, regularly visited the ill-fated Murray-Stewart trustees in Kirkcudbrightshire. In 1849 John Nicholson, a Durham ironmaster, was offered a carefully-phrased thirty-one-year lease of Cally lead and copper for a lordship of one-fourteenth. In 1850 Nicholson and William Muschamp, a Sunderland coalowner, leased all minerals (except gold and iron) for one-fourteenth (to be paid in cash if required), promising to employ at least six pickmen. And in 1851 and 1852 further copper and lead agreements were made with Sir Frederick and George Fowke. But in 1853 the Nicholson partnership assigned its rights to the Cally Mining Company (headed by William Winship, a Newcastle surgeon), which soon ceased working and renounced its interest in 1858.[76] Nevertheless, until its decline in the late nineteenth century, lead mining created substantial incomes for some landowners in west Scotland, the Pennines, Cleveland, north-west Yorkshire, the Midlands and Wales —men like the Duke of Cleveland in Teesdale, the Farrers of Clapham, R. J. More in Shropshire and the squires of Cardigan. The industry collapsed in the seventies and eighties through the exhaustion of many workings, competition from Spain, Germany and America and, perhaps, lack of capital for further exploration.

Other minerals generally paid smaller and rarer sums. A manganese quarry on John Paton's little Grandholme estate near Aberdeen produced £1,032 for the laird and his three partners in 1809; and in 1837 Paton's trustees let the enterprise to Isaac Cookson of Newcastle for nineteen years at £20 rent and a 15s tonnage charge.[77] Copper benefitted several squires in North

Wales, the Trent Valley and the South-West, but very few received such sums as the second Earl Grosvenor's annual £40,000 (which financed the rebuilding of Eaton) or the seventh Duke of Bedford's vast income from Devon Great Consols.[78] The Scottish shale-oil industry created opportunities for some men. 'Lairds, forgetful of their rural amenity', complained one commentator in 1866, 'await with anxiety the performance of the borers, with their mineral "prospecting apparatus".'[79] Tin long continued to provide widely differing sums to some Cornish owners.[80] And alum and other salts produced small payments to such proprietors as Lord Zetland in Cleveland and the Cholmleys at Whitby.[81] Numerous other holes in the ground provided some profit for landowners. But coal and iron remained by far the most lucrative minerals.

Mining ventures resulted in many different experiences for landowning families. Some squires inevitably failed at the very start of their first optimistic attempts. A little mine on Walter Spencer-Stanhope's Horsforth estate in the West Riding ended with a disaster in 1806.[82] In the same county the Greenwoods of Swarcliffe Hall hoped to exploit the coal occasionally found at Birstwith, but John Greenwood's shaft of 1820 and a mining company's explorations ten years later were unsuccessful.[83] And, of course, even if the preliminary work succeeded, a mineral 'take-off' did not inevitably lead to 'self-sustained growth'; bad surveying, unsuspected geological difficulties and even market changes could permanently harm small undertakings and cause income fluctuations which small landowners could tolerate less easily than magnates like Lord Durham.

The Clerks of Penicuik experienced virtually every turn of fortune. The venturesome Sir John's descendants maintained his mines on their 13,000 acres in Midlothian and Peebles, though generally with little personal control. In 1844 Sir George, the politician fifth baronet, was mortified by a prosecution under Ashley's Act of 1842. 'I regret extremely to learn that, notwithstanding my particular directions to the contrary, women have been permitted within the last three months to work in my colliery at Loanhead and that it appeared that Mr G. Grieve, the

manager of the colliery, had connived at this breach of the law,'
he told Seymour Tremenheere, the mines inspector, threatening
to dismiss both Grieve and the women's husbands.[84] This was
not Clerk's only difficulty, however. In 1850 he let the Loanhead
minerals, except those already feued, to R. B. Wardlaw-Ramsay
of Whitehill (who, by the seventies, drew £7,506 from 7,500
Scottish acres and £2,312 from mines) and in 1865 to the Shotts
Iron Company (for thirty-one years at a rent of £200 rising to
£500 from the fifth year). When the company ignored the exception, the eighth baronet sued it, in 1874, for additional wayleaves.
By 1878, during the iron depression, the income of £920 was still
'nearly double the fixed rent', through royalties of one-ninth or
one-eighth on coal, 9d per 22½cwt of raw blackband ironstone
(and 1s 6d if calcined), 6d (or 9d) on other ironstone, 6d on limestone and fireclay and 1d wayleaves on 'foreign' minerals. But
local inhabitants secured a legal prohibition of calcination at
Penicuik, and in 1882 the ironstone charges were cut to 4½d and 3d,
thus reducing royalties by £257 to £1,314 by 1888. After paying
£9,292 between 1884 and 1892, the company ended its lease in
1898, despite large royalty reductions in 1884.[85] Although the
Clerks owned coal, iron and shale (let to the Midlothian Oil
Company in 1884), court cases inaugurated by local residents
against the activities of both laird and lessees made it increasingly
difficult to maximise the potential mineral income.

In west Cumberland several squires, notably the Senhouses of
Netherhall and the Curwens of Workington, sought to emulate
the Lowthers' example. Humphrey Senhouse unsuccessfully
tried to develop Ellenborough coal from 1721. His son Humphrey
created the town of Maryport between his harbour and his park
from 1749, helped to promote a blast-furnace in 1754 and in 1755
joined a group in leasing the Earl of Egremont's Broughton coal.
The Broughton lease was assigned to John Christian of Unerigg
Hall in 1763 in return for large payments to Egremont and the
partners. Harbour dues, wayleaves, urban rents, partnership receipts and modest sums (for the third Humphrey, from 1791)
from Ellenborough coal considerably augmented the Senhouses'
income, eventually amounting to about half of their £3-4,000 in
the mid-nineteenth century. They also caused controversy with
Christian, who complained in 1781 of Senhouse's 'Jew bargen'

and 'dirty tricks'. Christian started to win this controversy, both in the courts and by leasing further Egremont coal. And in 1790 his wayleave and other problems were solved when he assumed the name of Curwen on inheriting his second wife's important Workington estates.

The Curwens had long developed their mineral and other properties. When Henry Curwèn died in 1778 he left a personal estate of £15,000, land worth £2,000 a year, four collieries, extensive royalties, ironstone works, Harrington harbour, boats and shares in trading ships. Four years later, when Christian married Isabella Curwen, the estate produced about £2,500 while the colliery profits averaged £5,500.[86] The mineral income was partly used to extend and improve the model estate; J. C. Curwen was a pioneer of Cumbrian agricultural reform. A varying number of pits were exploited at the Workington and Harrington collieries. Like Lonsdale, Curwen consulted the Buddles, and his son solicited Matthias Dunn's advice. The resulting income fluctuated considerably: Charles Udale, the agent, reported net ironstone profits of £472 in 1789 and £185 in 1795, while (of a gross income of £8,949) in 1809 ironstone paid only £40 and the collieries £3,331. In 1788 coal had contributed merely £83 to the estate's £3,808 income, and in 1794 Broughton and Unerigg coal profits of £1,289 had been cut by Birkby's loss of £187. Certainly the mines' progress was not continuous. In 1832 Dunn told Henry Curwen of the 'inferior value of [his] coals as compared with Whitehaven and other Neighbouring Collieries', particularly noting the expense of pumping, long conveyance and scattered workings, the 'limited quantum of the vend' and the 'rude and unimproved' techniques. Furthermore, Workington periodically suffered cataclysmic recessions, and in 1837 (Dunn's warnings against the reduction of pillars apparently having been ignored) the undersea workings were inundated by the Solway. The death-roll at this disaster undoubtedly influenced the decision to let the pits.

Difficulties did not end with the protracted negotiations over leases. In 1871 G. B. Forster reported to Edward Curwen that the Harrington lessees produced too little coal to meet their payments (though after draining and further sinkings 'the Royalty would exceed the fixed Rent'), that the Workington lessee (with only one pit working, the 'output . . . very limited' and a rent of £600) was in the same position, but that at Flimby (where the pit was 'comparatively exhausted' but the lessee had reached new deposits by drifts from a pit on Lowther land) 'they might expect the Rent to exceed the Minimum of £800 a year'. Curwen let further coal at Crossbarrow for £100. In 1875 H. F. Curwen inherited 7,128 acres in three counties, with a rental of £10,054 and a continuing mining interest. His Wythemoor colliery failed—according to R. W. Moore because of bad management rather than high charges; but even in 1910 Alan de Lancy Curwen owned 296 acres of minerals at Winscales and 721 acres under his own estate which were as yet unlet.[87]

Meanwhile, the Senhouses had continued their smaller Maryport ventures. The third Humphrey worked hard on colliery estimates, calculations and plans from his succession in 1770. James Spedding and William Brown recommended caution in 1781: there should be further trials 'before Mr Senhouse went further into any considerable expence in trying [Ellenborough] colliery'. In fact, Senhouse management was fairly brief, and the fourth Humphrey's son-in-law, Joseph Pocklington-Senhouse, let the colliery soon after inheriting the estate in 1842, selling the machinery for £888. There was an echo of former controversies in 1850 when Henry Curwen alleged that the Senhouses had worked his Flimby coal seven years previously; but he had to withdraw the complaint within days. The Senhouses still drew considerable royalties and continued to interest themselves in their colliery's affairs: in 1870 Pocklington-Senhouse consulted H. S. Stobart, a Darlington engineer, as to whether he should permit lessees to remove pillars. And wayleaves for carriage to Maryport harbour were also of some importance.

As early as 1775 the third Earl of Egremont, owner of Cumbrian coal at Bransty, Birkby and Aspatria, considered the possibility of evading Senhouse wayleaves by making the River Ellen navigable or driving a canal from Aspatria to Allonby, with a new harbour on the Solway. John Smeaton rather dampened enthusiasm by describing the difficulties and expense of improving the river (although if Senhouse, Sir James Lowther and other owners helped, 'it would be a proposition very worthy of Attention') and by preferring a waggonway to a canal.[88] Further inland, Sir Wilfrid Lawson, first baronet of Brayton and Isel, let collieries and limestone quarries to several firms. He also owned a Durham estate at Washington, where he let coalmines, coke ovens and industrial premises.[89] The landowners of west Cumberland certainly profited from their underground rights, but they included hard-headed businessmen for long accustomed to taking entrepreneurial risks.

Although by 1891 Lord Lonsdale was lessor of over half of Cumbrian coal (at an average royalty, according to different estimates, of 5·62d or 6·98d per ton, the latter figure including interest on the Lowthers' capital investment), other local owners were also considerable coal proprietors. Lord Muncaster, for instance, could use Cumberland and Lancashire coal rents to make up the long decline in receipts from his East Riding land (which was sold in 1878).[90] And the Egremonts, owners of vast properties in Cumberland, Devon, Somerset, Yorkshire, Sussex and Ireland (which produced some £250,000 a year for the eccentric third Earl in the 1830s), had very extensive coal, iron and lead rights on their 11,000 Cumbrian acres. On the third Earl's death in 1837 this empire was divided, the bulk passing to his eldest illegitimate son, the future Lord Leconfield. The Cumbrian property, which eventually passed to Leconfield and his brother, General Sir Henry Wyndham, included iron ore in fifteen places, coal in thirteen, lead in four and slate in one. Management of these mineral concerns was left to John and George Dixon of Whitehaven; and by 1864 coal, iron and lead paid the Baron £7,154, and in 1865 £7,554. As their meticulous correspondence testifies, the Dixons performed their task admirably.[91] And so did most of their kind.

Nineteenth-century landowners in every colliery area inevitably gained something from industrial development, even if the advantage arose simply from the classic extension of a local market. Those who owned coal benefitted more immediately. In Furness the ubiquitous Buccleuch, with only 369 acres, was overshadowed by Devonshire, heroically creating Barrow; but Buccleuch's coal was extremely valuable.[92] Lancashire coal also provided incomes for such owners as the Earls of Abingdon,

Bradford, Crawford, Derby and Sefton, the Bankes family of Winstanley, Roger Leigh (whose 2,337 acres in the county produced £25,000 a year in the seventies), Lord Alexander Gordon-Lennox (a co-heir by marriage of the Towneleys of Burnley) and Le Gendre Starkie of Huntroyde.

Northumberland and Durham minerals made fortunes for many landowners, headed by the Church, represented at different times by the Bishop, the Dean and Chapter and individual incumbents and by the Ecclesiastical Commission. Such peers as the Dukes of Northumberland and Portland and Lords Hastings, Ravensworth, Windsor, Howden, Carlisle, Grey, Durham, Londonderry, Eldon, Dunsany, Waterford and Boyne (who inherited the coal-pioneering Russells' Brancepeth estate by marriage and let its 10,000 coal acres for £12,000 a year in the fifties) received varied but often large sums. Other beneficiaries included the Hazelrigg, Blake, Ridley, Musgrave, Clavering, Eden and Milbanke baronets and such squirearchic lines as the Towneleys, the Claytons of Chesters, the Ellisons of Hebburn, the Bowes of Streatlam, the Blacketts of Wylam, the Edens of Beamish Park, the Shaftos of Whitworth, the Salvins of Burn Hall, the Surtees of Redworth, the Riddells of Felton Park and Swinburne Castle, the Wilkinsons of Hulam, Sheraton and Clennell and the Coulthursts of Gargrave in Yorkshire. Indeed, a list of North-Eastern coalowners is almost a roll-call of local landed families. The only variable in the almost automatic catalogue was the different degree of (generally aristocratic) estates' involvement in the industries which so widely sustained rural rent-rolls.

Many such owners had originally operated their own small pits, some of which had grown into considerable undertakings. For instance, the Liddells of Ravensworth were prominent as leaders of 'the Regulation' during the eighteenth century. The sixth baronet (created a Baron in 1821) was an early patron of George Stephenson and in 1843 was the principal owner of five collieries. Another family of pioneers, the Brandlings of Gosforth, owning six early nineteenth-century collieries before their financial collapse, were also technological innovaters: Robert William, a leader of the Durham industry, employed Robert Stephenson, while his brother Charles John owned the Middleton colliery near Leeds, where John Blenkinsop opened his cele-

G

brated railway in 1812. The Braddylls, landowners in Cumberland, Lancashire and Durham, had their estates surveyed in 1821, and Colonel T. R. G. Braddyll subsequently joined the great South Hetton Coal Company. Such north-eastern squires as Christopher Blackett, Sir Robert Eden, Sir William Chaytor and partners and Lord Howden and partners were still operating collieries in 1843. The Midland Mining Commission then asserted:[93] 'If we inquire into the general character for wealth and rank of the employers of mining labour on the Tyne and Wear, we shall find them to be the nobility and gentry and landed proprietors.' This view was, in fact, already obsolescent and was soon to become largely untrue.

Cleveland ironstone became important only from the mid-nineteenth century. Early ventures had failed, sometimes because of squirearchic hostility and sometimes despite landowners' keen participation. John Wharton of Skelton Castle, Whig MP for Beverley from 1802 to 1826, 'would not listen to any proposal' from late eighteenth-century prospectors. A voracious and venal constituency undoubtedly helped to promote his bankruptcy, and from the ending of his parliamentary immunity until his death in 1843 the squire was lodged in a debtors' prison. The tragic lesson was apparently taken to heart by his successor, J. T. Wharton: in 1891, despite the estate solicitor's denials, the local miners' leader alleged that Wharton's lead royalties were excessive.[94] On the other hand, W. W. Jackson of Normanby Hall hopefully sent ironstone samples to Newcastle for expert examination in 1811, only to be told that they were 'good for nothing'. A partnership worked on the estates of Sir John Lowther, Martin Stapylton of Myton and Sir William Pennyman of Ormesby from 1839, but failed within two years. After 1848, however, a major industry started to develop on the property of Lord Zetland, Anthony Maynard of Skinninggrove, Lord de L'Isle, Stapylton, G. W. Jackson and H. B. Darley of Aldby and Spaunton.[95]

The nineteenth-century growth of the old West Yorkshire coal districts and the massive development of South Yorkshire coal led to major increases in many owners' incomes. Coal enabled the financially embarrassed Earls of Mexborough to expand their property and resume their occupation of Methley Hall.[96] It provided three-quarters of the income (£13,000 from about 3,300

acres in 1873) of the Fullerton family of Thrybergh Hall.[97] It
brought nineteen firms to the Yorkshire and Lancashire properties
of the Radcliffe baronets of Rudding Park.[98] And it created great
wealth for the Armytage baronets of Kirklees Park; the 'New
Domesday' survey reported an income of £17,064 from 3,400
acres in 1873 and ten years later Sir George, fifth baronet,
had £8,700 from 3,274 acres. Armytage's son, Sir George John,
chairman of the Lancashire & Yorkshire Railway, sat on the Royal
Commission on Coal Supplies of 1901.[99] Even that unlikely squire
Richard Monckton Milnes (later Lord Houghton) of Fryston
Hall drew £916 from two collieries for six months in 1881; and
his son, the Marquess of Crewe, was a considerable coalowner in
Yorkshire and the Midlands.[100] Other recipients of West Riding
coal incomes included the Davison-Blands of Kippax Park, the
Beaumonts of Whitley Beaumont, the Lowther baronets of Swil-
lington, the Gaskells of Thorne House, the Hatfields of Thorp
Arch, the Thellussons of Brodsworth Hall, the Torres of Sny-
dale Hall, the Edmunds of Worsborough Hall, the Calverleys of
Oulton Hall, the Taylors of Scaftworth, the Thornhills of Fixby,
the Meynell-Ingrams of Temple Newsam, the Ferrands of St
Ives and the Warde-Aldams of Hooton Pagnell and Frickley.[101]
Among local peers the Duke of Leeds and Lords Conyers, Cardigan, Mowbray, Scarbrough, Savile, Hawke, Dartmouth, Rosse
and Effingham, and among lesser squires such established colliery
owners as the Stocks and Lister families of Shibden drew diverse
mineral incomes.[102]

In 1843 the Midland Mining Commissioners regretted that in
South Staffordshire 'the immediate employers of labour . . . and
many of the owners of mineral property also were men whose
fathers, if not themselves, had risen to their present situation
from the ranks—speculators who had become wealthy *per Saltum*
with the rapid progress of manufacturing prosperity'. Nevertheless, there were some large owners among the generally small
proprietors in Staffordshire and Worcestershire. The Duke of
Sutherland already received 'some thousands a year' from Braids
Hill royalties on the Trentham estate and, with Lord Stafford,
owned Shropshire minerals. Staffordshire minerals also benefitted
such owners as Lords Sidmouth, Dartmouth, Granville, Hatherton, Lichfield and Shrewsbury and the Sneyds of Keele Hall.[103]

And the Duke of Cleveland's income of £97,398 (from 104,195 acres) in the seventies included agricultural rents from eleven counties and Durham and Stafford coal royalties.

Nottinghamshire and Derbyshire iron and coal for long enriched many landowners, including several great magnates. Earl Manvers had £51,649 from some 38,000 acres in five counties in the 1870s, in addition to a growing mineral income. The Duke of Portland supplemented his rent-roll of £124,925 from 162,235 acres in eight counties by involvement in Nottingham and Scottish mines. The Duke of Newcastle (with agricultural rents of £74,547 from 35,547 acres in four counties) and the Montagus of Ingmanthorpe Hall (whose 27,265 acres in four counties paid £53,034) similarly increased already large incomes. Some such owners, like the Earl of Shrewsbury, the Willoughbys of Wollaton (from 1711 Lords Middleton), the Sitwells of Renishaw and the Spencers (eventually squires of Cannon Hall), were pioneer entrepreneurs. Others, like Viscount Melbourne, were apparently unbusinesslike.[104] Great and small, active and indolent, British landowners were extensively affected by mining developments.

Minerals, and especially coal, not only buttressed the fortunes of established landed families but also aided the rise of new gentry. The process was first and most noticeably demonstrated in north-eastern England. For instance, coal created the fortune of the Ridleys of Heaton and Blagdon, who received a baronetcy in 1756 and a viscountcy in 1900. They moved into Northumbrian Tory politics, as owners of some 10,000 acres, but until the succession of Sir Matthew, fourth baronet, in 1836, they retained many commercial interests.[105] The Cooksons of Neasham House and Meldon Park, the Cuthberts of Beaufront Castle, the Strakers of Stagshaw House, the Taylors of Chipchase Castle and the constantly rising Joiceys of Newton Hall and Ford Castle (who obtained a Liberal baronetcy in 1893 and a barony in 1905) all owed their social and economic status to coal. In the West Riding the Charlesworths of Chapelthorpe Hall and the Clarkes of Noblethorpe Hall became Tory squires through long involvement with colliery ownership and management (in the Charlesworths' case, on a large scale).

Similar examples might be found in each colliery district. Such great Scottish industrialists as the Bairds and Dixons, for instance, bought their way into substantial landownership. For the successful coal- or iron-master, purchases of land often served the double purpose of extending control over minerals and establishing a personal position within county society. Several nineteenth-century iron dynasties, like the Barkers of Albrighton, the Baldwins of Wilden, Stourport and Bewdley, the Guests of Canford, the Hardys of Dunstall and Chilham and the Walkers of Blythe and Beckford, re-established themselves as landowners. Richard Crawshay might assert in 1822 that 'I have but one pride, to be head of the iron trade, and land won't do that.' But even he resided at Ottershaw Park, while his elder brother William settled at Cyfartha Castle and Caversham Park.

Older families continued to use mineral incomes, at least in part, to pay off accumulated debts. When Ralph Sneyd's Staffordshire royalties increased in 1857 his agent was 'looking forward with great confidence to the time when they should be able to wipe off some of the debt'. Coal similarly aided even such great owners as Durham and Fitzwilliam. And Lord George Cavendish (later first Earl of Burlington) must have found £3,000 a year from his Furness blue slate quarries in the twenties as useful as his Devonshire cousins found their Yorkshire and Derbyshire lead profits or the Bedfords (more reluctantly) their income from copper. Coal royalties on occasion might save small estates from breaking up during periods of agricultural difficulties.[106]

Many landowners at least tried to run their mining ventures on traditional lines. In 1843 George Stephenson and F. Foster praised John Peile's management of Lonsdale's Whitehaven collieries, but added that 'notwithstanding this, however, it appears that not more than two-thirds of the coal is got, and at a former period that two-thirds were left in the workings'. The energetic Peile attacked the 'meagre report' on the ground that it contained nothing new. But in one sense the two Chesterfield engineers were representative of their kind and their age: their technical advice was supplemented by economic and local 'diplomatic' information. A Whitehaven–Workington–Maryport railway, they wrote, might be constructed for about £80,000, and[107]

It appears to us to be of the greatest importance to the Town of Whitehaven that this line should be made, [as] if it is not made there is no doubt in our minds that the Maryport Harbour will be so improved as to seriously affect the trade of Whitehaven. We should advise your Lordship and Mr Curwen to give the portion of your lands required for the Railway to a company for nothing, with a clause that no coal shall be carried upon it except that which may belong to your Lordship and Mr Curwen. We think this would be a considerable inducement in getting the whole of the inhabitants in Whitehaven who can spare any capital to get a company together, as they would certainly protect the interests of the Town by so doing.

Several owners were led by similar strategic considerations to participation in important transport undertakings.

In general, there appears to be no reason to suppose that aristocratic industrialists were less efficient than rival companies. A Lonsdale, Durham, Fitzwilliam or Dudley was no amateur dabbler in industrial affairs. But in curious ways traditional agricultural customs were often maintained. For instance, the Lowthers and Charlesworths provided occasional 'treats', reminiscent of estate celebrations, for their employees. The Fitzwilliams provided good houses, free coals, sickness and injury benefits and Christmas gifts, and the Londonderrys and Durhams also tried to act as benevolent employers. Tremenheere approvingly recorded such examples of paternalism.[108] The Duke of Portland's Kilmarnock undertaking, with its good houses, 'arrangements . . . for comfort, propriety and cleanliness', schools and kirks, benefit societies, savings bank and amiable industrial relations, seemed an eminently happy and respectable place in 1845, when Tremenheere also praised the managerial practices of the Bairds, Buccleuch, Fitzwilliam, J. D. Charlesworth and Robert Brandling, while condemning the state of Lister-Kaye's colliers. In 1843 Thomas Tancred maintained that

It appears a legitimate deduction . . . that the rank and wealth of the employers of mining labour has an important influence upon the welfare of the workmen . . . It is not unreasonable to imagine *a priori* that men of rank and capital will not condescend to adopt the shifts and expedients to which an inferior class of proprietors are as it were driven to resort. Besides, the former may be

generally presumed to have enjoyed a better education and also to
be more amenable to public opinion. Hence mining districts may
be expected to vary in regard to the general and customary treatment of the workmen according as the proprietors are generally
and on an average of greater or less rank and wealth. We have
seen that the butty system and the truck system are merely
methods of supplying a lack of adequate capital on the part of the
mineowner, and whatever exceptions there may be, I think it will
be found that the general customs prevailing in the treatment of
workpeople in any district will be established and regulated by
the sense of the majority of the great proprietors, and will be more
or less liberal and considerate according to the scale on which the
mining operations are conducted.

It is, of course, impossible to estimate whether and to what extent
some notion of the 'politics of deference' influenced such analyses.
John Dickinson, a mines inspector, told the 1852 Select Committee on colliery explosions that 'as a general rule the larger [mines]
were better managed than the smaller ones'. However, he maintained that 'the defective arrangement in the smaller collieries
[did] not always [arise] from a deficiency of pecuniary means, but
a wish to get the coals as cheaply as possible. There were [also]
some very large and wealthy coal owners who were extremely
careful in getting coals at a cheap rate.'[109]
Most owners and viewers were hostile to the miners' unions.
In Scotland, where the colliers were bound for life to their collieries until legislation of 1775 and 1799 (but where the law's
harshness was rarely employed), owners reacted quickly against
absenteeism and combination in 1797. A meeting was held with
the Crown lawyers 'to consider what steps ought to be taken for
counteracting [the miners'] proceedings'. Captain Andrew Wauchope, who attended the assembly, told Lord Balgonie that
'opinions were pretty similar in thinking the present Wages of
Colliers such that it would be highly improvident to raise them'.
The owners had decided 'to put in force the present Laws re-
specting Combinations' and to demand legislation to compel
miners 'to perform regular work as other Labourers'.
'As to fixing the Rate of Wages, I perfectly agree with your
Lordship that it is impossible to establish any general Rule',
Wauchope told Balgonie,

the principal thing would be (if possible) to prevent Coalmasters from suborning, enticing and bribing away other people's Colliers, restricting the Bounty or earnest money and requiring a Line from their former Employers declaring their time of Service being expired . . . I was happy to hear from different Reports that your Coalliers in Fife are a more orderly set of people than in other Countys, however you are not without your Plagues, you have got your *Mealmakers*.

North-eastern English miners were subject to a yearly bond, often broken by migration connived at by owners and managers.[110] Tremenheere was inclined to regret that union campaigns had, by 1845, induced many masters to cease yearly hirings, 'in order to enable them to discharge refractory men more readily'. He believed that annual contracts, by giving greater security, created confidence and improved industrial relations. But union activities remained unpopular even with landed industrialists. Lord Londonderry, a 'good' employer by the standards of the forties, earned a black mark in labour history by his stern measures against striking workers in 1844. Henry Morton, Durham's agent, and John Peile, the Lowthers' manager, were equally hostile to 'the pitmen's union', and Fitzwilliam threatened to close his collieries and dismiss unionists rather than yield to it.[111] Many such owners expressed surprise and regret that their relatively well-treated employees should join combinations against them; and their disappointment was not always feigned.

While it appears probable that landed mineowners were often 'better' employers than commercial partnerships, many eagerly sought to adopt all the *mores* of the business community. The bitter arguments between the Whig Curwens and Tory Senhouses in Cumberland provide one example. And George Bowes, an original 'Grand Ally', who constantly broke his Durham colleagues' agreement for quick eighteenth-century returns, was almost a prototype of the swashbuckling tycoon. His precedent was followed by John Bowes, illegitimate son of the tenth Earl of Strathmore, who continued family tradition by forming a great mining partnership in 1844 with C. M. Palmer (whose iron and shipbuilding enterprises he also aided) and making huge profits, later used to finance the Bowes Museum near Barnard Castle.[112]

Certainly, some landowners remained doggedly hostile to industry. 'The Account you give me of my timber and the Coal Pit', Cary Elwes, a Lincolnshire squire, told his Yorkshire agent, George Prissick, in 1758, 'has determined me to lay aside all intention of medling with either. As to the former it was only on supposition that it was the worse for standing, and *the latter I never much cared about, being no Schemer.*' He offered no help to mining ventures, though not absolutely forbidding them:[113]

> As to the trial for Coal which you tell me of [he wrote to Prissick in 1759], I have no objection to it on the terms you mention, and am willing to furnish them with the rubbish wood you speak of; but on no acc't will ever be concern'd in it so as to advance a shilling of Cash or be in the least in partnership, or be answerable for any miscarriage in the said adventure, but if the persons you mention make any thing considerable of it, I doubt but you will take care of my Interest on that supposition.

Such an attitude, however, seems to have become gradually rarer. A small Scottish laird, Admiral Keith Stewart, was more typical in thinking, in 1787, that it was[114]

> very much for my Advantage as a Land Proprietor that as many different Veins of Coal and Mines should be opened as possible both as to Establishing the Character of the Country as also Tending towards making Roads and bringing Inhabitants, but above all as a substantial encouragement to Iron Masters.

This more general reaction inevitably involved the landowner in many of the problems already instanced. Stewart himself was soon waging complicated contests with both other owners and his lessees.[115] At the furthest extreme, Lord Dundonald's 'sanguine expectations of retrieving the family estates by his discoveries led him to embark in a multitude of manufacturing projects'. His son, the tenth Earl, sadly described the result:[116]

> The motive was excellent; but his pecuniary means being incommensurate with the magnitude of his transactions, its object was frustrated, and our remaining patrimony melted like the flux in his crucibles; his scientific knowledge, as often happens, being unaccompanied by the self-knowledge which would have taught him that he was not, either by habit or inclination, a 'man of business'.

Much of the managerial and actuarial work on mineral estates was, of course, performed by (sometimes amazingly knowledge-able) consultants or (often fanatically loyal) stewards. One Lons-dale agent, John Bateman, even opposed the 'new practice' of holding a coroner's inquest on a pit-woman's death in 1803, as it might 'frighten the ignorant and discourage them from going into the Pits'. His successor from 1812, John Peile, could honestly tell Lonsdale in 1843 that [117]

> I have devoted my whole life exclusively to your Lordship's service day and night with pleasure to myself and I feel thankful in having enjoyed your Lordship's confidence and support for a term of years beyond that of any former predecessor and in having the good fortune to steer safely this great and weighty ship through many a storm.

Good and faithful servants were undoubtedly important. But ultimate decision-making rested with the owner, and there was considerable truth in the observations of G. P. Richards, the experienced Cardiff lawyer. 'I have long thought', he wrote in 1826,[118]

> a large fortune, coupled as it is with the hundred agents, lawyers and all the hangers-on usually attendant upon it, a great evil. I find myself more and more satisfied of this when I consider Lord Bute's expenditure in this way and if I were called on to pay out of the little pittance it has pleased Providence to bestow on me in the same proportion to my means as his Lordship I fear St Luke's would be my resting place.

From the viewpoint of the historian of landed estates, the landowner's connection with mineral ventures is seminal. Mineral trade was primarily responsible for the Duke of Bridge-water's canal, for the harbour undertakings of Lonsdale, Curwen, Senhouse, Londonderry, Bute, Eglinton, Lord Wemyss and others and for many landowners' initial involvement with the railways. Above all other factors, it led landed proprietors into association with industry. The fact that successful mine-operators, like other industrialists, purchased land—and often purely agri-cultural land—demonstrated an important non-economic cal-culation: a landed estate, appointment as JP and possible election for a parliamentary borough could be a sound social investment, producing dividends for a university-educated son with ambitions for a deputy-lieutenancy, a yeomanry commission and 'county' status. And mining, involving a rare mixture of great capitalists, small partnerships, landowner-lessors, landowning partners and aristocratic entrepreneurs, was an extraordinary catalyst. It created variegated but close links between Land and Industry, with vital social and sociological consequences. Its great extent, only now being explored and revealed by local researchers, must surely compel historians to re-examine some cherished and facile 'economic' explanations of political motivation. Above all, the notion of an inevitable dichotomy between Land and Industry, expounded for different reasons by sentimental hagiographers of noblemen and by 'liberal' extollers of 'dissenting academy' entrepreneurial virtue, appears to be at least doubtfully tenable. Whig and Tory, Free Trader and Protectionist, ancient dynasty and brash newcomer, Protestant, Anglican and Roman Catholic were equally affected by mineral development.[119]

NOTES

1 See J. U. Nef, *The Rise of the British Coal Industry* (2 vols 1932), passim.
2 William Green, 'The Chronicles and Records of the Northern Coal Trade . . .', *Trans North of England Institute of Mining Engineers*, 15 (1866), 202; R. L. Galloway, *Annals of Coal Mining and the Coal Trade* (1898), vol 1, 248; T. S. Ashton and J. Sykes, *The Coal Industry of the Eighteenth Century* (Manchester 1929), 4; P. M. Sweezy, *Monopoly and Competition in the English Coal Trade, 1550–1850* (Cambridge, Mass 1938), 24, 27; Edward Hughes, *North Country Life in the Eighteenth Century, 1: The North-East, 1700–1750* (1952), 233–50.
3 A. K. Hamilton Jenkin, *The Cornish Miner* (1962 edn), 32–5, 311.
4 See Arthur Raistrick and Bernard Jennings, *A History of Lead Mining in the Pennines* (1965), 189–98, 247–50.
5 Ashton and Sykes, *Coal Industry*, 175–8; W. Fordyce, *A History of Coal, Coke, Coal-Fields . . . Iron, Its Ores and Processes of Manufacture . . .* (1860), 50–1. For eighteenth-century examples, see G. W. Daniels and T. S. Ashton, 'The Records of a Derbyshire Colliery, 1763–1779, *Economic Hist Rev*, 2 (1929); W. H. B. Court, 'A Warwickshire Colliery in the Eighteenth Century', ibid, 7 (1937).

6   Fordyce, *History of Coal*, 139–40; Breadalbane Muniments (SRO) GD 112/18; Senhouse MSS by courtesy of Mr Roger Pocklington-Senhouse (CRO) 19/165.

7   PP, 41 (1893–4), [C 6980], *RC on Mining Royalties. Final Report*, 4; Fordyce, *History of Coal*, 51. See also *Mining Royalties and Rents in the British Empire* (1936), 12–23; J. H. Morris and L. J. Williams, *The South Wales Coal Industry, 1841–1875* (Cardiff 1958), ch 5.

8   Fordyce, *History of Coal*, 51–2; K. Neville Moss, 'Mining Leases', in *Historical Review of Mining* [1931], 321–33; John Clark, 'Minerals', in R. C. Walmsley (ed), *Rural Estate Management* (1948), 323–33; Sir R. A. S. Redmayne and Gilbert Stone, *The Ownership and Valuation of Mineral Property in the United Kingdom* (1920), passim; PP, 41 (1893–4), 5–24.

9   Broughton and Cally Muniments (SRO) GD 10/1246.

10 Fordyce, *History of Coal*, 93; information kindly communicated by Sir William Lowther, Bt.

11 PP, 41 (1893–4), 79.

12 PP, 36 (1890), [C 6195], *First Report of the RC . . . [on] Mining Royalties*, 1, 156; Cmd 360 (1919), *Coal Industry Commission Report*, II, 584, 596, 603, 607, 618, 626, 648, 653.

13 Draycott Hall MSS by courtesy of Mrs M. S. Radcliffe (NRRO) ZLB, Allison-Littlefair correspondence, May–Aug 1836.

14 Hamilton Bruce Muniments (SRO) GD 152/196, G. P. Richards to O. W. Tyndale, 14 & 28 Jan 1826, J. Clayton to Bute, 24 May 1847.

15 John Bateman, *Great Landowners of Great Britain and Ireland* (1879 edn), 66; Cmd 360, II, 698, 653; Fordyce, *History of Coal*, 45, 76, 90; William Rees, *Cardiff: A History of the City* (Cardiff 1962), 126, 146; E. D. Lewis, *The Rhondda Valleys* (1963 impr), 68–9, 84, 201, 218; Sir D. H. Blair, *John Patrick, 3rd Marquess of Bute* (1921), 2–3; John Strawhorn, *The New History of Cumnock* (Cumnock 1966), passim; Blair of Blair Muniments (SRO) GD 167/4E, memorandum by Capt W. F. Blair, 3 Jan 1868. Bute's Welsh royalties rose from £10,765 in 1848 to an average of £55,969 in 1871–5 (Morris and Williams, *South Wales Coal Industry*, 120–5).

16 J. L. Carvel, *One Hundred Years of Coal. The History of the Alloa Coal Company* (Edinburgh 1944), 58–9.

17 Blair of Blair Muniments, GD 167/4A, James Methven to Robert Patrick, 10 Oct 1838. I am indebted to Mr J. R. Hume for this reference.

18 PP, 36 (1890), 72.

19 Clerk of Penicuik Muniments (SRO) GD 18/1155, J. Clark memorandum, 5 Feb 1875.

20 See David Spring, 'The English Landed Estate in the Age of

Coal and Iron, 1830–1880', *Jour Economic Hist*, 11 (1951); 'The Earls of Durham and the Great Northern Coalfield, 1830–1880', *Canadian Hist Rev*, 33 (1952).

21 Earl of Crawford and Balcarres, 'Haigh Cannel' (Manchester Statistical Society 1933). I am indebted to the Earl of Crawford and Balcarres, KT, GBE, for help.

22 Bateman, *Great Landowners*, 107; Alan Birch, 'The Haigh Iron-works, 1789–1856', *Bull John Rylands Lib*, 35 (1952–3); Crawford, 'Haigh Cannel'.

23 Wentworth Woodhouse Muniments, by courtesy of the Earl Fitzwilliam and the Trustees of the Fitzwilliam Settled Estates (SCL), passim; J. T. Ward, 'The Earls Fitzwilliam and the Wentworth Woodhouse Estate in the Nineteenth Century', *Yorkshire Bull Economic and Social Research*, 12 (1960).

24 Archibald and Nan L. Clow, 'Lord Dundonald', *Econ Hist Rev*, 12 (1942), *The Chemical Revolution* (1952), 393–423; Earl of Dundonald, *The Autobiography of a Seaman* (1861), 21ff; R. H. Campbell, *Carron Company* (Edinburgh 1961), 60.

25 Bateman, *Great Landowners* (1883 edn), 168, 334; Arundel Castle MSS by courtesy of His Grace the Duke of Norfolk, EM, KG and the Sheffield City Librarian (SCL) S 180–2, 190, 205, 521, SP 59; G. P. Jones, 'Early Industrial Development', in D. L. Linton (ed), *Sheffield and its Region* (Sheffield 1956); PP, 36 (1890), 77–8.

26 Cmd 360, II, 672, 689–90, 698, 658.

27 PP, 8 (1830), *Report of the SC of the House of Lords on the State of the Coal Trade*, 31; PP, 36 (1890), App B, 161–99. See also Lord Percy of Newcastle, *Some Memories* (1958), 14 and lists in PP, 18 (1871), iii [C. 435–II], *Report of the Commissioners appointed to inquire into the several matters relating to Coal in the United Kingdom*, App 27, 17–55.

28 PP, 13 (1843), *Midland Mining Commission. First Report. South Staffordshire*, xv.

29 See R. L. Galloway, *A History of Coal Mining in Great Britain* (1882, intro B. F. Duckham, 1969), 93–100; Fred Bland, 'John Curr, Originator of Iron Tram Roads', *Trans Newcomen Soc*, 11 (1932); David Spring, *The English Landed Estate in the Nineteenth Century: Its Administration* (Baltimore 1963), passim; F. M. L. Thompson, *English Landed Society in the Nineteenth Century* (1963), 171–5; J. T. Ward, 'West Riding Landowners and Mining in the Nineteenth Century', *Yorks Bull*, 15 (1963); Sidney Pollard, *The Genesis of Modern Management* (1965), 63–4, 268–9; B. F. Duckham, 'The Emergence of the Professional Manager in the Scottish Coal Industry', *Business Hist Rev*, 43 (1969).

30 Arundel Castle MSS (SCL) S 214, Curr to Norfolk, 23, Norfolk Curr, 27 Oct 1801.

31   Robert Bald, *A General View of the Coal Trade of Scotland* . . .
     (Edinburgh 1812 edn), 8–10; Carvel, *One Hundred Years in
     Coal*, 11–131, passim; PP, 72 (1874), iii [C 899], *Scotland,
     Owners of Lands and Heritages*, 42; Bateman, *Great Landowners*
     (1879 edn), 291. The various creations of the Mar earldom were
     re-examined by the House of Lords in 1875, and two distinct
     lines were eventually recognised.
32   P. Ford, 'Tobacco and Coal: A Note on the Economic History of
     Whitehaven', *Economica*, 9 (1929); J. E. Williams, 'Paternalism
     in Local Government in the Nineteenth Century', *Public Ad-
     ministration*, 33 (1955), 'Whitehaven in the Eighteenth Century',
     Econ Hist Rev, 2S, 8 (1956); Galloway, *History*, 92–100,
     Annals: vol 1, 216–18; D. Swann, 'The Pace and Progress of
     Port Investment in England, 1660–1830', *Yorks Bull*, 12 (1960);
     W. Parson, W. White, *History, Directory and Gazetteer of the
     Counties of Cumberland and Westmorland* . . . (Leeds 1829), 202,
     228, 235–49, 337–9; Lowther MSS by courtesy of the Earl of
     Lonsdale (CRO) D/Lons/47, 45 (Peile to Lonsdale, 14 Dec
     1843) and MS 'History of the Whitehaven Collieries'; PP, 36
     (1890), 175, 177.
33   Spring, 'Earls of Durham'; T. Y. Hall, 'The Extent and Prob-
     able Duration of the Northern Coalfield', *Trans N Eng Inst
     Min Eng*, 2 (1854); PP, 18 (1871), iii, App 27; Marchioness of
     Londonderry, *Frances Anne* (1958), passim; Cmd 360, II,
     631–2.
34   PP, 18 (1871), iii, App 27; Cmd 360, II, 703.
35   PP, 18 (1871), iii, App 27; Nostell MSS by courtesy of the
     Lord St Oswald, MC; Cmd 360, II, 689–90; PP, 13 (1843),
     cxlv, 11–12, 131; A. L. Kennedy, *My Dear Duchess* (1956), 69;
     Fordyce, *History of Coal*, 152–3; Gervas Huxley, *Lady Eliza-
     beth and the Grosvenors* (1965), 9; Georgina Battiscombe, *Mrs
     Gladstone* (1956), 14, 61, 65; D. A. Wray, *The Mining Industry
     in the Huddersfield District* (Huddersfield 1929), 23.
36   Bateman, *Great Landowners* (1879 edn), 136; PP, 13 (1843),
     xiii, xxi, cxlvii–cl, 45, 52–3, 56, 131; PP, 18 (1871), iii, App 27,
     140, 142; Cmd 360, II, 615–16. See also T. E. Jones, 'The
     South Staffordshire and North Worcestershire Mining District
     and its Relics of Mining Appliances', *Trans Newcomen Soc*, 11
     (1930–1); Fordyce, *History of Coal*, 154.
37   Frickley Hall MSS by courtesy of Col R. J. P. Warde-Aldam,
     TD, T. Goulding to W. Aldam, 11 Feb 1850; J. T. Ward, 'The
     Squire as Businessman: William Aldam of Frickley Hall (1813–
     1890)', *Trans Hunter Arch Soc*, 8 (1962).
38   Leven and Melville Muniments (SRO) GD 26/5/368/1, A. Fyfe
     to J. Kyd, 5 Oct 1812.
39   W. T. Jackman, *The Development of Transportation in Modern
     England* (Cambridge 1916), vol 2, 471–2, n 4; Rees, *Cardiff*,

150; Cmd 360, II, 653–7, 648, 698–9, 603, 607; A. H. John, 'Iron and Coal on a Glamorgan Estate', *Econ Hist Rev*, 8, (1943), *The Industrial Development of South Wales, 1750–1850. An Essay* (Cardiff 1950), 8–10, 36–7.

40 A. H. Dodd, *The Industrial Revolution in North Wales* (Cardiff 1951 ed), 17–18, 21, 102, 131–228, passim; Marquess of Anglesey, *One-Leg* (1963 edn), 20, 356.

41 Bateman, *Great Landowners* (1879 edn), 61; PP, 18 (1871), iii, App 27; PP, 41 (1890–1), [C 6331] *RC on Mining Royalties. Second Report*, 336.

42 Bateman, *Great Landowners* (1879 edn), 197; C 6331, 323–4; Cmd 360, II, 617–20.

43 PP, 18 (1871), iii, App 27; Bateman, *Great Landowners* (1879 edn), 464; Cmd 360, II, 640–2.

44 PP, 18 (1871), iii, App 27; Fordyce, *History of Coal*, 11–12; James McKechnie and Murray Macgregor, *A Short History of the Scottish Coal-Mining Industry* (Edinburgh 1958), 42–5.

45 Bald, *Coal Trade in Scotland*, 18–19. See also, T. C. Smout, 'Scottish Landowners and Economic Growth, 1650–1850', *Scottish Jour Political Economy*, 11 (1964).

46 J. R. M. Butler, *Lord Lothian* (1960), 146.

47 Frank Atkinson, 'Some Northumberland Collieries in 1724', *Trans Arch and Antiq Soc of Durham and Northumberland*, 11 (1965), *The Great Northern Coalfield, 1700–1900* (Barnard Castle 1966), passim.

48 PP, 72 (1874), iii; Bateman, *Great Landowners* (1883 edn), passim; Ian Anstruther, *The Knight and the Umbrella* (1963), passim.

49 Pollard, *Genesis of Modern Management*, 67–9; PP, 18 (1871), iii, App 27.

50 Wharncliffe Muniments by courtesy of the Earl of Wharncliffe (SCL), passim.

51 Joseph Wilkinson, *Worsborough* (1872), 247; Joseph Hunter, *South Yorkshire* (1831), vol 2, 281; Vernon-Wentworth Muniments, by courtesy of Major C. J. Vernon-Wentworth (SCL), Thomas Boultbee's accounts.

52 Spencer-Stanhope Muniments by courtesy of Mr S. Fraser (SCL); A. M. W. Stirling, *Annals of a Yorkshire House* (1911), vol 2, 79–82; J. T. Ward, ' "Old" and "New" Bradfordians in the Nineteenth Century', *Bradford Textile Soc Jour* (1965).

53 Fordyce, *History of Coal*, 86; Lewis, *Rhondda Valleys*, 69.

54 Leven and Melville Muniments, GD 26/5/370, Keith to Balgonie, 7 July, 3 Oct 1800.

55 Ibid. GD 26/5/319, 333, 335, 368/1 (Anderson report, 14 Dec 1801).

56 Ibid. GD 26/5/368/1 (Puncheon report, 16 May 1804), 371/1–3, 372, 374, 368/2 (Bald report, 8 Jan 1817); Cmd 360, II, 658.

57 Lane-Fox MSS by courtesy of Col and the Hon Mrs F. G. W. Lane-Fox (LCL), LIX, 6; LXXIV, 35; LXXXIV, 2; LXXXVIII, 56; CX, 13, 18; J. T. Ward, 'The Saving of a Yorkshire Estate: George Lane-Fox and Bramham Park', *Yorks Archaeological Jour*, 42 (1967).

58 Netherby MSS by courtesy of Sir Fergus Graham, Bt, KBE; David Spring, 'A Great Agricultural Estate: Netherby under Sir James Graham, 1820–1845', *Agricultural History*, 29 (1955); J. T. Ward, *Sir James Graham* (1967), 70.

59 Tennyson d'Eyncourt MSS (LAO) 2 TdE/H/1/23, Yarborough to Tennyson, 6 Feb 1801. I am indebted to Dr G. Jackson for this reference.

60 Wentworth Woodhouse Muniments, passim.

61 *Trans N Eng Inst Min Eng*, 1 (1853), iv; 4 (1856), 109; PP, 36 (1890), 77–8; Cmd 360, II, 672, 674, 690, 698, 656.

62 Fordyce, *History of Coal*, 105–6, 159; Hamilton Bruce Muniments, GD 152/196, Bute to Tyndale, 4 Jan 1847.

63 Campbell, *Carron Company*, 32, 46, 49, 205–10, 289; Blair of Blair Muniments, GD 167/4A, Miller to Speir, 29 Dec 1836; PP, 72 (1874), iii, 169, 178; Bateman, *Great Landowners*, 410.

64 *Digest of Evidence given before the RC on Coal Supplies, 1901–1905*, 1 (1905), 18, 241, 266; PP, 86 (1890), 51–2, 55, 57–61, 74–80; PP, 41 (1890–1), [C 6529] *RC on Mining Royalties, Third Report*, 126–8.

65 Blair of Blair Muniments, GD 167/4B, C, E, passim; Bateman, *Great Landowners* (1879 edn), 41; PP, 72 (1874), iii, 18. See also R. H. Campbell, 'The Iron Industry in Ayrshire', *Ayrshire Arch and Nat Hist Soc Collections*, 2S, 7 (1966).

66 Blair of Blair Muniments, GD 167/4E, Alexander to Blair, 15 Apr, Blair memoranda, Apr, Alexander to Blair, 28 Dec 1865; Bateman, *Great Landowners* (1879 edn), 6, 70. Professor Campbell has shown that some early charges were very low: R. H. Campbell, 'Investment in the Scottish Pig Iron Trade, 1830–1843', *Scott Jour Pol Econ*, 1 (1954).

67 PP, 41 (1890–1), [C 6529] 201; Tremenheere's Report (1845), 17; Pollard, *Genesis of Modern Management*, 73–4.

68 Bolton Abbey Estate MSS by courtesy of the Duke of Devonshire, MC; Robert T. Clough, *The Lead Smelting Mills of the Yorkshire Dales* (Leeds 1962), 19, 70, 76; Arthur Raistrick, 'The Lead Mines of Upper Wharfedale', *Yorks Bull*, 5 (1953), 'The Mechanisation of the Grassington Moor Mines, Yorkshire', *Trans Newcomen Soc*, 29 (1953–5); information kindly communicated by Mrs E. E. Yorke.

69 Clough, *Lead Smelting*, passim; Raistrick and Jennings, *History of Lead Mining*, passim; Arthur Raistrick, *Mines and Miners in Swaledale* (Clapham 1955).

70 Draycott Hall MSS, ZLB, accounts.

71 Chaloner MSS by courtesy of the Lord Gisborough (NRRO) ZFM, passim; J. W. Walker, *Wakefield, Its History and People* (Wakefield 1934), 457; Joseph Wilkinson, *Worthies, Families and Celebrities of Barnsley and the District* (1883), 19.

72 Chaloner MSS, ZFM/56B, 209–13, 206.

73 Thomas Sopwith, 'On the Lead Mining Districts of the North of England', *Trans N Eng Inst Min Eng*, 13 (1864); Raistrick and Jennings, *History of Lead Mining*, 148–52, 201–2; A. E. Smailes, *North England* (1960), 68, 144.

74 Bretton Hall MSS by courtesy of the late Viscount Allendale, KG, CB, CBE, MC; J. T. Ward, 'The Beaumont Family's Estates in the Nineteenth Century', *Bull Inst Historical Research*, 35 (1962).

75 *The Times*, 14 Feb 1907.

76 Broughton and Cally Muniments, GD 10/1247–52. By 1873 the mines paid only £20. (PP, 72 (1874), iii, 120.)

77 Burnett and Reid Papers (SRO) GD 57/358.

78 See Thompson, *English Landed Society*, 89, Spring, *English Landed Estate*, 43.

79 *Glasgow Morning Journal*, 7 Feb 1866. I am indebted to Dr J. Butt for this reference.

80 J. Rowe, *Cornwall in the Age of the Industrial Revolution* (Liverpool 1963), passim.

81 John Marley, 'Cleveland Ironstone', *Trans N Eng Inst Min Eng*, 5 (1857); K. A. MacMahon, *Roads and Turnpike Trusts in Eastern Yorkshire* (York 1964), 34.

82 Philemon Slater, *History of the Ancient Parish of Guiseley* (1880), 284.

83 William Grainge, *The History and Topography of Harrogate . . .* (1882), 429–30; information kindly communicated by Mrs M. Greenwood and Mr B. C. Greenwood.

84 Clerk of Penicuik Muniments, GD 18/1151, Clerk to Tremenheere, 16 Feb 1844. Several other owners faced similar difficulties in preventing breaches of the 1842 Act.

85 Clerk of Penicuik Muniments, GD 18/1154–5 (John Geddes's report, 15 July 1878), 1156–7; Bateman, *Great Landowners* (1879 edn), 367. On the early history of the Clerks' mineral interests, see B. F. Duckham, 'Some Eighteenth-Century Scottish Coal Mining Methods', *Industrial Archaeology*, 5 (1968); 'Life and Labour in a Scottish Colliery 1698–1755', *Scott Hist Rev*, 47 (1968).

86 Hughes, *North Country Life*, 2: *Cumberland and Westmorland, 1700–1830* (1965), passim; Senhouse MSS 19/165; C. Roy Hudleston, 'An Eighteenth Century Squire's Possessions', *Trans Cumberland and Westmorland Antiq and Arch Soc*, ns 57 (1958). On the West Cumbrian coalfield, see *Trans N Eng Inst Min Eng*, 8 (1860), 13 (1864).

H

87   Curwen MSS by courtesy of Mr J. N. St G. Curwen and Mrs I. M. Chance (CRO) D/CU/5/99, 100, 106, 108, 6/22, 38 (Dunn's report, 26 Dec 1832), 56 (Forster's report, 25 Feb 1871), 147; Galloway, *Annals*, vol 2, 143–4; Bateman, *Great Landowners* (1879 edn), 112; C 6529, 22; Parson and White, *Cumberland and Westmorland*, 212, 284.

88   Senhouse MSS 19/6, D 5 (Spedding's and Brown's report, 31 July 1781), 19/165, 245 (Curwen to Senhouse, 10, 20 Sept 1850), D 5 (Stobart's report, 2 May 1870; Smeaton to Egremont, 19 Oct 1775). The Senhouse estate remained small, amounting to only 890 acres, rented at £2,558 in 1873.

89   Lawson MSS by courtesy of the Lawson Estate Trustees (CRO) DL/24/19.

90   Pennington MSS by courtesy of Sir William Pennington-Ramsden, Bt (ERRO) DDWA, passim; C 6331, 261–2; C 6529, 23; C 6980, 84.

91   Leconfield MSS (Cockermouth Castle) by courtesy of the Lord Egremont, D/Lec/92, 93, records of J. A. Dixon, 1, 53, 69.

92   S. Pollard, 'Barrow-in-Furness and the Seventh Duke of Devonshire', *Econ Hist Rev*, 2S, 8 (1955); J. D. Marshall, *Furness and the Industrial Revolution* (Barrow 1958), passim. In 1857 the Kirklees Hall undertakers paid royalties of £6,000 to Muncaster and £2–3,000 to Buccleuch (whose surface rent was only £150), while Lord Burlington (who became the 7th Duke of Devonshire in 1858) had £8,000 from the Schneiders (Fordyce, *History of Coal*, 152).

93   Bateman, *Great Landowners* (1879, 1883 eds), passim; Fordyce, *History of Coal*, 63–100; Hughes, *North Country Life*, vol 1, passim; Galloway, *History*; *Annals*, vol 1, passim; T. Y. Hall, 'On the Rivers, Ports and Harbours of the Great Northern Coalfield', *Trans N Eng Inst Min Eng*, 10 (1862); Green, *Northern Coal Trade*; PP, 13 (1843), civ–cviii; R. V. Taylor, *Biographia Leodiensis* (1865), 302–3; W. G. Rimmer, 'Middleton Colliery, near Leeds (1770–1830)', *Yorks Bull*, 7 (1955); E. Kilburn Scott, 'Memorials to Pioneer Leeds Industrialists', *Trans Newcomen Soc*, 11 (1932).

94   Marley, 'Cleveland Ironstone'; W. W. Bean, *Parliamentary Representation of the Six Northern Counties . . .* (Hull 1890), 744–7, 768; C 6529, 75, 118.

95   Fordyce, *History of Coal*, 141–5; Marley, 'Cleveland Ironstone'; Darley MSS by courtesy of Mr G. Wardle Darley (ERRO) DDDA.

96   Taylor, *Biographia Leodiensis*, 490. I am indebted to the Earl of Mexborough for information.

97   J. T. Ward, 'Portrait of a Yorkshire Squire', *Yorks Arch Jour*, 11 (1960). I am indebted to Mrs C. E. Gardner-Smith and Mr J. R. R. Fullerton for information.

98 Rudding Park MSS and information kindly communicated by Sir Everard Radcliffe, Bt, and Capt J. E. B. Radcliffe, MC.

99 PP, 72 (1874), [C 1097–1], *Owners of Land, England and Wales . . . Return*, vol 2, 3; Bateman, *Great Landowners* (1883 edn), 15; Spring, *Landed Estate.*

100 Crewe-Milnes Muniments by courtesy of the late Marchioness of Crewe (SCL).

101 Ferrand MSS by courtesy of the late Col G. W. Ferrand, OBE (YAS and Cartwright Memorial Museum, Bradford); A. G. Ruston and D. Whitney, *Hooton Pagnell . . .* (1934), 118–22, 231. I am indebted for information to Mrs H. M. Beaumont, Sir William Lowther, Bt, Mrs Mary Ward, the Hon E. L. Jackson, Mr J. Towneley Taylor and Major Hugo Meynell, MC.

102 Leeds MSS by courtesy of the late Duke of Leeds (YAS); Wilkinson, *Worsborough*, 253; C 6529, 126–8; T. W. Beastall, 'A South Yorkshire Estate in the late Nineteenth Century', *Agricultural Hist Rev*, 14 (1966); Wray, *Mining Industry in Huddersfield*, 23; information kindly communicated by Mr W. D. Danwell, the Marquess of Ailesbury, DSO, the Earl of Cardigan, the Lord Savile, the Lord Hawke, the Earl of Rosse, MBE, and Mr E. P. Stocks.

103 PP, 13 (1843), civ, lxxxv, 97–8; David Spring, 'Ralph Sneyd: Tory Country Gentleman', *Bull John Rylands Lib*, 38 (1956).

104 Bateman (1879, 1883 eds), passim; J. D. Chambers, *The Vale of Trent, 1670–1800* (Cambridge 1957), 6–9; A. Raistrick, E. Allen, 'The South Yorkshire Iron Masters (1690–1750)', *Econ Hist Rev*, 9 (1939); Spring, *Landed Estate*, 126; David Smith, *Industrial Archaeology of the East Midlands* (Dawlish 1965), ch 5.

105 See Norman McCord, A. E. Carrick, 'Northumberland in the General Election of 1852', *Northern History*, 1 (1966).

106 On the ever-expanding Bairds, see A. M. Macgeorge, *The Bairds of Gartsherrie* (Glasgow 1875); G. E. Sleight, 'Ayrshire Coal Mining and Ancillary Industries', *Ayrshire Coll*, 2S, 7 (1966); Crawshay quoted in John, *Industrial Development of South Wales*, 39; Andrew Thompson to Ralph Sneyd quoted in Spring, *Landed Estate*, 128–9; ibid, 43; Parson and White, *Cumberland and Westmorland*, 715; Ruston and Whitney, *Hooton Pagnell*, 231.

107 Lowther MSS, D/Lons/45, Stephenson and Forster to Lord Lowther, 9 Sept 1843, Peile to Lords Lonsdale and Lowther, 14 Dec 1843.

108 Lowther MSS, passim; Frank Machin, *The Yorkshire Miners. A History*: 1 (Barnsley 1958), 69–70, 29; Lady Londonderry, *Frances Anne*, passim; Fordyce, *History of Coal*, 92–3. On Tremenheere, see R. K. Webb, 'A Whig Inspector', *Jour Mod History*, 27 (1955).

109 Tremenheere's Report (1845), passim; PP, 13 (1843), ciii; PP, 5 (1852), *Report from the SC on Coal Mines*, 65.

110   Printed circular, Edinburgh, 27 Dec 1797; Leven and Melville
      Muniments, GD 26/368/2, Wauchope to Balgonie, 17 Jan 1798.
      On the Dundee Radical George Mealmaker, see W. Norrie,
      Dundee Celebrities (Dundee 1873), 22. For examples of coal-
      masters' attitudes to bonding and 'poaching' of miners, see
      Campbell, *Carron Company*, 65–6; Hughes, *North Country Life*,
      vol 2, 176–7; Pollard, *Genesis of Modern Management*, 171;
      P. L. Payne, 'The Govan Collieries, 1804–05', *Business History*,
      3, no 2 (1961); D. Large, 'The Third Marquess of Londonderry
      and the End of the Regulation, 1844–45', *Durham University
      Jour*, 51 (1958). On Scottish mining labour, see B. F. Duckham,
      A History of the Scottish Coal Industry, I: 1700–1815 (Newton
      Abbot 1970), ch 9–10.

111   See Tremenheere's Report (1845), 14, 26, 39; Lady London-
      derry, *Frances Anne*, 232–6; Frederick Engels, *The Condition of the
      Working Class in England*, in *Marx and Engels on Britain* (Moscow
      1953), 292; A. J. Taylor, 'The Third Marquess of Londonderry
      and the North Eastern Coal Trade', *Durham Univ Jour*, 48 (1955);
      David Spring, 'Agents to the Earls of Durham in the Nineteenth
      Century', ibid, 54 (1962); Lowther MSS, D/Lons/45; Wentworth
      Woodhouse Muniments; Machin, *Yorkshire Miners*, vol 1, passim.

112   Ralph Arnold, *The Unhappy Countess* (1957), 13–15, 176, 197
      and passim.

113   Cary-Elwes MSS (LAO), Cary Elwes's letter books, Elwes to
      Prissick, 19 June 1758, 24 Apr 1759. See G. Jackson, 'Cary
      Elwes, Lord of Brigg', *Lincolnshire Historian*, 2, no 12 (1965);
      cf John, *Industrial Development of South Wales*, 36.

114   Seaforth Muniments (SRO) GD 46/17/7, Stewart to J. L.
      McAdam, 2 Dec 1787.

115   J. R. Hume, J. Butt, 'Muirkirk, 1786–1802', *Scottish Hist Rev*,
      45 (1966). See also J. W. Tweedie, 'Mines', in J. E. Shaw,
      Ayrshire, 1745–1950 (Edinburgh 1953), 233–4; J. T. Ward,
      'Ayrshire Landed Estates in the Nineteenth Century', *Ayrshire
      Collections*, 2S, 8 (1969).

116   Dundonald, *Autobiography*, 23.

117   Bateman to Lonsdale, quoted in Pollard, *Genesis of Modern
      Management*, 205; Lowther MSS D/Lons/45, Peile to Lonsdale
      and Lowther, 14 Dec 1843.

118   Hamilton Bruce Muniments, GD 152/196, Richards to O. W.
      Tyndale, 15 Oct 1826.

119   In addition to persons whose help is acknowledged above, I am
      greatly indebted to Professor S. G. E. Lythe, who made valuable
      comments on this paper, and to Mr M. Y. Ashcroft, Mr John
      Bebbington, Mr Frank Beckwith, Miss A. G. Foster, Mr
      Norman Higson, Mr F. G. B. Hutchings, Mr John Imrie,
      Mr B. C. Jones and Mr Wilfred Robertshaw, who have helped
      me in various ways.

3

Ulster Landowners and the Linen Industry

W. H. CRAWFORD

It is surprising that Ireland has not attracted the attention of more economic and social historians in Great Britain. Content to accept what Dr Cullen has described as 'facile generalisations about the Irish economy to which we have become accustomed',[1] based all too often on studies of the nineteenth century, they have not seriously examined Ireland within the larger framework of the British Isles. In American history the grafting of British civilisation on an alien culture, the influence on the colonists of their early struggle to establish themselves, and the effect of mercantilism on the colonial economy, have been studied, but in Irish history the surface has only been scratched. In the context of contemporary discussions about the origins of the Industrial Revolution the sudden appearance and rapid growth of an important linen industry in Ireland must attract serious attention.[2] The Irish Sea separated two different worlds and so the factors in the rise and development of the linen industry in such a colonial atmosphere, where its promotion with government support and under the aegis of the Linen Board was designed originally to strengthen the Protestant interest, differ in degree from those of a comparable industry in Britain. As Professor Charles Wilson has said: 'The . . . expansion of the Irish linen trade forms a remarkable chapter in the economic history of the eighteenth century.'[3]

When William Hincks in 1783 published a set of twelve engravings depicting the various processes in the manufacture of Irish linen, he dedicated the first to the Lord Lieutenant, the second to the members of Parliament, the third to the trustees of the Linen Board and a further eight to various noblemen; only

the twelfth and final engraving was inscribed to the linen merchants and manufacturers. Although Hincks was more concerned
with potential patrons than with eulogies, any student of Irish
life, aware of the influence of the landowner and the 'big house'
in the community, would be inclined to accept these dedications
at their face value: to him they are evidence of the authoritative
role played by the landlord in the development of the linen industry. This view, however, would be an over-simplification,
especially of social conditions in the province of Ulster, which
was recognised as the home of the industry. It is time therefore to
attempt an assessment of the influence of Ulster landowners in
the rise of the linen industry; but the evidence has revealed that
its rise seriously affected the influence of these landowners by
encouraging the growth of an energetic and independent middle
class, while it increasingly weakened the power of the landowners
to control the development of their estates.

The birth of this industry lay in the Restoration period. Although previously the Irish had produced linen cloth for home
consumption, they had exported considerable quantities of yarn
only.[4] Indeed this yarn surplus was one of the most important
factors in attracting the immigration of skilled weavers from
Britain into northern Ireland. In 1682 Colonel Richard Lawrence who had managed a linen manufactory for the Duke of
Ormonde at Chapelizod near Dublin, wrote:[5]

> the Scotch and Irish in that province [Ulster] addicting them-
> selves to spinning of linen yarn, attained to vast quantities of that
> commodity, which they transported to their great profit. The
> conveniency of which drew thither multitudes of linen weavers,
> that my opinion is, there is not a greater quantity of linen pro-
> duced in like circuit in Europe: and although the generality of
> their cloth fourteen years since was *sleisie* and thin, yet of late it is
> much improved to a good fineness and strength.

Settlement in Ireland was an attractive prospect to many British
tradesmen; according to the English House of Lords in their
petition of 1698 against the Irish woollen manufacture, 'the
growing manufacture of cloth in Ireland, both by the cheapness
of all sorts of necessaries for life, and goodness of material for
making of all manner of cloth doth invite your subjects of
England, with their families and servants, to leave their habita-

tions to settle there'.[6] Land was very cheap in Ireland: on the Brownlow estate in north Armagh, where many immigrants from northern England settled, lands outside the town parks were let in the 1660s for 18d per acre and did not double in value until the first decade of the eighteenth century.[7] At the same time religious persecution drove many Scottish Covenanters into Ireland and it was probably responsible for the large number of Quakers among the immigrants from the North of England who settled in the Lagan valley.[8] These people found themselves at home in the Nonconformist atmosphere and in the exercise of their trades were untrammelled by English gild restrictions. Into this energetic and enterprising community was injected a Huguenot contribution of capital, new equipment and new techniques, with the official approval and support of the Dublin Government.[9]

At least some of the Ulster landowners recognised the opportunities which had been presented to them. As early as the 1680s it had been forecast that by the linen manufacture 'Ireland will soon be so enriched that in probability the price of land will bear double the value that it doth at present so that the nobility and gentry will be great gainers in particular'.[10] The weakness of the landlords' position was their lack of capital to invest in the industry. William Molyneux wrote to John Locke in 1696 that the noblemen and gentry had been admitted into a joint-stock corporation to promote the linen industry 'more for their countenance and favour than for any great help that could be expected either from their purses or their heads'.[11] If they had any spare capital he did not expect them to invest it in linen. Yet some of the landowners did offer the immigrant tradesmen encouragement and leases on favourable terms. In the town of Lurgan, county Armagh, which was described in 1682 as the greatest centre of the linen manufacture in the north,[12] Arthur Brownlow granted beneficial leases to tradesmen[13] and deliberately stimulated the industry on his estate. He founded a linen market and until it was soundly established he bought up all the webs which were brought to it: at first he had lost money but later he made great profits.[14] As a result Lurgan recovered very rapidly from the effects of the Williamite wars, with an increasing population, reflected in the building of more houses in and around the market place and in the extension of both the Anglican and Quaker houses of worship, so that in 1708 it was 'the greatest mart of linen manufactories in the North, being almost entirely peopled with linen weavers'.[15] A few miles away, Brownlow's young neighbour, Samuel Waring, who had taken a tour through Flanders and the Low Countries about 1688, brought over a number of Flemish weavers from the Low Countries and settled them in Waringstown.[16] Crommelin's Huguenot colony in Lisburn was established with the support of Lord Conway who granted the French the site for their church:[17] Lisburn was probably chosen by them because of its location in the heart of the linen-manufacturing area. Its destruction by fire in 1707 checked its progress, so that some of the weavers went to Crommelin's brother's settlement at Kilkenny and others 'lodged themselves in Lurgan'.[18] Yet the town was very soon rebuilt and in a short time regained its position as one of the chief markets in Ulster.

The landlords of counties Cavan and Monaghan were responsible for planting the industry in those counties. Dean Richardson, writing in 1740 to the famous scholar and antiquarian Walter Harris, referred to the success of the industry about Cootehill in county Cavan:[19]

> a good market house, a large market kept on Fridays in which there is plenty of provisions and abundance of good yarn and green cloth sold. There is a great number of weavers and bleachers in this town and neighbourhood and no less than ten bleach yards the least of which bleaches a thousand pieces of cloth every year. All which was brought about by means of a colony of Protestant linen-manufacturers who settled here on the encouragement given them by the Honble. Mr Justice Coote, who with a great deal of good management took care to have this new town so tenderly nursed and cherished in its infancy that many of its inhabitants soon grew rich and brought it to the perfection which it is now at; to which if we add the great pains that he took and the expense he was at in propagating this profitable branch of our trade thro' other parts of the kingdom he may justly be called the Father of the Linen Manufacture in Ireland.

The success of the industry in county Monaghan was attributed to several gentlemen:

> The linen manufacture has made great progress in this county since the year 1703 by the industry and care of several gentlemen

and particularly of Edward Lucas of Castleshane, Esq., who first introduced it, and for many years employed workmen and kept them under his own inspection.

Lucas is said to have introduced French and Dutch looms for his workers. Afterwards William Cairnes of Monaghan followed this example and settled this manufacture in the town of Monaghan.[20] About this period the industry seems to have established itself throughout the rest of the province. There is evidence of a linen exhibition in Strabane in 1700, when local people were awarded prizes for their skill.[21] In Coleraine the London-based Irish Society in 1709 had declined to encourage the manufacture of linen cloth,[22] and yet by an Act of 1711 the name 'Coleraines' was applied to linens seven-eighths yard wide.[23] In 1708 Antrim was 'enjoying a considerable linen trade'.[24] In the Ballymena and Cullybackey area the first bleachgreens date back to about 1705.[25] The introduction of the weaving of diapers and damasks into north Down is ascribed to James Bradshaw, a Quaker from Lurgan who was persuaded by Robert Colville, the squire of Newtownards, to settle in that town in 1726.[26] The linen industry was also given credit for signs of prosperity in Larne where it was reported that 'a piece of forty hundred cloth manufactured in this town was made a present of to her Royal Highness the Princess of Orange at her wedding [in 1734][27] by the Trustees of the Linen and Hempen Manufactures being the finest then ever made in this Kingdom'.[28]

The success of these ventures induced the belief among landowners that any region could be improved by the introduction and expansion of the linen industry. Dean Henry, writing in 1739, noted that there was considerable trade in the linen manufacture throughout county Fermanagh, although Belturbet in county Cavan and not Enniskillen, the county town, was the chief market for counties Fermanagh and Cavan. He added, however,[29]

> these places might with a little encouragement be made rich by the linen-manufacture. Enniskillen might be a chief mart for it, the soil and flats about it being very good and convenient for bleachyards and the waters of Lough Erne having hereabouts a particular softness and sliminess that waters the flax and bleaches the linen in half the time that it can generally be done in other waters. It is not to be doubted but the happy national spirit for

carrying on this manufacture and other useful branches of trade will in process of time exert itself properly along this lake as it has already done in other places.

Unfortunately his dream never materialised.

About this time a number of serious attempts were made by landowners to sponsor the foundation of large manufactories. The most impressive to contemporaries was Lord Limerick's project at Dundalk, where in 1736 the Huguenot de Joncourt established a factory for making cambric;[30] it was probably in connection with this scheme that Harris noted in 1744 that a colony of fine diaper weavers had 'lately' been transplanted from Waringstown to Dundalk.[31] The Archbishop of Armagh,

> Primate Boulter . . . aided them materially by corresponding on their behalf with the government, as also in his office as one of the Trustees of the Linen Board; and, in addition to these efforts, he assisted in raising a subscription of £30,000 for the benefit of the settlement, which Lord Limerick encouraged in every way, by promising houses for the workmen, ground for the factory and a grant of ten acres for the sowing of flax.

It was later claimed that in a few years they had produced £40,000 worth of cambrics and lawns and that with the Board's help they had started a manufactory of black soap for the bleaching industry.[32] Although the factory was in operation in 1755 it had failed by 1776.[33] It was probably the initial and much discussed success of the Dundalk venture which impelled Sir Robert Adair of Ballymena to write to John Reilly in Dublin in 1741:[34]

> I entreat you may if by any means possible to send me down by next post or the post following at farthest a proper draft of a subscription paper for establishing here a linen manufactory which can be done to great advantage in this place considering the many engines I have now fully fixed for that purpose which I am sure at present exceeds any in the Kingdom that is yet done.

A linen manufactory was built in Hillsborough, county Down, by Lord Hillsborough, who later tried without success to encourage William Coulson of Lisburn to set up a damask factory there.[35] The most famous of these schemes were not established in Ulster however, although Ulster experts and weavers were settled on the lands: they were Sir Richard Cox's great enterprise in Dunmanaway, county Cork[36] and Lord Shelburne's costly project at Ballymote in county Sligo.[37]

In contrast with the failure of these enterprises, sophisticated in their organisation and supported by substantial amounts of capital, was the growing success of the industry in Ulster where it had developed mainly on domestic lines. To the Lagan and upper Bann valleys the development of the industry brought increasing wealth, and competition forced up the value of land steeply. The conditions which the industry in this region required were explained by an agent in 1764 when advocating a scheme for the improvement of the estate and town of Rathfriland in county Down. In the first place, he pointed out, it was essential for the landlord to provide adequate market facilities. Then in order to persuade linen-drapers to settle in the town and to build good houses, leases in perpetuity needed to be given for building plots, while the town parks could be let for profit for fixed periods; manufacturers of brown linens should be preferred when land was being let, not only because their competition would push up rents but also because they would stimulate the local markets for food, clothing and candles. As the whole tenantry paid their rents by some branch of the linen trade and were therefore not dependent on the land for their livelihood, only small areas needed to be leased to each individual at their full value, and so there would be no profit from sub-letting. On this point the agent noted:[38]

> The manufacturers of brown linen in the neighbourhoods of Waringstown and Lurgan, whose stock is barely sufficient to keep their looms in work and support their families, will give twenty shillings or a guinea per acre for a small farm with a convenient house thereon, and even at that price find it difficult to get proper accommodation . . .

Since the closing years of the seventeenth century the houses in the town of Lurgan had been set in leases renewable for ever, but country leases to Protestants were for the term of three lives (the Penal Laws prevented Catholics from holding leases of more than thirty-one years). With the appearance of the bleach-mills requiring a more substantial investment of capital, linen-drapers demanded much better terms. Harris attributed the success of the industry around Waringstown to the encouragement of long tenures:[39] in Waringstown five leases made to linen-drapers in 1720 and 1730 were for sixty-one years, but after 1736 leases were freeholds.[40] Because of a minority between 1739 and 1747, it was not until 1748 that a spate of freeholds was granted to linen-drapers in the Lurgan area: these took the form of three life leases renewable for a peppercorn, and the linen-drapers paid substantial fines for them.[41]

Some landowners found at this time that their estate entails or marriage settlements prevented them from leasing land in free-hold: both Lord Donegall in Belfast and Lord Hillsborough in north Down could grant leases of no more than three lives or forty-one years.[42] It was therefore the landowners who success-fully passed through Parliament two bills, which became Acts in 1764 and 1766, to enable themselves to break estate entails in order to grant leases of land not exceeding fifteen acres 'for one or more lives renewable for ever or for any terms of years' for the purpose of making or preserving a bleach-green.[43] The substance of this provision was quoted by the agent John Slade to his master, Lord Hillsborough, in 1786, in an attempt to persuade him to grant a freehold lease to Messrs William and John Orr for a large cotton manufactory at Hillsborough to employ from two hundred to four hundred weavers and three times that number of women and children in spinning. Although, however, they pro-posed 'to expend in building for their manufactory only at least £600, and if it succeeds to build handsome houses for their own habitation', and although they did in fact purchase a house, they soon left the area because they had no lease.[44]

Landlords were stimulated, however, by the success of the industry and the attendant prosperity of the province, to indulge in schemes for town building, which produced important changes in the character of towns in this area. Harris recorded in 1740 that in the villages of Greyabbey and Saintfield in county Down proprietors had specifically built good houses 'for the habitation of manufacturers'.[45] Yet the finest achievements were the creation of the modern towns of Hillsborough in county Down about 1740 and Cookstown in county Tyrone about 1750. Lord Hillsborough gave[46]

> great encouragement . . . to linen manufacturers. His Lordship has already erected two ranges of commodious houses, to each of

which are annexed a garden and park of five acres, with ground
for bleach greens at a convenient distance, and plenty of firing in
the adjacent mosses.

William Stewart of Killymoon Castle executed in Cookstown
what has been described as 'one of the boldest attempts at town
building during the whole of Ulster's history':[47] the magnificent
main street, 130ft in width and beautified with trees, runs in a
straight line for a mile and a quarter. To provide water for the
linen bleachers, he dammed a ravine above the town and so har-
nessed the river which was taken by a race to drive both corn-
mills and bleach-mills.[48] Although the scheme was never
completely realised, Cookstown and Dungannon, in which Lord
Ranfurly had encouraged enterprise, were, with eight bleach-
yards apiece, the chief centres of the industry in county Tyrone in
1802.[49]

While many of these improvements remain as memorials to the
efforts of the landlords the most symbolic of all was the market
house or linen hall. In Lurgan, 'the greatest market for fine linens'
in the north, a market house built soon after the Restoration
served until its destruction by fire in 1776 and was subsequently
replaced by a linen hall.[50] In 1728 Dublin white linen hall was
built on the same lines as Blackwell Hall,[51] the London centre of
the woollen industry, suggesting that it was designed to fill a
similar role in the Irish industry. The first linen hall (for brown
or unbleached linens) in Belfast was built in 1738 with the help
of Lord Donegall, who granted £1,500 towards its construction.[52]
By 1755 Lisburn (built by the Marquess of Hertford), Downpatrick (the de Clifford family), Strabane (the Earl of Abercorn),
and Cookstown (Stewart) had their own halls or at least special
facilities provided in the market house.[53] Coleraine had two linen
halls (one on each side of the River Bann) built in the last decade
of the century, but because of the rivalry between their respective
sponsors neither was used and the linen market was held in the
street: the Marquess of Waterford had sponsored the erection of
one, while a minor local landlord named Stirling built the other.[54]
In Londonderry the Hamilton family built a linen hall, but the
Inspector-General in 1817 frowned on the Hamilton charge of 2d
per web.[55] Ballymena, Armagh, Newry, Limavady, Banbridge,
Kircubbin, Ballynahinch, Rathfriland and Dungannon all had

linen halls before 1810, most of which had been provided by the proprietor of the town.[56]

Resident landlords often displayed an intelligent interest in their markets and some landlords gave premiums to tenants for the production of high quality flax, yarn and cloth. It was said of Lord Hillsborough and William Brownlow:[57]

> Both these landowners were well-known as being the most liberal patrons of flax-culture, flax-spinning and linen-weaving, as these industries existed among the tenantry of their respective estates. They gave liberal premiums for the largest and finest growths of flax produced by their tenants; . . . Once a year three different classes of prizes were given, on the market day preceding Christmas, for the best 'bunches' of linen-yarn, and the prizes consisted not of money but of dress patterns, as well for maids as for matrons.

Such interest in the trade was remarked on in 1817 by the Inspector-General appointed by the Linen Board for Ulster, James Corry: in Ballygawley, county Tyrone, he found that the proprietor of the town, Sir John Stewart, distributed premiums every market day 'among the weavers who bring webs to the market of the best quality and in the greatest number—those premiums generally amount to £3, half of which is paid by the shopkeepers of the place, and the remainder by himself'.[58] These demonstrations of enthusiasm tended to be confinded to those landowners who believed that their encouragement would be reflected in their rentals and often evaporated if this object was not speedily realised.

It was not only landlords who were genuinely interested in the welfare of the industry on their estates that applied regularly to the Linen Board for allocation of spinning wheels and reels: some felt it incumbent on themselves to get as many as possible, even if it was only to demonstrate the extent of their influence in high places. In an amusing letter about the profits of office in Dublin, Charles Coote of county Cavan commented in 1748[59]

> the business as usual is a series of jobs, the pleasure ends in awkward minuets and romping country dances; we begin to scramble for wheels and reels tomorrow and as soon as it is over I return to my much better business or more agreeable idleness

in the country . . . if I get a tolerable harvest of wheels and reels
I shall go home rejoicing.

His cynicism was justified, because the Linen Board did not
trouble even to keep track of the wheels. Robert Stephenson, the
most able critic of the Board's undertakings, exposed this abuse
when he heartily condemned the Linen Board's foolishness[60]

> to bestow money as cheerfully as we do, for spinning wheels,
> thousands of which lie idle and are spoiling for want of use in the
> garrets and outhouses of gentlemen, because they have neither
> material nor proper persons to employ them; and here we may
> reasonably enquire after spinning wheels, there being about
> 7,000 of them given away annually in three afore-mentioned
> provinces (Munster, Leinster and Connaught); how are they
> employed?

In the areas where the industry was increasing many landowners
took full advantage of the grants. William Brownlow's account
books show that between 1771 and 1792 he received from the
Linen Board at least £200 towards the purchase of wheels and
looms: he was allowed £1 15s 0d each for thirty-three looms in
the years 1775-7 and his rentals note more than twenty looms
given to tenants. Five shillings was the grant for each wheel. In
1754 the absentee Earl of Abercorn's agent asked him, 'Will your
Lordship be pleased to direct me how I shall dispose of the
wheels [50 wheels and 10 reels], whether your Lordship would
have them spun for, or divided amongst the poorer sort of
tenant?'[61]

In a countryside where the linen industry flourished such gifts
were considered as an investment in the estate, since they enabled
poor tenants to pay their rents and reduced the number dependent
on the parish.[62]

In the train of the linen industry came a revolution in com-
munications in the north which seems to have got under way in
the 1730s. The landlords were the foremost sponsors of this revolution and were active in presenting schemes for constructing
roads and canals to open up the undeveloped countryside to
trade and industry. They forced through an active policy of road
construction, putting pressure on the parish vestries to improve
local roads, submitting presentments to the grand juries for

county roads, or promoting turnpike trusts. Harris commented on county Down in 1744:[63]

> As these roads cannot be well-repaired by the statute or day labour of the welders [sic] only, so the gentlemen of the county, who wish well to the commerce of it, now think it worth their attention to repair them by a county charge, which has been done to good advantage in other places.

The system of statutory labour was finally abolished in 1766. The roads from Dundalk to Banbridge and from Banbridge to Belfast had been placed under turnpike trusts by Acts of 1733, and two years later trusts were created for the roads from Newry to Armagh, Lisburn to Armagh, and Banbridge to Randalstown. For lack of sufficient revenue to pay interest on debentures and wages to officials even before the consideration of repairs, the turnpike roads tended to deteriorate more rapidly than the new county roads:[64] Arthur Young commented in 1776 that the turnpikes were as bad as the by-roads were admirable.[65]

As early as 1699 the idea of a canal from Lough Neagh to Newry was seriously examined by a group of landowners which included Arthur Brownlow and Samuel Waring,[66] and the region was mapped for the purpose in 1703 at the instance of several members of the House of Commons;[67] again in 1709 Thomas Knox of Dungannon petitioned Parliament for its construction but without any success.[68] The increasing exploitation of coal deposits in east Tyrone added much more weight to their arguments and with the foundation of the 'Commission of Inland Navigation for Ireland' in 1729 official approval was given to the scheme. Work commenced in 1731 but the first cargoes of coal from Coalisland in county Tyrone did not arrive in Dublin until 1742: even so it was the first major inland canal in the British Isles.[69] The section of the Lagan canal from Sprucefield near Lisburn, to Lough Neagh was completed in 1794, cost £62,000 and was constructed almost entirely at the Marquess of Donegall's expense.[70] The Strabane canal, first suggested to the Earl of Abercorn in the early 1750s[71] was not constructed until 1796: the then Marquess bore the total cost of £11,858.[72] Although these eighteenth-century canals did play an important role in promoting the growth of the regions they served, they were eclipsed by the rapid expansion of the railway network in the mid-nineteenth century.[73] It is significant, however, that Ulster landowners were prepared to advance so much for improvements in Ireland.

Some of the Ulster landowners were among the most active members of the Board of the trustees of the Linen and Hempen Manufactures which had been established in 1711 to regulate the industry, to spread the knowledge of methods and technique throughout the country and to subsidise worth-while projects. The Board did tackle these tasks with enthusiasm but without sufficient knowledge of the trade; it did not ensure that the terms of its grants were fulfilled and so money was wasted; and in spite of its measures to encourage the industry in the south, the slump of the early 1770s almost obliterated the industry outside Ulster. Yet if the Linen Board had been more effective and able to regulate the industry as it pleased, there was a serious danger that its inexperience and lack of knowledge combined with an increasingly inflexible and bureaucratic approach to problems, would have imposed a straight-jacket on the industry. It was for instance, fortunate for the industry that the Board was unable to enforce such of its regulations as concerned the reeling of yarn, the dimensions of cloth and the time and method of bleaching.[74] The trade carried on by 'jobbers'[75] and 'keelmen' on the fringe of the industry was impossible to regulate and regularly condemned as illegal and yet it played an important role in serving the remoter districts and encouraged enterprise among the smaller dealers: it was reckoned in 1821 that in Armagh market, then one of the most considerable in the north, more than one-third of the dealers were 'keelmen'.[76]

The Linen Board enjoyed great authority in its early years, especially when the Ulster landowners were most busily engaged in its support. They were very active in the House of Commons particularly on committees which discussed the linen trade and relevant matters.[77] Only through the landlords could the rising class of drapers make its demands heard. It was Brownlow of Lurgan who introduced the Linen bill of 1762 to regulate both the bleachers and the brown linen market[78] and in 1766 Thomas Knox of Dungannon (later Lord Ranfurly) wrote to Thomas Greer:[79]

I

I . . . think myself much honoured by the respectable body of
Linen Drapers, that thought proper to fix on me to present their
memorial to my Lord Lieutenant. I beg you will assure them
from me that I did with pleasure this day deliver it, and had the
strongest assurance from his Excellency that he would recommend it to the Linen Board with all his power, which gives me
reason to hope we shall succeed.

John Williamson, an eminent linen-draper from Lisburn, re-
sented the condescending attitude adopted by the trustees when
Henry Betty of Lisburn and himself tried to salvage the Linen
bill of 1762 when it was dropped by the Commons:[80]

We have carried everything we wished for. Very full boards of the
trustees have sat nearly every day and tomorrow there is to be a
final settlement. It is, however, my opinion that we would never
have got a patient hearing, but would have been condemned and
abused, had it not been for Lord Hillsborough, who has been our
patron, our friend and adviser, in all cases. He received us as his
children and since we came here he has laboured for us night and
day, the effect of which has been that we are now treated with the
highest respect by people who, when we came here, were ready to
insult us . . . Many of the noble lords here would not vouchsafe to
look on us, even though we worshipped them; they would suffer
our cause to fail even though their own estates and the whole
kingdom were equally involved in the same.

Williamson, who was presented by the merchants of Dublin and
London and by the linen-drapers with a piece of engraved silver
plate in recognition of his work on the 1764 Linen Act, was
punished for his presumption by the Linen Board who refused
to grant him a white seal although every other bleacher in the
kingdom had been furnished with one: the Board did not reply
to a memorial submitted by the drapers on Williamson's behalf
and after a further petty insult Williamson went to live in
London.[81]

Yet the landowners in Ulster were themselves well aware of
the growing importance and influence of the linen-drapers. On
the Brownlow estate in north Armagh the most important men
in the community were the wealthy linen-merchants and they
were independent enough for Brownlow to cultivate their
friendship and regard. During the 1761 election he had to quieten

the fears of his partner Sir Archibald Acheson that their opponents the Caulfields were sounding out possible support among
the Lurgan merchants and linen-drapers: Brownlow's local
agent, the linen-draper Jemmy Forde, had to make it clear to
Maziere and Ruddle, two fellow linen-drapers who were disposed to listen to the Caulfields, that Brownlow was engaged to
support Acheson and would have to share the expenses of the
poll if one was necessary. Brownlow himself warned Acheson:[82]

> the people of substance here would, to be sure, wish to be con-
> versed and to appear of consequence, which they cannot be with-
> out an opposition, and on that account grumble a little at your
> going on so smoothly but I shall take all the care in my power to
> make that ferment subside, and so strengthen your interest.

In 1783 Thomas Knox of Dungannon professed friendship in his
letters to the draper Thomas Greer, while apologising for being
unable at the time to repay a loan of £1,000.[83] In Strabane an
even more powerful landowner, the Earl of Abercorn, had during
the 1760s the greatest difficulty in his attempts to secure control
of the corporation of Strabane, the chief town within his estates.[84]

The increasing authority of the drapers may have been responsible for the initial collapse of the 1762 bill over the clauses
designed to regulate bleachers,[85] but the real clash between the
Linen Board and the drapers came twenty years later in 1782 over
'Mr Foster's' Act.[86] The bleachers and drapers had been consulted by a parliamentary committee before the bill was drafted
and they expected a renewed campaign to tighten up the administration of the 1764 Act against the frauds of the brown-
sealmasters (who examined unbleached linen), but they found
that the whole burden of the Act was directed against them: although their trading reputation as responsible merchants should
have guaranteed their products, they were to be held liable and
punished for dealing in poor quality cloth. As white-sealmasters
they were to be strictly regulated: they would have to take an
oath to obey all the Board's rules and each man would have to
provide not only bonds of £200 for his conduct but also two
sureties who would guarantee him and bind themselves for similar
sums. Although these clauses provoked angry reactions, the most
serious of all was the Linen Board's demand that each sealmaster

had to perfect a warrant of attorney confessing judgement on the bond. This step would enable the Linen Board to adopt the simplest, quickest, and most economical method of securing all fines it might levy on the sealmasters: it would not be necessary to sue the sealmasters as by their warrant they had already admitted their liability to pay. The white-sealmasters objected that both the oath and the warrant bound them to obey without question any Act which the Board might introduce in the future no matter if they faced thereby the loss of their trade and the destruction of their livelihood, and several petitions on these lines were laid before Parliament.[87]

The drapers were angry when they learned that their memorials, supported by their testimony before the Board, had been rejected out of hand and that instead a meeting of only five trustees on 23 July 1782 had decided to enforce the Act imposing a fine of £5 for each illegally sealed web; so they decided at meetings held in Lisburn, Lurgan and Newry that they would buy no more brown linens. At a meeting held by the Ulster drapers in Armagh on 5 August following, 437 drapers decided not to carry on trade until they obtained an assurance from the Linen Board that they would not be required to take the new oath or give any other than the usual simple bonds for their conduct. They further resolved[88]

> That whoever acts contrary to the general sense of the trade ought never to be considered as one of our body, or a friend to the linen manufacture of Ireland; nor will we on any pretence whatsoever bleach any linen for such persons who will not strictly and uniformly adhere to this our general determination.

In face of this opposition fifteen trustees (including only one of the original five and not John Foster, the real author of the measure) met two days later in Dublin, took into consideration the resolution at Armagh and revoked the order of 23 July on the grounds that no words appeared in the Act authorising or requiring the administering of the oath: if this was the case, however, it was a loop-hole in the Act.[89] A meeting at Newry three days later refused still to resume trade, on the grounds 'that the Linen Board have not yet given the trade satisfaction sufficient to enable them to proceed to business with safety'.[90]

At the same time, however, the drapers had found their own

loop-hole in the Act and were trying 'to procure five trustees who will join in issuing seals without putting the sealmaster to the severe qualifications required by the present Act of Parliament'. Five was the minimum number of trustees required by the Act to authorise appointments.[91] Brownlow and Sir Richard Johnston were joined first by Lords Hillsborough and Moira and then by John O'Neill of Shane's Castle (all Ulster landlords) as the five trustees.[92] The Board had been forced to surrender. There is no doubt that, like the Irish Volunteers, the northern drapers had adopted the language and attitudes of the American rebels with success: the lesson had not been lost on John Nevill, the self-appointed advocate of the drapers' cause: 'the stubborn perseverance of enforcing an Act of Parliament lost Britain the greater part of her dominions; there is no reason to believe that the experiment will be attempted on the trade of Ireland'.[93]

From this time the independence of the northern drapers became more pronounced. Later in the same year it was decided to build a white-linen hall in Ulster to sell white linens in the heart of the manufacture: it was unnecessary to send linens to Dublin when they could be shipped from Belfast or Newry.[94] Underlying these valid arguments was a certain resentment felt by the Ulster drapers against the authority of the Dublin factors and this was expressed in the grumble that the government in Dublin paid more attention to the views of the Dublin factors than to those of 'the most eminent drapers in the country'.[95] By 1785 white-linen halls were open in Belfast and Newry: although the Newry hall soon failed that in Belfast grew steadily at the expense of Dublin.[96]

The Act of Union (1800) saw the end of the Irish Parliament and a subsequent decline in the influence of the Board of Trustees: Dublin was no longer the centre of government which attracted active personalities and it became more and more divorced from the industry. The Board was still the guardian of the linen trade but now its meetings were very sparsely attended and in some years there was not a quorum of twelve.[97] It was run by John Foster (now Lord Oriel) and its secretary James Corry, both of whom showed energy and initiative in making grants for the erection of scutch mills to prepare flax for the spinners.[98] Yet they could only subsidise but not initiate changes in the industry. One of the arguments used by an English manufacturer to dissuade an Irishman thinking of establishing a spinning mill at Dundalk in 1801 was that 'the premium to be expected from the Linen Board would be of little importance compared with the eligibility of the scheme':[99] the optimism of the mid-eighteenth century had submitted to the realistic assessment of the nineteenth. The Board itself was increasingly under fire for inefficiency, jobbery and ostentation:[100] even Foster was forced to recognise the justice of these criticisms when he complained in 1819:[101]

> It strikes me that the flax seed inspectors ought not to take advantage of the two Acts of 1802 and 1804 to do an act to put money in their own pockets without any advantage to the trade or any additional security against the sale of bad seed to the grower.

It is not surprising that one of the fiercest diatribes against the Board came after its decease from the Lisburn historian of the industry, Henry McCall (1805–97):[102]

> The Board of Trustees—the supreme authority on all questions—issued their decrees with the pomposity of three-tailed bashawism. Their dogmas dare not be disputed; and the secretary of that formidable cabinet, Mr James Corry, made his tour of the provinces in semi-regal state, the county inspectors, the deputies, and sealmasters forming his body-guard in every market town which he honoured with a visit. All this complicated and cumbrous machinery was kept in motion at great cost, and it was only when forward men arose and stood against such mischievous meddling, that the trade was emancipated from its trammels.

The forward men had their reward in 1828, when the government withdrew its grants from the trustees and the Linen Board ceased to function.

Yet early in the nineteenth century the domestic linen industry reached its peak and played a very important role in the economy of the Ulster countryside. The rapidly increasing population was already pressing hard on the resources of the land in Ireland; emigration had eased the pressure on Ulster but modern industry had scarcely made its appearance and natural controls had not yet operated to check the growing numbers. As a result many small farmers and their families were forced to take up the linen industry to make a living, although as contemporary observers noted, weavers might earn no more than day labourers.[103] The organisation of the industry in Ulster had become so efficient that it was able to cope with the increasing production of the remoter areas and to give the North the relative appearance of prosperity which so impressed travellers after their experiences in the south of the country.[104]

How the linen industry and changing conditions on the land interacted may best be learned from an examination of four distinct regions. Around Belfast by 1800 the majority of handloom weavers relied on manufacturers for regular employment and the supply of raw materials, so that the cotton industry was replacing the linen industry and encouraging many men to break their final ties with the land.[105] Away from the coast, however, in north Armagh and west Down observers were surprised to find that highly skilled linen weavers were often independent of the manufacturers and still farmed smallholdings. Further south in Cavan and Monaghan such smallholdings were usually leased directly from landlords by weavers of coarser linens and were the prevalent features of the rural scene. In the rest of the linen country—in counties Antrim, Londonderry, and Tyrone—the weavers were usually cottiers dependant on weaving to supplement their earnings on the land. On the verge of poverty lived the weavers in mountainous districts, compelled to rely on the markets for their supplies of flax and thread which they themselves could not produce.[106]

The heart of the industry lay in the triangle between Lisburn, Armagh and Dungannon and there the independent craftsmen secured small parcels of land in the vicinity of a good market town as they were able to pay a higher rent than any farmer who was prepared to earn his living by farming alone. A study of estate rentals and leases on Brownlow's manor of Derry shows that when leases expired the previous sub-tenants had been taken on as full tenants because they were able individually to offer a higher rent than a middleman.[107] In this way Brownlow and landlords who adopted a similar policy had been able to take advantage of the rising value of rents but they were prepared in turn to grant to good tenants long secure leases instead of mere tenancies at will. The landlords' readiness to lease holdings direct to sub-tenants forced out the middleman or the original holder of the grand lease who was thus deprived of what had been a valuable and easy source of income. As a result there were in this region by 1800 very few substantial farmers and even fewer minor gentry: most of the gentry owed their prosperity to wealth acquired from trade or the professions or indirectly from the profits of the linen industry.

Although observers like Arthur Young and Sir Charles Coote were convinced that in such circumstances agriculture must suffer as the skills of weaving and farming could not be combined,[108] the weaver took a different view. If he grew his own flax he could employ the skill of his womenfolk to spin the very fine threads needed for his cambrics and lawns while he had turbary rights and enough grass for one or two cows: on a farm of ten acres two cows would supply a family with milk for a year and one hundred-weight of butter to sell in the market. It is not surprising then that the linen country was noted for its dairy farming and supplied the Lagan valley and Belfast.[109] Here the weaver knew too that he could turn to farming during slumps in the industry which occurred more frequently as the market for expensive fine linens was more liable to saturation than that for coarse linens; he was also able to cushion himself against the fluctuating price of oatmeal, his chief article of diet, especially during bad seasons. Coote himself did admit that he believed 'that the people would rather have nothing to do with agricultural pursuits if the markets were more numerous and constantly supplied with provisions': besides, too much farming rendered their hands unfit for weaving fine linens.[110]

In south Armagh, Cavan and Monaghan, the southern counties of Ulster, where the population density often exceeded 400 persons to the square mile, the lot of the farmer-weavers was harder. The weavers manufactured the cheaper coarse linens while their farming was very poor and reflected none of the more modern techniques. Of the barony of Tullaghonoho in county Cavan Coote reported:

> Here there is no market for grain . . . They breed but very few horses here, and less of black cattle; tillage is their principal pursuit, and they cultivate now no more of provisions than they require for themselves, their great concern is flax-husbandry and the linen-manufacture,

and complained:

In so many thousand acres now occupied by very poor weavers
we rarely see better than black oats, of an impoverished grain,
which are capable of yielding the finest wheat, or could certainly
be converted to the best sheep-walk.

Pressure of population had reduced the weavers to subsistence
level and the standard of agriculture to such a condition that the
landlords did not attempt to introduce improvements and often
did not even trouble to renew leases but permitted them to continue as tenancies at will after they had lapsed.[111] The tenants on
the other hand, feared that improvements would only mean increased rents and tithes.[112]

In this region there were also many cottiers; but cottiers were
much more numerous in the northern counties of Antrim,
Londonderry and Tyrone, where they were employed by farmers
and manufacturers. These counties contained a larger percentage
of more substantial farmers than anywhere else in the province
and in the Bann and Foyle valleys they farmed some of its best
agricultural lands. Young noticed in 1776 that the farmers in
north Londonderry concentrated on farming and gave out to
weavers the yarn their womenfolk had spun.[113] Dependant on
such farmers or on linen manufacturers for employment, the
cottier tenants secured scraps of land on which to graze a cow and
grow potatoes and although they were given no title to the land
they paid for it exorbitant sums or worked for their landlord.[114]
Whether their employer was a manufacturer or a farmer the cottiers were at his mercy in their pursuit of a livelihood and they
were exploited: of county Londonderry in 1802 it was reported:[115]

In many districts the cottier could not hold out but for the liberal
wages of linen merchants and other gentlemen . . . I assure the
reader that the grass of a cow, which three or four years ago was
valued at 20s is now raised to two guineas even on the bare moors
where the poor animal is tethered and where she has better
opportunity of grinding her teeth on the sand than of filling her
belly with pasture.

Often they owed arrears of rent to their employers. When farmers
wanted to consolidate and improve their farms it was easy for
them to remove cottiers since they had no rights to their land.
One observer noticed in 1813 that the population of Omagh was

increasing 'not only on account of the linen and other manufactures there carried on, but also by reason of the people here, as
almost everywhere, being driven from their farms into towns by
monopolizing farmers'.[116] But the small provincial towns could
not absorb such large-scale immigration.

Such was the condition of the industry throughout Ulster on
the eve of the introduction of machinery. The first dry-spinning
mills had appeared in Ulster soon after 1800 but for twenty years
they made little progress because of the low cost of labour in
Ireland: indeed the spinning women were often forced to cut
their losses by disposing 'of the worked article for less than the
raw material cost them', and it was said that the women regarded
it as 'an alternative to idleness' rather than a paying pursuit.[117]
When the more efficient process of wet-spinning displaced dry-
spinning the domestic industry soon vanished with a consequent
decline in the rural standard of living. Soon after 1850 the introduction of the power-loom finally destroyed the livelihood of the
handloom weavers.[118] Their numbers declined so rapidly that by
the early twentieth century only the finest damask tablecloths
were still woven by hand.

Irish landlords had promoted the linen industry to improve
their estates: that they succeeded in Ulster their substantial
rentals will testify. This does not mean that the tenants on their
estates benefitted to the same extent. To the region bounded by
the triangle of Belfast, Armagh and Dungannon where skilled
weavers from England, Scotland and France had congregated,
the industry brought increasing wealth but in the surrounding
counties it had become by 1800 a means of supplementing farming incomes and with the rapidly increasing population had arti-
ficially inflated the value of lands where improved methods of
farming had never been adopted: there it depressed the standards
of agriculture and the subsequent decay of the domestic linen
industry left these remoter districts in comparative poverty. It
may be true also that the spread of the industry had hastened the
collapse of the manorial system originally introduced into
Ulster by the English government and the planters early in the
seventeenth century, but before we can make a judgement, much
more detailed investigation of estate records will be required:
linked with this is the problem of land tenure and the evergreen

topic of Ulster tenant right and its origins. There is no doubt, however, that the rise of the linen industry produced from the descendants of yeoman and tradesmen a new wealthy class which in 1782 successfully challenged the authority of the Linen Board to dictate the conditions under which the industry should operate. It would be interesting to find out the extent to which linen-drapers were involved in the United Irishmen as their successful opposition to government interference in industry may have been reflected in a radical approach to politics. To the Ulster linen industry must be attributed the creation of conditions in which the cotton industry flourished for a time and indeed it played an important part in laying the foundations for Belfast's rise to eminence in the nineteenth century. With the subsequent establishment of the factory system in the linen industry, however, the landlord's interest in it faded.

NOTES

1   L. M. Cullen, 'The value of contemporary printed sources for Irish economic history in the eighteenth century', *Irish Historical Studies*, 14 (1964), 155.

2   The only full-scale treatment of the industry in the eighteenth century is contained in Conrad Gill, *The Rise of the Irish Linen Industry* (Oxford 1925, reprinted 1964). See also E. R. R. Green, *The Lagan Valley, 1800–1850* (1949) and *The Industrial Archaeology of County Down* (Belfast 1963).

3   C. Wilson, *England's Apprenticeship, 1603–1763* (1965), 198.

4   Rawlinson MSS (BLO) D 921, fo 147, (transcript in PRONI) T 545 (8), 'Proposals for the cultivation of flax and hemp in Ireland' (undated, but Dr Cullen believes that internal evidence points to a date early in the 1680s).

5   Richard Lawrence, *The Interest of Ireland in its trade and wealth stated* (Dublin 1682), vol 2, 189–90.

6   House of Lords' address to King William III, 9 June 1698 published in A. Young, *Tour in Ireland* (A. W. Hutton, 1892), vol 2, 193.

7   Brownlow MSS (PRONI) T 970, Arthur Brownlow's lease book.

8   There were strong Quaker communities in Lisburn and Lurgan: their first meeting in Ireland was formed in 1653 at Lurgan by William Edmundson, a Cromwellian soldier. See Quaker meeting records (PRONI T 1062 and Mic 16).

9   Gill, *Irish Linen Industry*, 16–20.
10   'Proposals for the cultivation of flax and hemp in Ireland', 10.
11   Quoted in W. R. Scott, 'The King's and Queen's Corporation for the linen manufacture in Ireland', *RS Antiq Ire*, 5S, 11 (1901), 371.
12   William Brooke to Dr William Molyneaux, published in 'An account of the Barony of O'Neiland, Co Armagh, in 1682', *Ulster Journal Arch*, 2S, 4 (1898), 241.
13   Arthur Brownlow's lease book, 87. Lurgan Quaker Records note a 1695 lease of a tenement in their account of the rebuilding of the meeting-house. Both the Quakers and Brownlow regarded these leases as copyholds: they were not fee-farm grants but leases for three lives renewable on the fall of each life with fixed rents and renewal fines and subject to the usual duties of the manor, especially suit to courts and mills.
14   Thomas Molyneux, 'Journey to the North, August 7th 1708', in *Historical Notices of old Belfast and its Vicinity* (ed R. M. Young, Belfast 1896), 154.
15   Molyneux, 'Journey to the North', 154.
16   E. D. Atkinson, *An Ulster Parish* (Dublin 1898), 49.
17   H. McCall, *Ireland and her Staple Manufactures* (3rd edn, Belfast 1870), 40.
18   Louis Crommelin to Duke of Ormonde, 24 May 1707, *Ormonde Calendar*, ns, no 4, 299.
19   Lodge MSS (APL) Bundle no 35, 'Cavan' in bundle of Topographical and Statistical returns from various respondents sent to Walter Harris and the Physico-Historical Society of Ireland circa 1745.
20   Lodge MSS, Bundle no 35, 'Monaghan'. Mr William Cairnes, a Dublin merchant, bought the Blaney estate in county Monaghan in 1696; two of his brothers were London merchants. See H. C. Lawlor, *A History of the Family of Cairnes or Cairns* (1906), 82, 83.
21   Abercorn MSS (PRONI) D 623/47; this is confirmed by Molyneux, 'Journey to the North', 159.
22   A. Marmion, *The Ancient and Modern History of the Maritime Ports of Ireland* (1855), 383.
23   9 Anne c 3.
24   Molyneux, 'Journey to the North', 156.
25   H. C. Lawlor, 'Rise of the Linen Merchants in the Eighteenth Century', *Irish and International Fibres and Fabrics Journal*, 7 (1941), 11; 8 (1942), 44.
26   W. Harris and C. Smith, *The Antient and Present State of the County of Down* (Dublin 1744), 56; Green, *County Down*, 29; Londonderry Estate MSS (PRONI) D654/LE36A/10 and D654/LE31/1.
27   In 1734 Anne, Princess Royal as eldest daughter of King George II, married the Prince of Orange.

28 William Henry, 'Henry's Topographical Descriptions' (a bound manuscript in APL), 142

29 Henry, 'Topographical Descriptions', 96

30 Gill, *Irish Linen Industry*, 154.

31 Smith and Harris, *County of Down*, 104.

32 D. C. Purdon communication to *Journal of the Historical and Archaeological Association of Ireland*, 3rd S, 1 (1868), 17–20.

33 Young, *Tour*, vol 1, 115.

34 Adair MSS (PRONI) D929/F4/1/15.

35 Smith and Harris, *County of Down*, 95; H. McCall, *Ireland and her Staple Manufacture*, 126.

36 *A Letter from Sir Richard Cox, Bart, to Thomas Prior, Esq, showing a sure method to establish the Linen Manufacture* (Dublin 1749).

37 Young, *Tour*, vol 1, 223–30; Greer MSS (PRONI) D1044/52.

38 PRONI/T 1181/1.

39 Smith and Harris, *County of Down*, 105.

40 Leases made by Samuel Waring and recorded in the Registry of Deeds, Dublin:

Book 72, p 43, no 49626 to Thomas Factor including bleachyard for 61 years	(1730)
Book 69, p 321, no 48537 to Mark Gwyn, linendraper, for 61 years	(1732)
Book 62, p 4, no 41615 to Thomas Waring for 61 years	(1729)
Book 62, p 4, no 41616 to Henry Close for 61 years	(1729)
Book 64, p 504, no 44915 to John Murray, linendraper for 61 years	(1730)
Book 84, p 356, no 60015 to Thomas Waring for ever	(1737)
Book 87, p 174, no 61151 to John Houlden, linendraper, for ever	(1736)
Book 114, p 340, no 79161 to Robert Paterson	(1744)
Book 121, p 98, no 82221 to Samuel Paterson for ever	(1745)

41 Brownlow MSS (at present in the custody of Messrs Watson & Neill, Solicitors, Lurgan)

Brownlow to David Maziere for land in Derrymacash and Derryadd	(1755)
Brownlow to James Bradshaw for land in Drumnakelly	(1750)
Brownlow to Henry Greer for land in Dougher	(1759)
Registry of Deeds Book 139, p 68, no 92984 to Henry Greer	(1749)
Registry of Deeds Book 135, p 452, no 92216 to James Greer	(1749)
Registry of Deeds Book 143, p 208, no 96608 to David Ruddell	(1750)
Registry of Deeds Book 143, p 209, no 96611 to James Forde	(1750)
Registry of Deeds Book 193, p 106, no 127135 to Ben Hone	(1757)

42 Donegall MSS (PRONI) D 509/129. Downshire MSS (PRONI) D 607/259A, John Slade to Lord Hillsborough 20 Feb 1786.

43 3 Geo III, c 34 and 5 Geo III, c 9, s 4.

44 Green, *Co Down*, 26.

45 Smith and Harris, *County of Down*, 49, 71.

46 Ibid, 95.

47 G. Camblin, *The Town in Ulster* (Belfast 1951), 81.

48 Article in *Mid-Ulster Mail*, 12 Sept 1925 [PRONI/T 1659].
49 J. McEvoy, *Statistical Survey of the County of Tyrone* (Dublin 1802), 138–9, 158.
50 Lurgan town lease no 103. It is surprising that Arthur Young who visited the linen market a month after the fire did not comment on it.
51 Gill, *Irish Linen Industry*, 79–81.
52 R. M. Young (ed), *Town Book of Belfast, 1613–1816* (Belfast 1892), xii.
53 Pococke, *Tour in Ireland in 1752* (ed G. T. Stokes, Dublin 1891), 13 (Downpatrick); Abercorn Irish agents' Letters (held at Baronscourt, Co Tyrone). Copies in PRONI T2541/1A1/2/31 and 34.
54 James Corry, *Report of a tour of inspection through the province of Ulster* (Dublin 1817), App 94. PRONI D699/5. Will of Robert Rice, 6 Oct 1800.
55 Corry, *Report*, App 91.
56 Ibid, App 12 (Dungannon), 59 (Banbridge), 71 (Ballynahinch), 75 (Kircubbin), 83 (Ballymena); Marmion, *Maritime Ports of Ireland*, 314 (Newry); E. M. Boyle, *Records of the town of Limavady, 1609–1808* (Londonderry 1912), 98; S. Lewis, *A Topographical Dictionary of Ireland* (1837), vol 1, 68; vol 2, 498.
57 W. J. Green, *A Concise History of Lisburn and Neighbourhood* (Belfast 1906), 30.
58 Corry, *Report*, 76. See also his reference to Monaghan (75) and Enniskillen (84).
59 Charles Coote to Earl of Abercorn, 31 March 1748 (Abercorn MSS, T2541/1A1/1D/13.
60 [R. Stephenson], *Remarks on the present state of the linen manufacture of this Kingdom* (Dublin 1745), 13. Stephenson's career and his considerable influence over the policies of the Linen Board are examined in some detail in Gill, *Irish Linen Industry*, 96–7.
61 Abercorn MSS, T2541/1A1/2/44, 175.
62 R. Stephenson, *Considerations on the present state of the linen manufacture* (Dublin 1754), 21.
63 Smith and Harris, *County of Down*, 77.
64 *Commons' Jn Ire*; VII, 51, 112, 113, 192; VIII, 468, 495, 501–2 (dealing with the problems of the Lisburn to Armagh turnpike).
65 Young, *Tour*, vol 2, 7. See also vol 1, 116.
66 Waring MSS (PRONI), D 695/51, Arthur Brownlow to Samuel Waring, 27 August 1699.
67 Waring MSS, D695/M/1.
68 W. A. McCutcheon, *The Canals of the North of Ireland* (1965), 63.
69 Ibid, 11, 20.
70 Ibid, 45.

71 Abercorn MSS, T2541/1A1/2/149.
72 McCutcheon, *Canals of North of Ireland*, 86.
73 Ibid, 16.
74 Gill, *Irish Linen Industry*, 150–1.
75 'Jobbers' bought webs in outlying markets to sell them in the chief centre of trade: their existence was vital to the small markets. Gill, *Irish Linen Industry*, 170–2.
76 'Keelmen' were dealers who bought cheap coarse cloths in the local markets and retailed them in Britain. J. Corry, *Report on the measuring and stamping of brown linen sold in public markets* (Dublin 1822), App, 174–5.
77 *Commons' Jn Ire*, III, 31, 251; IV, 13, 337; V, 228.
78 McCall, *Ireland and her Staple Manufactures*, 74.
79 Greer MSS, D1044/92.
80 McCall, *Ireland and her Staple Manufactures*, 74, 75.
81 Ibid, 84–7.
82 Gosford MSS (PRONI), D1606/1/21 March 1761. .
83 Greer MSS, D1044/692. See also D1044/677A.
84 Abercorn MSS. The correspondence for 1764 contains many references to this struggle since it lasted throughout the year.
85 McCall, *Ireland and her Staple Manufactures*, 74.
86 Gill, *Irish Linen Industry*, 206.
87 Massereene MSS (PRONI) D207/28/3, 99, 100, 101; Greer MSS, D1044/899. The row is discussed in detail in John Nevill, *Seasonable remarks on the linen trade of Ireland* (Dublin 1783).
88 Massereene MSS, D207/28/3.
89 Ibid, D207/28/99.
90 Ibid, D207/28/100.
91 21 & 22 Geo III, c 35, s 9.
92 Massereene MSS, D207/28/100; Greer MSS, D1044/899.
93 Nevill, *Linen Trade of Ireland*, 39.
94 Ibid, 68, 69; Greer MSS, D1044/900.
95 Nevill, *Linen Trade of Ireland*, 52.
96 Gill, *Irish Linen Industry*, 189–91.
97 Massereene MSS, D207/28/272.
98 Ibid, D207/28/249A.
99 Ibid, D207/28/113.
100 Ibid, D207/28/249A.
101 Ibid, D207/28/214.
102 McCall, *Ireland and her Staple Manufactures*, 243.
103 E. Wakefield, *An Account of Ireland* (1812), 700.
104 J. C. Beckett, *The making of modern Ireland, 1603–1923* (1966), 180.
105 Green, *Lagan Valley*, 99.
106 McEvoy, *County of Tyrone*, 200.
107 Table to show changes in the size of holdings on the Brownlow estate (1755–85):

	0–5 acres	5–10 acres	10–20 acres	20–50 acres	50–100 acres	100 + acres
1755	10	31	55	55	34	14
1765	14	34	75	49	35	13
1775	27	52	83	42	19	11
1785	56	114	113	53	12	5

Note: Of the leases in 1785 eight were perpetuities, 196 were for terms of three lives, 78 for thirty-one years and 9 for twenty-one while 60 had no lease. In 1765 and 1775 the number of tenants without a lease had been 10.

108   Young, *Tour*, vol 2, 215–17; Sir C. Coote, *Statistical survey of the county of Armagh* (Dublin 1804), 261–7.
109   Green, *Lagan Valley*, 142.
110   Young, *Tour*, vol 1, 134.
111   Sir C. Coote, *Statistical survey of the county of Cavan* (Dublin 1802), 108–9, 151, 157.
112   Rev J. Hall, *Tour through Ireland* (1813), 116–17.
113   Young, *Tour*, vol 1, 165.
114   McEvoy, *County of Tyrone*, 99–100. Rev J. Dubourdieu, *Statistical survey of the county of Antrim* (Dublin 1812), 147.
115   Rev G. V. Sampson, *Statistical survey of the county of Londonderry* (Dublin 1802), 298.
116   Hall, *Tour through Ireland*, 118.
117   Wakefield, *Account of Ireland*, 684; Green, *Lagan Valley*, 116.
118   J. H. Johnson, 'The population of Londonderry during the great Irish famine', *Econ Hist Rev*, 2S, 10 (1957), 272.

4

The Denisons and Milneses: Eighteenth-Century Merchant Landowners

R. G. WILSON

The old textbook discussion of eighteenth-century change in terms of two largely distinct movements—the Industrial and Agrarian revolutions—has now lost much of its meaning. This heterogeneity has been ceaselessly pared away during the last twenty years in the attempt to provide a total explanation of our industrial progress in the complex terms of economic growth. The traditional account of agrarian change particularly has undergone radical reappraisal. The achievements of Young's and Sinclair's countless 'improvers' are now seen not so much as an endless catalogue of exemplary endeavour but as part and parcel of the transformation in industry, transport and trade.[1] This does not suggest that the historian's application of the economist's tools to the problem of eighteenth-century change has in any way diminished the significance of agrarian developments. Only recently Professor Rostow has stressed that 'an increase in agricultural production and productivity plays a multiple role in economic development which can hardly be overestimated.[2] One aspect of this multiple role, emphasised by a growing number of studies since 1951[3]—the direct ancestors of this volume of essays —has been the contribution which the landowners made to industrial progress as well as agricultural improvement. This essentially bridging function of the landowner was stressed in a recent synthesis of these studies: 'in some vital spheres of the economy, in mining, iron and transport as well as in agriculture, the landlord's contribution was itself crucial to the process of expansion'.[4]

So persuasive has been this line of argument that the latest account of the Industrial Revolution has suggested that capital accumulated from estate income was the 'most likely source of additional savings in the middle and later eighteenth century', and that this provides one explanation of the sudden spurt of industrial investment after 1780.[5] This hypothesis advancing the landowner's participation in productive investment seriously questions the explanation that a considerable proportion of industrial enterprises were floated by profits accumulated in the home and export trades. It is suggested that this percolation of commercial profits into the key growth industries must not be exaggerated: 'The first goal of many a merchant was the acquisition of a landed estate with a stately home, and an unknown proportion of all mercantile profits in the eighteenth century was poured into this form of conspicuous consumption.'[6] Such an interpretation at first sight suggests an analysis of the merchant's place in eighteenth-century comedy rather than of his role in the economy. Two points, however, are relevant. It is impossible, at least at the moment, to answer Clapham's question 'how representative?' The evidence that has come to light tends to confirm Professor Flinn's view. Secondly we should therefore shift our line of inquiry from a sole preoccupation with the merchant's connections with industry. If we regard agricultural advance as being part and parcel of industrial change then we should look upon the merchant as being an innovator in the agrarian sector.

It is necessary that we bear in mind Adam Smith's remark that the merchants who became landed proprietors 'were the best of all improvers'. Unfortunately the paucity of work completed on eighteenth-century commercial activities in Britain makes it impossible to provide precise conclusions about the mercantile contribution to economic advance during this period. Generalisations abound, detailed investigations are few. This paper attempts some tentative answers—from an admittedly narrow base (the two principal merchant houses in the West Riding of Yorkshire)[7] —to the questions of the merchant's motivation in purchasing land, his approach and contribution to estate management, his integration with traditional county society and the effect of his migration on the industry and town where he had acquired his fortune.

Answers to the question of the merchant's motivation in land purchase have almost always been stated in terms of social and political advancement. William Denison's[8] letter books suggest that an economic incentive provides a sounder explanation.[9] The mere enumeration of the numerous properties in his will indicates a curious piecemeal acquisition which does not square with the socio-political integration and aggrandisement argument. When he died in 1782 he left no fewer than seven estates to his younger brother Robert.[10] Besides the valuable patrimonial estate in Leeds there were properties in four counties: Ossington and Sutton-on-Trent (Notts); Kelstern and Calsthorpe (Lincs); Beswick and Rimswell (East and North Ridings); Potterton Hall (West Riding); Coatham, Grindon and Chilton (Co Durham). One central large estate would have served Denison's purpose better were his ambitions purely to emulate the great landowners.[11]

On the other hand this somewhat haphazard accumulation reflects two considerations. Firstly there is the personal element. William Denison was born into an easy affluence. He was the descendant of a long line of West Riding clothiers who had made broad cloths for generations at Great Woodhouse, a village on the edge of Leeds.[12] As the name was common in the Leeds area, the early genealogy of the family is difficult to disentangle.[13] Certainly, however, around 1700 the family leapt into sudden prominence when they abandoned cloth-making to take up the export of Yorkshire cloth. In the next forty years, at a time when the Leeds and Wakefield woollen merchants were finally gaining full control of the Yorkshire export trade, and the Portuguese and Mediterranean trade was rapidly expanding, the Denisons made a fortune. Cossins's 1725 map of Leeds, its margins embellished with the more impressive of the merchants' dwellings, shows Robert and Thomas Denison occupying two fine Georgian houses at the North Town End.[14] William followed in the family tradition, and the firm became one of the most important in the Yorkshire cloth trade.[15] He was so sure of his standing in the town and trade that he could refuse the mayoralty of Leeds no fewer than four times in the 1750s.[16] William's independence, illustrated by this celebrated piece of truculence, was reinforced by the fact that he remained unmarried. In no way did this lessen his diligence in the cloth export firm, but it meant that there was not the same incentive to create a first-class consolidated estate. Secondly the estates were in some degree purchased out of current earnings by the merchant house, and this probably limited the size of property purchased at any given period. As a large surplus built up—and unlike later manufacturing concerns the capital required by the larger export houses in Leeds probably never exceeded £20,000 before 1782—Denison looked around for the best possible investment.[17]

If the size and scattered nature of William Denison's properties reflect his personal and financial arrangements we must look elsewhere for the motivational factors which led him to this new departure. There was perhaps a certain element of emulation not of the neighbouring gentry but of his wealthier fellow merchants. For the latter a country estate was the ultimate seal of success. In Leeds itself William Milner and James Ibbotson had bought notable West Riding estates from the Fairfax family, although in both cases they themselves had continued in business, and their acquisitions had been reserved for their children's pleasures.[18] Certainly there was no question of Denison neglecting business in Leeds to spend time in country pursuits. To the end William was extremely conscientious, prepared to haggle with the clothiers over the smallest detail, supervise his cloth dressers and make occasional trips abroad to visit his contacts. Moreover not only was he head of the largest woollen cloth exporting firm in Yorkshire, but also in 1772 he joined the important city merchant house of Sir George Colebrooke and Josiah Smith.[19] It was seldom that he saw his estates more than once a year and such visitations were brief. In 1779, when he tried to evade serving as High Sheriff of Nottinghamshire he wrote to the Speaker of the House of Commons, Sir Fletcher Norton, 'Nor do I call myself an inhabitant of that county for tho' I have a large house upon my estate and keep an old woman there to light fires for its preservation, I have never been in Nottingham 14 days per ann. since I purchased it, and then only upon business.'[20] And Ossington, William claimed, was his favourite estate. What leisure time he had was spent taking the waters each spring at Bath, for with advancing years he was laid up each winter in Leeds with gout for increasingly long periods.

Although William purchased his first estate in Lincolnshire in

1759 the factors which influenced this departure and subsequent ventures emerge from a perusal of his only surviving letter books, which cover the years 1777–81. The firm's involvement by the 1770s appears to have been entirely in the Italian market. And, as William stressed, the worst slump in the Yorkshire woollen industry during the eighteenth century, that of 1778–83, was due not merely to the fact that the American market was closed but that the French entry into the war in March 1778 had ruined the Mediterranean trade. The hesitancy of the British Government to protect merchant shipping resulted in insurance rates rising to 18–20 per cent. The cost of sending goods, especially cheap Yorkshire woollens, by the overland route to Italy via Ostend or Hamburg through Germany was prohibitive. Denison ceaselessly lamented that things had been very different during the Seven Years' War and he echoed the entire commercial world's dissatisfaction with Lord North when he concluded that the Prime Minister knew 'no more of trade than a child'.[21] In Leeds the firm was at a virtual standstill: 'an exporter of woollen goods at present had better lend his money at one per cent Interest than trade with it up the Straits [of Gibraltar]'.[22] Two ships which had sailed from Hull in May 1778 had proceeded no further than Gibraltar by the following February.[23] In spite of the fact that the price of cloth was falling sharply in the cloth halls, Denison felt he was better doing nothing at a time when insurance costs were high, exchange rates unfavourable and remittances behind hand. He summarised his position when he wrote to his nephew, 'my capital during the year 1778 had better have been at 2 per cent interest than in trade . . . and 1779 promises no better success, tho' goods are cheap'.[24]

As debts came in William curtailed his orders with the clothiers and his purchases in the cloth halls, and began to investigate the best available investment opportunities. He considered three outlets: annuities, government stock and land. In 1779 he was exploring opportunities for the negotiation of suitable annuities. For a number of years William had occasionally speculated in this field, and in 1779 he agreed to let Lord Chesterfield have £4,800 on an undisclosed annual repayment. In the following year, however, he was writing, 'Little money to be made in the annuity business—only with trustworthy private gentlemen.

Foley's family have robbed the publick near £300,000 that way.'[25]
His doubts came too late. When the executors settled his
brother's estate in 1789 they commented that both William and
Robert Denison had been lax in keeping their annuity accounts—
many of the annual payments were unpaid—and it was reckoned
that Lord Chesterfield, Lord Seaforth and Lord Foley together
owed them £9,881.[26] The second and third investment cate-
gories were more important. In these difficult years William constantly weighed the monetary return of Consols against land.
Rents fell sharply after 1778 and large arrears were forcing the
necessitous to sell. In the winter of 1777–8 Denison was offered
several West Country estates at Bath, and in the following autumn
he was considering properties in Lincolnshire and the East and
West Ridings, but as he told a York land agent, 'If I can't make
four per cent or upwards in elegible purchases my spare money
will go into the funds.'[27] As the war dragged on and the depression
deepened rents fell further—William reduced his by 20 per cent
in the spring of 1780—and the value of land in some places fell by
as much as one-third. As the land market became increasingly
uncertain, the problem of management, outlay and rent arrears
weighed heavily with William: 'I will not purchase unless I can
do it upon as good terms as I enjoy in the funds which is 5 per
cent clear of all charges and expences whatsoever, where I have
no delays, no disappointments, no bad Tennants, nor no
Stewardships.'[28] The yield of government stocks rose sharply
between 1777 and 1780, from an average of 3·7 per cent in 1777
to 5·0 per cent in 1780.[29] By early 1780 William realised that his
trading surplus was nowhere so well invested as in stocks producing 5 per cent. The difficulty was to obtain them. He was prepared to advance £10,000 to £12,000 in January 1780, but only
£6,000 was accepted.[30] In February 1781 he wrote demanding
£20,000 worth of that year's issue.[31] Yet in spite of persistant
letters to John Robinson at the Treasury to remind him that his
distant relative Joseph Denison, the banker, had been allowed
his full quota of £100,000, he was only allowed £5,000, of his
£20,000 application. As he concluded to his banker, 'those that
get such large sums have a private ear to either my Lord North's
or Robinson's ears especially when the loan is advantageous'.[32]
    The evidence on Denison's monetary transactions in these

three years confirms the view that his estates were purchased as the best outlet for his surplus cash. Only a narrow range of investments were considered: in 1759 and 1768 he believed land to be the better speculation; in 1780 and 1781 the return on government stocks was more attractive. Denison's attitude was significant in two respects. Firstly, land was viewed entirely in the utilitarian terms of improvement and return. Distance, tradition, beauty mattered little; the most rapturous adjective which flowed from William's pen was 'fair'. Rents and improvement potential were of greater interest. Moreover he was prepared to resell his property; in January 1779 he was offering Ossington and Sutton for sale at £60,000. 'It always seemed to me to be a favourite Estate of my Broths.', wrote Robert Denison, 'and never imagined he wo'd part with it at any rate . . . I know my bror. will abate nothing of the last price sett, nor will he take it, if the value of money sho'd alter.'[33] Property was never once considered for its built-in social guarantees or political advantages—William well knew he could have afforded any pocket borough he chose. His wealth and position in Leeds gave him a sufficient status. Secondly, he eschewed any form of industrial investment either in transport improvements or the West Riding woollen and coal industries. The executor's accounts of Robert's will showed that not a penny found its way outside land, annuities, government stock and of course the firm itself. Here then on the threshold of Britain's industrialisation was a merchant who, according to the traditional interpretations, should have been channelling surplus earnings into industrial enterprises of one form or another, completely ignoring this outlet. And William Denison was extremely rich by any contemporary standards—the Leeds papers estimated his fortune between £500,000 and £700,000 when he died in 1782.[34] Few early industrialists' wealth could compare with this. Yet his actions are entirely explicable: his was the classic but common merchant's attitude that one pursued one's trade vigorously but did not become involved in industry. It was far easier when depression frequently came to curtail activities as a merchant, than it was to keep going as a manufacturer. The minimum capital was employed: surplus earnings were canalised into the safest and most easily realisable outlets—land and government stocks.

If we argue that the processes of agricultural and industrial change in the eighteenth century are conterminous, and accept the generalisation that many wealthy merchants were ultimately more concerned with the acquisition of a landed estate than continuing their interest in industry, then we must consider the contribution which these newcomers made to the development of contemporary agriculture. An analysis suggests two divergent approaches. If we accept Adam Smith's premise then we concern ourselves with questions of the innovational aspects of his landownership. Did the fact that the merchants approached the problems of landownership without being inhibited by the weight of agricultural tradition, that they came out of their counting houses and applied stricter criteria of accountability to their new projects, lead to an improved form of estate management? Or on the other hand was this large injection of commercial capital into the agricultural sector dissipated by lack of knowledge, inefficient control and the demand for quick returns? William Denison's experience provides answers to both these lines of inquiry.

In the eighteenth century the division between town and country, industrial and agrarian pursuits, was difficult to draw. Merchants and manufacturers who knew nothing of the ways of the land were rare. William Denison came to landownership with a knowledge drawn from his family's management of their small, but valuable, properties in Leeds,[35] and with the advice of his kinsman, Thomas Denison, who managed the Sheffield family's estates in Lincolnshire.[36] It was an acquaintance with agriculture which was sufficient to stop William making grave errors, yet it did not imply a traditional involvement which might have curtailed the vision of his plans. His attitude to farming illustrates this point. When in 1781 he was unable to let a 600-acre farm— 'esteemed one of the prettiest farms in the county of Lincoln'— at an economic rent, he was forced into stocking it with 120 Scots beasts and sowing 50 acres of turnips. At the outset of his ventures he was writing gloomily to his steward, 'farming I think is a bad plan . . . I wish instead of turning grazier I had thrown a hundred guineas into the River before I began'.[37] His reaction was exactly that of a West Riding merchant to cloth manufacture: the problems of supervision made it too troublesome to consider. Mercantile theory was translated into agrarian practice. This meant that his concept of estate ownership appeared curious to the traditional landowning community. Property was not conceived in terms of providing a current income to maintain a social role, but of consolidating realisable assets. His practice was to buy land cheaply and then by extensive improvement rapidly to increase its value. Ossington was bought for £34,000 in 1768, and as we have seen William briefly considered selling the estate for £60,000 in 1779. As Robert Denison wrote to the prospective purchaser, who offered £58,000, 'he has laid out an Immensity of money in building planting and improving the Estate and has cut down very little timber only some offall decayers that the woods are better by some thousands than they were when he had it'.[38] Yet money was not poured into improvements without thought. Change was achieved in three ways: by planning the tenants' farming practices; by planting and conservation in the woods; and, in the case of Ossington, by improvements to the house and park.

Far the biggest obstacle to improvement came from the tenant farmers themselves. William read the latest manuals of estate improvements; he knew every advantage to be derived from draining, manure and clover seeds. In convincing the farmers of these benefits, however, his books were less helpful. To enforce improvement he had recourse to leases which contained written cropping agreements. This scheme, admirable in securing quick change, relied upon a generous landlord, the integrity of the farmer and a high level of agricultural incomes. Unfortunately the evidence for William's tenant agreements relates to the period 1778–81 when prices were falling and rents as much as two years in arrears, so that there was considerable difficulty in enforcing the system. The correspondence is a continuous catalogue of quarrels, legal actions and forced possessions. William's relations with Joseph Iveson, who farmed at Beeston (Leeds), were not untypical of those subsisting between landlord and tenant on all the Denison estates. Iveson had allowed the farm during his five year's lease to become 'a disgrace to husbandry'. At first William merely gave detailed advice. His instructions on laying down Danby Ing to permanent pasture reveal the demands he placed upon his tenants:

Fallow it in 1780, cleanse it well, and drain it well with durable drains, and lime it with two chaldron of Knottingby lime per

acre, sow it down with Barley in the spring 1781, and 8lbs., of
white clover and two quarters of hayseeds per acre, manuring it
the winter after the Barley crop, with 20 good cart load per acre
—when I think it will do you some service this may be expensive
but the profitts will center in your own pockett.

In the following spring nothing had been done, and William was
attempting to force Iveson into paying £125 for the 500 cart loads
of manure of which he computed the grassland had been deprived.
Then William demanded 'immediate satisfaction', for Iveson's
'other breeches of covenant'. The quarrel disappears before three
arbitrators nominated to give the landlord satisfaction.[39] On the
Durham estate there were attempts to compel a penalty clause of
£5 for every acre ploughed contrary to agreement.[40] Difficulties
stemmed from two causes. The farmers themselves, both in the
scale of their outlook and in the scope of their pockets, were un-
prepared for the pace of change dictated. At Ossington the
tenants had to be threatened with paying for the lime they did not
spread, although two loads per acre were provided free of charge.
Secondly, in spite of the fact that William was careful in insisting
that his tenants had adequate financial security, the position of
the majority of them was precarious during these years of
stress.

It would be misleading, however, to dwell entirely on the problems which faced Denison. The framework for improvement was
created. Facilities were extended which few other landlords provided: farm buildings were repaired and extended; clover seeds
and hedging plants were supplied; free lime made available at the
nearest river port, the tenants being responsible only for carting
and spreading. Farms at least in county Durham were 'underlett
in order to gett 'em into good condition'.[41] Loans were occasionally granted. William's policy was that he was 'always ready
to show any reasonable indulgence to a good Tennant'.[42] Wider
schemes that were beyond the scope of the single farm unit were
undertaken. The Ossington and Durham estates were drained,
and enclosures of these estates, both without parliamentary sanction, appear to have been completed in the 1770s.[43]

In 1779 Robert Denison noted that his brother had increased the
valuation of the 370 acres of woodland at Ossington by several
thousand pounds in his ten years' ownership. Admittedly timber

prices rose steadily throughout the 1770s, and Ossington timber always found a good market in Leeds. Yet improvement of the woods was more than a mere question of revaluation; it was achieved by a carefully-balanced policy of felling and replanting. Some 15–16 acres of young trees were cut each summer for hop poles and stakes. Heavier timber was floated down the Trent to Gainsborough. William was using Ossington oak for building in Leeds during 1781, and his tenters were supplied from the same source. There was continuous replanting of softwood at both Ossington and Beswick. Oaks were considered unsuitable at the latter: 'I don't think that the growth of oak timber in a clay soil pays one per cent, for the Interest of the money therefore few people in their senses will cultivate it.' In 1781 10,000 trees were planted at Beswick, and the quantity of elms raised in 1780 was so prodigious that William had 'a notion we may have some claim for the Prize Medal given annually by the Society of Agriculture'.[44]

With Denison's constant consideration for his return on capital outlay the improvement of his houses came far lower on his list of priorities than it did with those of other contemporary estate owners. Of the three country houses he owned—Ossington, Potterton and Beswick—there is evidence of improvements only at Ossington, although even here the chronology of change is difficult to establish with any precision.[45] The house was valued at £2,000 in 1759, yet twenty years later Robert maintained it was worth £10,000 and would cost £15,000 to build.[46] Denison's steward reported building in 1769. On the other hand John Denison's major additions after 1785 do not suggest that his uncle's alterations were extensive.[47] Evidence, however, for the improvement of the park and gardens between 1779 and 1781 is abundant. William was obviously impressed with Thornes House (a sketch plan exists at Ossington), built by John Carr in 1779–81 for James Milnes of Wakefield. Not to be outdone among the West Riding merchants William invited Carr to submit designs for a large circular peripteral temple in 1780, and Richard Cotton of Haigh near Barnsley was asked to supply the ironwork for a hot-house at Ossington similar to the one he had constructed for Milnes. An order was placed for 3,500 sq yd of glass and six horses were bought to cart 460,000 bricks from Newark for the garden walls.[48] In effect William was already planning for his

nephew, as he himself could enjoy such extravagant embellish-
ments for a mere two weeks in the year.

Arthur Young might have applauded the zeal with which
William Denison pursued the copy-book plans of the 'new-
husbandry'. When we turn to the question of estate management,
however, there is no similar yardstick of comparison. Although
manuals for the instruction of land agents and stewards existed,
no uniform practice of management emerged.[49] As a practical
science it was largely empirical. Most landowners had their own
ideas of improvement. The influence of land agents in estates
where the landlord was non-resident (the large minority of
estates) can easily over emphasise their significance in general.
The running of the Denison estates is interesting in that although
the landlord was non-resident on his estates, the agent wielded
little influence. Admittedly the estates posed peculiar problems.
Time was a more important consideration than money in that the
pressure of William's commercial commitments meant that
visitations to individual properties were short and infrequent.
Moreover William's concept of estate management was borrowed
directly from his merchanting experience. Not only was the abuse
that was common between merchant and clothier extended to
farmers and estate workers, but also the meticulous attention to
detail, that was necessary for every successful woollen merchant
in the absolutely non-standardised cloth trade, was applied to the
running of the Denison estates. As the woollen export trade was
of necessity largely carried on by correspondence, William believed he could manage his properties by the same method. That
the farmers were unused to this form of communication, and
were men of modest understanding never appears to have entered his head. Business in Italy, estate improvement in England
could both be achieved by the same means.

Certainly the formal machinery of management existed. William appears to have been well served both by Robert Arthington,
an extremely able Quaker, and Miles Dawson, a professional
agent who was employed in 1778 at a salary of £100.[50] Yet both
men had their difficulties. The far-flung nature of the estates in
four remote counties made constant supervision impossible.
Arthington was obliged to spend most of his time in Leeds, Dawson appears to have acted only in a part-time capacity. In effect

they saw little more of the estates than when they toured them annually with their master. Neither of them had a free hand. William himself wrote instructions to each tenant individually, and Dawson at least was not always sure of William's detailed intentions. Day-to-day oversight was in theory maintained by the chief tenant on each estate. The burden was heavy. He was bombarded with constant letters about cropping, rents and arrears. He was expected to report all developments in the village and on individual farms. Affairs at Ossington were placed in the hands of the head woodman. Of Hayes's abilities as general estate foreman William had scant faith: he believed him to be both a poor salesman and a bad overseer. Yet for some reason he was never replaced, although William seemed unable to discipline him effectively for long. That the curate was used as a general unpaid informant of affairs emerges from William's attempt to find a replacement in 1778:[51]

> I yett want a clergyman if I can meet with one to my liking of the turn and disposition of Mr Clay, who used to keep the town in pretty good order, had an eye to the game and wou'd have acquainted me if anything materiall went wrong to the prejudice of the Estate. I have had many offers from mere clergymen but they appeared to me to be totally ignorant of everything but their book.

The new incumbent when installed into the living was not cooperative. When told that the new orchard at Ossington was wrongly planted, he wrote promptly back saying that he was unable to risk his health in superintending the planting of trees.[52] Denison's instructions from Leeds became increasingly strongly worded. Hayes and William Ancliff, the gardener, were entirely, if easily confused. And the latter found the directives so tiresome that he and his labourers spent all day drinking at Sutton feast and 'put down both his own and their labour to my account'.[53]

If William Denison's approach to estate management has some novel features, the problems he faced were those which faced all improving landlords. Certainly the geographical dispersion of the estates and non-residence did not make administration easy, but the real hindrance to his ambitious improvement schemes was traditionalism. The farmers' practices were rooted in infallible

custom, their monetary resources limited, their readiness to take
advantage of new opportunities circumscribed by several factors.
The estate workers found the application to effort which their
new squire demanded irksome, and the fact that he was absent
for at least fifty weeks in the year allowed them by and large to
pursue their old ways. In his knowledge of the 'new husbandry'
William was well abreast of current discussions, but whereas the
old squirearchy knew the limitations of their tenantry and servants, William was not prepared to admit their shortcomings.

No one has questioned Malachy Postlethwayt's contention that
'the mercantile station . . . affords as large a prospect for opulent
acquisition as any other; and estates got by trade have, perhaps,
been far more numerous than those by anyway whatsoever'.[54]
Yet the extent to which the landowning merchant integrated
himself with traditional county society has always been more de-
batable. Was he the stock figure of the eighteenth-century comedy
of manners: the fish out of water, proud of his wealth, careful
with his money, devoid of taste, accomplishments and polish? Or
was his passage into the world of Squire Western less painful
than a perusal of these plays would suggest?

The discussion has tended to overlook two pieces of evidence.
Firstly historians have accepted the landowners' views on the
merchant community as being identical with their unfavourable
reaction to the new manufacturers after the 1770s. There was in
fact a marked discontinuity. Many of these manufacturers, like
Arkwright, Strutt and Peel were entirely self-made men without
a recognised place in the hierarchy of eighteenth-century social
order.[55] We come now to the second point. In contrast with the
new industrialists it must be remembered that the merchants who
embarked upon large-scale landownership already had considerable status in the urban community, a status based upon their
pre-eminent position in town society. In Leeds their standing
was defined by a delicately balanced series of factors. The key to
success was ultimately wealth: riches that stood comparison with
the neighbouring gentry and wealthier clergy. Because merchanting was a lucrative profession restrictions to entry were enforced
by educational and formal training requirements. This meant in

practice that the merchants were largely drawn from families already prominent in the Yorkshire cloth trade or from recruits whose fathers were able to afford a long and expensive apprenticeship with one of the bigger export houses in the town. This selective and costly form of education together with the fact that landed families frequently turned their younger sons into trade meant that many merchant families had an additional status conferred through their connections with the local gentry. Further recognition came with nomination to the closed corporation, as a trustee of the advowson of Leeds parish church, and possibly ultimately as mayor of the borough.[56] Some merchants were singled out by the conferment of a title (never more than a baronetcy), or more frequently by their appointment as county JPs and occasionally as High Sheriff of the county.

William Denison could fulfil most of these criteria of acceptance. Like his cousin, Sir Thomas Denison,[57] he was probably educated at Leeds Grammar School, although the more important part of his training was the apprenticeship he served with the family firm and his sojourn abroad learning languages and visiting his father's customers. Certainly his family connections were of no great social standing—Robert Denison's will left, 'To such poor relations who are half couzens the sum of Ten Pounds each' —although they had been exporting cloth since the 1680s and were prominent in town affairs after 1700. But long before he bought his first estate in Lincolnshire, William was a highly respected figure in Leeds, in the Yorkshire woollen industry and the West Riding itself. Later he was to extend his knowledge of the business world through his connections with the London merchant community. And for many years, especially during the struggles in America, he was frequently seeing the Yorkshire MPs and those merchant members concerned with trade affairs, on problems concerning the woollen industry.[58]

Yet the extent to which William's vast commercial repute guaranteed his acceptance amongst landed society in Nottinghamshire and Lincolnshire is difficult to determine. As we have noted William spent little time on any of his estates. Moreover he was not interested in any of the traditional pursuits of the country gentleman. Brother Robert occasionally entertained a shooting party at Ossington, but William was more interested in the preservation of his fences and trees than his game. When a neighbour hunted Ossington woods in the summer of 1777 and rode through the farmers' standing corn William demanded prosecution, begged the tenants to give information and assured Hayes that he would bear the latter 'harmless against all charges'. Later fox-traps were set in the woods on William's instructions. It probably therefore came as no surprise to him, when Hayes reported that on ordering someone hunting out of the plantations he had been told his master was 'no gentleman'. At Kelstern there were similar incidents.[59] Even to the farmers whose interests he was protecting he appeared a strange if awesome landlord, annually descending on his distant estates, rich as Croesus, impatient of delay, suffering no fools, bent on improvement at all costs.

By the employment of more tangible criteria William's social acceptance would appear to be complete. The year following his purchase of Ossington he was appointed a Justice of the Peace for Nottinghamshire and in 1779 he was nominated High Sheriff of the county. This advancement suggests two interpretations. It might reflect the shortage of candidates for offices which are usually considered by historians to carry considerable social prestige. That such a reading of the evidence is not impossible comes from a description of Nottinghamshire given by Sir George Savile of Rufford: 'The idea I gave Lord Rockingham of this county was four Dukes, two Lords and three rabbit warrens, which I believe, takes in half the county in point of space.'[60] Certainly the impression left by William's candidature for shrievalty is that he was the slowest of the three persons whose names were traditionally submitted to the King to withdraw his nomination.[61] This does not diminish William's standing in the county. He was old and gout racked. He neither wanted office, nor was he interested in the county's social round. Had he wished to cut a figure in Nottinghamshire he might easily have done so. Robert had grander social aspirations. When he died, three years after William, his executors were instructed to provide, 'Sir Thomas Gascoigne Bart, a diamond mourning Ring of the value of one hundred pounds, to Sir Thomas Blackett Bart, Messieurs Bosvilles and my other friends of Distinction a mourning ring each of the value of five guineas at the least.'[62] When their nephew, John Wilkinson (he assumed the name of Denison in 1785), succeeded to the estates in 1785 he set up an establishment at Ossington that many Nottinghamshire squires must have envied. The old woman who had lit fires for its preservation was replaced by a staff which included six male servants and a French butler.[63] Sir John Soane made plans for altering the front of Ossington, remodelling the interior to provide a picture gallery and constructing a tower in the park.

It is possible to draw some general conclusions from William Denison's excursions into landed society, although the fact that his experiences were entirely personal makes this a somewhat speculative exercise. The merchant's social acceptance was based on his wealth and his experience. In William Denison's case there was recognition of his frequent contact with ministers and MPs on matters concerning Yorkshire industry and questions of finance, acknowledgement of his position as the doyen of West Riding traders. Above all his wealth commanded respect. Before gout made such trips impossible, William travelled abroad most years in France and Italy in his own coach; there were frequent sojourns in Bath and London, and occasionally York.[64] Yet in the eighteenth century wealth was not necessarily equated with vulgarity. There was a uniformity of upper class taste in Georgian England which eased the merchant's transference into the landowners' ranks. In Leeds William lived in a modest town house in Kirkgate opposite the Assembly Rooms. The rooms contained a fair collection of Italian pictures and books, yet at the end of the yard were huddled together the counting house, dressing and packing shops, stables and a vast dung-hill.[65] At Ossington, however, William furnished the house 'in neat fashionable taste'. He and Robert were portrayed full length in the grand manner by Gainsborough and Romney respectively. When William died in 1783 Robert commissioned the country's leading sculptor, Joseph Nollekens, to produce two statues:

a Monumental Statue at full length to the memory of my late Brother agreeable to his Directions and also shall set up and finish in the said Mausoleum opposite to and upon a similar plan or device with that to be erected to the memory of my said late brother a Tomb or Monumental Statue to my memory and I will that not less than the sum of one thousand pounds shall be laid out and expended in the compleating and finishing of such

L

Tombs or Monuments and that such farther sums shall be applied for that purpose as will be necessary to finish the same in the most compleat manner.

And although the executors appear to have scrapped the plans for the mausoleum, the statues now command John Carr's church which Robert built in the woods at Ossington. There was a strong element of emulation in Robert's grandiose schemes— Nollekens had executed a similar statue of the Marquess of Rockingham for Wentworth Woodhouse in 1774—but the result was ostentatious not vulgar.[66] Such catholic patronage of the arts suggests a taste which no contemporary could have faulted. The only point that separates the Denisons and the average north-country squire in such matters is that whereas the latter were un-likely to afford even a half-length Gainsborough portrait, still less a Nollekens memorial, William and Robert Denison could proudly sit to two of the leading painters of their day, and plan their park with the North's most fashionable architect. This fusion of interest and unity of taste much facilitated the inte-gration of the landed and mercantile communities. It accounts for the large number of prosperous merchants who were prepared to abandon trade, or at least provide their sons with a comfortable rent roll, for the pleasures and stability of country life.

The account of the Milnes family is essentially similar to that of the Denisons.[67] Claiming descent from the smaller Derbyshire gentry the Milneses settled in Wakefield around 1700 to earn their livings in the Yorkshire woollen trade and their reputations as solid Unitarian merchants.[68] Wakefield was a pleasant market town at the extreme south-eastern tip of the West Riding cloth-producing area. With the improvement of the River Calder at the beginning of the eighteenth century the town became increas-ingly important as a corn and wool market, and maintained its position, second only to Leeds, as a cloth-exporting centre.[69] The small handful of merchants that dominated the town's economic life (Wakefield unlike Leeds and Halifax was never an important centre of production itself) shared the new prosperity they created. No family took a larger portion than the Milneses. By the outbreak of hostilities with the American colonies they were the closest rivals of the Denisons in the latter's claim to be the largest export house in the Yorkshire cloth trade. The various branches of the family lived in great comfort in splendid town houses in Westgate.[70] But by 1770 their wealth, accumulated in three generations of trade with Russia, allowed them to open up social and political horizons far beyond the narrow confines of a market town, and to shift their base from the respect of Yorkshire Unitarianism and the West Riding commercial community to the shifting sands of social London.

The firm in 1770 was run by three Milnes brothers: Pemberton, Robert and James. Over the next twenty years the virtual monopoly that the family had secured in the Wakefield trade was relaxed. As the aphorism current in Wakefield around 1800 put it, 'The Milnes were, the Heywoods are, the Naylors will be.'[71] Partly the relaxation was a question of family circumstances, largely it was a matter of choice. Firstly Pemberton Milnes's only daughter married the second son of Archbishop Drummond of York in 1775.[72] Pemberton settled £20,000 on her, and shortly afterwards bought himself an estate at Bawtry to live in the style appropriate to the match. Gradually he spent more and more time in the politics of the Yorkshire Association, gaining *pari passu* the reputation of having 'drunk more port wine than any gentleman in Yorkshire'.[73] Secondly Richard Slater Milnes (1759–1804), Robert's son, after an education at Glasgow University, was elected MP for York in 1784 on the Yorkshire Association's ticket opposing the Fitzwilliam interest.[74] Thirdly James Milnes (d 1805) pursued a similar course to that of his cousin Richard. Walter Spencer-Stanhope writing in May 1796 noted that, 'This morning James Milnes bought the Borough of Shaftsbury for 15,000 gns.'[75] As more and more time was consumed in political pursuits and the social round of Yorkshire and London the cloth firm was inevitably neglected. To a certain extent their financial dependence on its well-being was lessened by their marriages. Richard and James Milnes married the two daughters and co-heiresses of Hans Buck, a well-to-do Unitarian cloth-merchant in Leeds. Their dowries were reputed to be 'upwards of £100,000 each', and through their mother they inherited the Great Houghton estates.[76] Moreover their predisposition for the joys of landed society was unhampered by their upbringing, their work or their sober Unitarian wives. James Milnes commissioned John Carr to build Thornes House in 1781, presumably on part of the proceeds of his newly acquired wife's dowry. Robert Milnes bought the Fryston Hall estate in 1786 and immediately had the house refaced in the Italian manner.[77] But the Milnes's style of living was advertised far beyond the Wakefield district. Not only did they sit to Romney and Reynolds for full-length portraits, and George Stubbs paint Richard Milnes riding to hounds, but they set up establishments in London which were the wonder of their West Riding neighbours.[78] The dinner James Milnes gave for 200 in 1801 in honour of George III's birthday, with rare fruits from his hot-house in Wakefield—'one of the most extensive in the Kingdom'—indicates the scale of his operations.[79]

When Richard Milnes died in 1804 he had the good sense to leave his estates to his wife during her lifetime. She made some attempt to keep them going, run the family firm in Wakefield and educate her children. The task was difficult. Although her elder son, Robert (1784–1858) seemed full of promise (he was offered a seat in the Cabinet at the age of 25) it was a promise which never matured.[80] A neighbour wrote, 'he was a wild, unstable creature, at one time devoting his days and nights to reading, at another giving them up to play, at another entirely engrossed in shooting'.[81] Thomas Carlyle commented more perceptively that he had 'many many remarkable things about him, all loose and distracted. If they were only braced up and fibred together he would be a very distinguished man.'[82] In fact Robert Milnes quickly withdrew from political life to become a respected, if unconventional Yorkshire squire. The second son Rodes brought the family to the verge of ruin. At first he drove to Wakefield two or three times a week to look after the business, but soon his association with the Prince Regent and the Turf demanded his full attention.[83] As the Victorian biographer of his nephew wrote, with as little censure as he could muster, 'he was addicted to gambling, betted freely on his own horses and played a prominent part in the gaieties alike of York and London. His racing associate was Mr Petre of Stapleton, and their stable won the St Leger no fewer than five times in the eight years between 1822 and 1830.'[84] It is not a distinction one usually associates with the scion of a leading Unitarian merchant family. And as we continue to peruse Sir Wemyss Reid's prim account of Rodes Milnes and Lord Glasgow stationing themselves in an inn window at the conclusion of York races, inviting every passer-by to join them in a bottle of wine, the textbook image of the tireless endeavour of the dissenters in their business pursuits begins to lose some of its precision, and at the same time the suspicion grows that the continuity between eighteenth-century trade and nineteenth-century industry has been much overstressed by historians.

In conclusion we must make some attempt to analyse the results of the merchant's transference from commerce to landownership. It is possible to consider the problem in two ways: to estimate the effect of his withdrawal on the trade and town in which he made his living; to examine the special nature of his contribution to British landed society.

As to the former it would create a mistaken impression to conclude that many Yorkshire woollen merchants went the way of the Milneses and Denisons, just as few merchants followed Benjamin Gott's footsteps into factory ownership. The majority was prepared neither to take the trouble nor make the heavy outlay that was necessary in the adoption of the new system after 1790. Yet the merchant was not able to continue as before for the competition of the manufacturers (frequently former clothiers, dyers, cloth dressers etc) and changing conditions in the woollen trade tended to force him out of business. Some carried on until disaster overtook them; the majority, especially the wealthier element, found a safer and more remunerative outlet for their capital, usually, but not always in the purchase of a country property.[85]

The significance of the Denison and Milnes examples was that here were the two largest firms in the industry virtually withdrawing their capital from trade at the crucial stage of the first period of rapid industrialisation. And by the standards of the early industrialists they had unlimited financial resources. William Denison ploughed far more money into land than Benjamin Gott and the Wormalds expended in establishing the first factory in the woollen industry. The emulation of the Denison and

Milnes example on a lesser scale throughout the Yorkshire woollen trade suggests that Mantoux's assertion that there was 'a gradual transformation of commercial to industrial capital' and Charles Wilson's similar conclusion that 'capital came to industrialists in need from merchants of an older generation . . . Everywhere there is unbroken continuity', are an oversimplification of the position, at least in the West Riding.[86] One might also argue that the merchants had an entirely conservative outlook (expressed with vigour in their evidence before the major inquiries into the woollen industry in 1806 and 1821), that they refused to contemplate innovation, that they were lacking the entrepreneurial qualities necessary to lead the industry through its transition from a domestic into a factory-based system of production.[87] The cumulative effect of their refusal was important. In an analysis of the causes which led to the economic decline of Wakefield after 1800, C. E. Cammidge wrote,[86]

> It is a well-known fact that at the time when manufacturers began to excite considerable attention in the West Riding, the aristocracy of Wakefield, who had already made their fortunes, refused to permit mills or factories to be established here, they were well content to ride in their carriages and fours, and attend the markets in other towns, but would not have manufactures brought to Wakefield. Indeed they went so far as to have inserted in the indentures of apprenticeship, that those thus bound should not exercise their trade etc. within seven miles of Wakefield, and soon this aristocracy left Wakefield altogether.

In Leeds, where the business community was larger and there was not the same reliance on a single industry, the merchants were unable to ossify developments to this extent. Moreover the town had been declining in importance as a centre of cloth production as early as the 1770s. Yet even as a marketing and finishing centre its position was being undermined by the 1820s. The factory manufacturers marketed their own output; merchant communities and finishing establishments appeared in Bradford, Huddersfield and even the lesser centres after 1815. The relative decline in Leeds's key position in the Yorkshire woollen and worsted industries might partly be explained by the long established merchant houses' refusal to contemplate large-scale change.

Turning to a consideration of the merchant's contribution to landownership in the eighteenth century we cannot argue that it was, in any large degree novel. The predilection of the wealthy town dweller for a place in the country was as old as the development of urban society itself. These newcomers to the land had always brought a fresh approach to its problems. Yet the impact of the increasing number of wealthy merchants who came to buy estates in the eighteenth century was important in two respects. Firstly at a time of accelerating change in agricultural practices large amounts of capital were being channelled from trade into land. Whether economic progress would have been more rapid had this capital been expended in developing the industries in which it had been accumulated is a question we have already posed. Admittedly some of this capital found its way into lavish social expenditure, but where the merchants were engaged in active improvement, as possibly the majority were, the transference of capital was not unproductive. The only large-scale alternative considered by the merchants in their investment schemes was government securities. And it is feasible to argue that the expansion of productive capacity was more rapidly achieved by expenditure in land than in 3 per cent Consols. The second point stresses that development in many similarly acquired estates to those of the Denisons and Milneses had wider social implications. The significance of change went deeper than the fact that they became country gentleman and gave their children such fine educations that they became more genteel than the gentry themselves. Of John Denison's eleven sons one became Speaker of the House of Commons (Viscount Ossington), another Governor-General of Australia and a third Bishop of Salisbury.[89] Robert Milnes refused the Chancellorship of the Exchequer at the age of twenty-five. Here in microcosm was the process essential for continuity in English society: in Europe there was nothing quite like it, but in Britain this amalgam blurred countless social distinctions. On the one hand traditional landed society easily assimilated these wealthy merchant families; on the other the contribution of the new element was critical in the revitalisation of England's upper classes during the readjustments of the nineteenth century. Moreover the process was continual. In three generations the initial dynamism of the Denisons

and Milneses was, by and large, expended. Lord Ossington was a
somewhat diffident Speaker, 'neither brilliant nor conspicuous';[90]
Lord Houghton was the most effete gentleman in Victorian
England.[91] The new red blood in landed society was being in-
fused by the great Victorian industrialists.

NOTES

1 P. Deane, *The First Industrial Revolution* (1965), 50. For a dis-
sentient view see J. D. Chambers and G. E. Mingay, *The Agricultural Revolution 1750–1880* (1966), 1–2: 'It is no explanation of
the Agricultural Revolution to regard it as simply the rural
counterpart of the transition to industrialism, the agrarian side of
the medal of the Industrial Revolution.'

2 W. W. Rostow (ed), *The Economics of Take-Off into Sustained
Growth* (1963), 13.

3 Ie. Since David Spring's pioneer article 'The English Landed
Estate in the Age of Coal and Iron: 1830–1880', *Journal of
Economic History*, 15 (1951), 3–24.

4 G. E. Mingay, *English Landed Society in the Eighteenth Century*
(1963), 201.

5 M. W. Flinn, *The Origins of the Industrial Revolution* (1966),
44–5.

6 Ibid, 46.

7 The Denisons in Leeds and the Milneses in Wakefield.

8 1714–82.

9 Denison MSS (UNL), De/H 45, 46. The two letter books cover
the period April 1777–May 1781. William Denison died ten
months after the last entry. It is impossible to assess how many
letters were copied into these books for although they range over
all sections of Denison's activities, others of a more confidential
nature went directly into the 'Great Book' which has not been
traced.

10 1720–85.

11 Will of William Denison proved at York, June 1782. It is impossible to date the exact chronology of Denison's purchases from
his surviving papers. Kelstern was brought in 1758–9. Ossington
and Sutton in 1768 for £34,000 and Beswick for £55,000 in the
same year. (Glentworth in Lincolnshire was considered at
£58,000, but turned down.) In 1806 the 3,309 acres at Ossington
and Beswick produced £4,126 per annum (De/B21); in 1879
W. E. Denison of Ossington owned 6,309 acres in Nottinghamshire and Lincolnshire only, J. Bateman, *The Great Landowners
of Great Britain and Ireland* (1879 edn).

12 LCA, DB/36. These papers show the Denisons' slow progression from cloth-making at Woodhouse in the 1580s to Thomas Denison's first tentative commercial venture in the 1680s.

13 Even the account of the descent of the family after 1785 is thoroughly confused in R. V. Taylor, *The Biographia Leodiensis* (1865), 180–1.

14 J. Cossins, *A New and Exact Plan of Leeds* (1725).

15 Thomas Hill noted in Jan 1782 that the Denisons were the largest export house in Leeds: 'Extract from an old Leeds Merchant's memorandum Book, 1770–1786', *Publications of the Thoresby Society*, 24 (1919), 37.

16 J. Wardell, *The Municipal History of the Borough of Leeds* (1846).

17 Robert Denison left £20,000 as a sufficient capital for his nephews to continue the firm in 1785. See also R. G. Wilson, 'Leeds Woollen Merchants: 1700–1830', unpublished University of Leeds PhD thesis (1964), 92–4.

18 Ibid, 315–21.

19 *Leeds Intelligencer*, 3 Oct 1773.

20 De/H 35, 6 Feb 1779. A similar letter was despatched to the Duke of Newcastle on the same day.

21 Ibid, letter to George Prescott MP, 24 Dec 1780.

22 Ibid, letter to – Crofts, 24 Feb 1779.

23 Ibid, letter to J. Wilkinson, 13 Feb 1779.

24 Ibid.

25 Ibid, letter to Richard Bignell, 20 May 1780.

26 De/H 47, 'Report and Statements of the Transactions of ye executors of ye will of ye Deceased Robert Denison Esquire' [1789].

27 De/H 45, letter to Joseph Butler, 20 Nov 1778.

28 Ibid, letter to Sam Field, 5 June 1780.

29 T. S. Ashton, *Economic Fluctuations in England, 1700–1800* (1959), 187.

30 De/H 45, letters to George Prescott MP, 17 Jan, 13 Mar 1780.

31 Ibid, letter to John Robinson MP, 24 Feb 1781.

32 Ibid, letter to George Prescott MP, 18 Jan 1781.

33 Ibid, Robert Denison to William Cartwright, 12 Jan 1779.

34 *Leeds Intelligencer*, 16 April 1782; *Leeds Mercury*, 30 April 1782. When Robert Denison died in 1785 his executors reckoned that besides the seven estates, his money in the funds, trade, and debts due to him totalled £140,972. Of this £31,562 was invested in 3 and 4 per cent Consols.

35 The Leeds estates, which included residential property, a colliery and corn mill besides some 200 acres of land, produced £1,736 per annum in 1837. They were not extended by purchase after William Denison's death, but their rentals increased sharply from the 1780s onwards. In 1810 their annual value was reckoned to be £1,029, and their sale value £39,670 (De/H 24, 41–2).

36 Thomas Denison was chief tenant at Normanby and agent for the Lincolnshire estates of the Sheffields from 1749 to 1775. In 1776 his widow Elizabeth farmed 1,738 acres (Snape's 'Survey of the Sheffield Estates', 1776). I am grateful to Dr G. Jackson and Mr M. H. Kirby for this information.

37 De/H 45, letters to George Bygott, 13 May 1780; to Miles Dawson, 2 March 1781; to Jas Sharpley, 11 & 25 April 1781.

38 Ibid, Robert Denison to William Cartwright, 12 Jan 1779.

39 The above account is drawn from Denison's letters to Iveson dated 14 Sept 1778, 17 May, 1 Oct, 4 & 12 Nov 1779.

40 Ibid, letters to John Mowbray, 28 April, 4 May 1779.

41 Ibid, letter to Joseph Butler, 20 Nov 1778.

42 Ibid, letter to John Buxton, 24 Jan 1780.

43 Ibid, letters to J. Outram, 17 May 1777; to Matthew Webster, 28 Oct 1777; to John Hayes, 20 April 1781. See also J. D. Chambers, *Nottinghamshire in the Eighteenth Century* (1932), 346.

44 This paragraph is based on letters to John Hayes, 20 Nov 1778, 25 Jan 1779; to John Pate, 12 Feb 1779, 31 Jan 1781; to William Gray, 15 Nov, 17 Dec 1777, 10 Dec 1778, 12 & 24 April 1781.

45 Potterton was extensively altered in the late eighteenth century, but it is not clear whether this was during the ownership of William Denison or his nephew Edward Wilkinson, who succeeded to the Potterton estate in 1785. N. Pevsner, *The Buildings of England, Yorkshire: The West Riding* (1959), 396–7.

46 De/H 45, Robert Denison to William Cartwright, 12 Jan 1779.

47 I am grateful to Lieutenant-Colonel W. M. E. Denison for allowing me to see the architectural drawings at Ossington.

48 De/H 45, letters to Richard Cotton, 13 Jan 1781 and Robert Millington, 9 April 1781.

49 There is a brief account of the problems of estate management in S. Pollard, *The Genesis of Modern Management* (1965), 25–30.

50 De/H 45, letter to Miles Dawson, 2 May 1778.

51 Ibid, letter to William Cartwright, 22 Dec 1778.

52 Ibid, letter to the Rev J. Charlesworth, 15 Jan 1780.

53 Ibid, letter to John Pate, 31 Jan 1781.

54 M. Postlethwayt, *Dictionary of Trade and Commerce* (3rd edn 1765), see under 'merchant'.

55 Witt Bowden, *Industrial Society in England Towards the End of the Eighteenth Century* (1925), ch 3.

56 R. G. Wilson, 'Leeds Woollen Merchants', 12–48, 339–92.

57 R. V. Taylor, *Biographia Leodiensis*, 169–70.

58 Denison's particular merchant friends in Parliament were Edwin Lascelles of Harewood, 'Governor' Thomas Pownall and George Prescott of Theobalds Park (Denison's banker); see Sir L. Namier and J. Brooke, *The History of Parliament, The House of Commons: 1745–1790* (1964), vol iii, 22–3, 316–18, 324–5.

59 De/H 45, letters to John Hayes and Richard Hutton, JP, 6 Sept 1777; to Wm Ancliff, 27 Nov 1779; to J. Boucheret, 21 Nov 1780.
60 Quoted in J. D. Chambers, *Nottinghamshire in the Eighteenth Century*, 82.
61 De/H 45, letters to the Duke of Newcastle and Sir Fletcher Norton, MP, 6 Feb 1779.
62 Will dated 3 Nov 1783 in the Denison MSS.
63 De/B 22, a, b.
64 De/H 45, letters to John Hawkins, 9 April 1777; to W. Cartwright, 12 Aug 1777.
65 De/H 21.
66 The executors' accounts of Robert's Will (De/H 47) show that Nollekens was paid £921 for the two statues between 1785 and 1787 and John Carr £104 14s, 'In full for his plans attendance etc., at Ossington in 1782, 1783, 1784.' See also R. Gunnis, *A Dictionary of British Sculptors, 1660–1851* (1954), 276–7; Sir Bernard Burke, *A Visitation of the Seats and Arms of Noblemen and Gentlemen of Great Britain and Ireland* (1855), vol i, 121.
67 Narratives, frequently erroneous in detail and emphasis at least about the family before 1780, are to be found in Sir T. Wemyss Reid, *The Life and Letters and Friendships of Richard Monckton Milnes*, 2 vols (1890) and J. Pope-Hennessy, *Monckton Milnes, the Years of Promise 1809–1851* (1949).
68 Reid, vol 1, 3 and Pope-Hennessey, 7 suggest that the Milneses came to Wakefield from Chesterfield around 1660; J. W. Walker, *Wakefield, Its History and People* (1934), 397, 410, maintains that Robert Milnes (1671–1738) and his brother John settled in Wakefield around 1700. Certainly by 1745 evidence makes it clear that the Milneses were well established in the West Riding cloth trade.
69 R. M. Hartwell, 'The Yorkshire Woollen and Worsted Industries, 1800–1850', unpublished Oxford DPhil thesis (1956), 216–20; J. Aikin, *A Description of the Country from Thirty to Forty Miles around Manchester* (1795), 579.
70 Reid, 3–4; H. Clarkson, *Memories of Merry Wakefield* (1889), 46; A. M. W. Stirling, *The Letter Bag of Lady Elizabeth Spencer-Stanhope* (1913), vol 1, 117–18; *Leeds Intelligencer*, 30 April 1804.
71 J. W. Walker, *Wakefield*, 397.
72 *Leeds Intelligencer*, 28 Nov, 5 Dec 1775.
73 A. M. W. Stirling, *Annals of a Yorkshire House* (1911), vol 2, 195. I. R. Christie, 'The Yorkshire Association, 1780–4: A Study in Political Organisation', *Historical Journal* (1960), vol 3, 144–61; N. C. Phillips, *Yorkshire and English National Politics, 1783–1784* (1961), 48.
74 Namier and Brooke, *History of Parliament*, vol 3, 142.
75 Stirling, *Annals*, vol 1, 285 n.
76 *Leeds Intelligencer*, 3 March 1778; *Leeds Mercury*, 5 June 1781.

77 *Leeds Mercury*, 17 July 1787; H. M. Colvin, *A Biographical Dictionary of English Architects 1660–1840* (1954), 124.

78 J. Pope-Hennessy, *Monckton Milnes, Years of Promise*, 7.

79 *Leeds Mercury*, 13 June 1801; *The Gentleman's Magazine*, 72 (1802), 1,163 records that Mrs James Milnes was attended to an early grave by 36 servants each carrying lighted torches.

80 H. Clarkson, *Merry Wakefield*, 47; Pope-Hennessey, *Monckton Milnes, Years of Promise*, 7–9; Reid, *Life of Richard Monckton Milnes*, 9–19.

81 Stirling, *Letter Bag*, 119.

82 Pope-Hennessy, *Monckton Milnes, Years of Promise*, 10.

83 Stirling, *Letter Bag*, 120–1.

84 Reid, *Life of Richard Monckton Milnes*, 37.

85 R. M. Hartwell, 'Woollen and Worsted Industries', 288–324; R. G. Wilson, 'Leeds Woollen Merchants', 119–21, 176–83.

86 P. Mantoux, *The Industrial Revolution in the Eighteenth Century* (1961 edn), 62; C. Wilson, 'The Entrepreneur in the Industrial Revolution in Britain', *Explorations in Entrepreneurial History*, 7 (1955), 130.

87 See the evidence of William Cookson, John Hebblethwaite, and Jeremiah Naylor in *Select Committee . . . [on] the State of the Woollen Manufacture in England*, PP, 3 (1806), and William Lee and Jeremiah Naylor in *Select Committee on the Laws Relating to the Stamping of Woollen Cloth*, PP, 4 (1821).

88 C. E. Cammidge, *A History of Wakefield and its Industrial Fine Art Exhibition* (1866), 8. See also J. Wilkinson, *Worthies, Families and Celebrities of Barnsley and the District* (1883), 163.

89 *Complete Peerage*, vol 10, 188–9; *DNB*, vol 5 (1908), 802–8. See also F. Boase, *Modern English Biography* (1965 imp), vol 1, 858; vol 5, 72–3.

90 *DNB*, vol 5 (1908), 804.

91 Richard Monckton Milnes (1809–85) first Lord Houghton, was grandson of Richard Slater Milnes. See T. W. Reid, *Life of Richard Monckton Milnes* and J. Pope-Hennessy *Monckton Milnes, the Years of Promise* and *Monckton Milnes: The Flight of Youth, 1851–1885* (1951).

5

Landowners, Mining and Urban Development in Nineteenth-Century Staffordshire

R. W. STURGESS

To the tired railway traveller looking out of the window near Walsall or Stoke-on-Trent stations, Staffordshire is a county of terraced houses, smoke and, particularly, of industry. It would take a great effort of his imagination to perceive a connection between the landowners of rural Staffordshire and the pre-eminent industries of the Potteries and Black Country. The object of this essay is to show the strong influence that agricultural income and rural matters played in the decisions of landowners to exploit the minerals lying under their estates and to develop for building their land which pressed against the bursting towns of the nineteenth century.

It must be stated at the beginning that this essay is not a comprehensive survey of mining and urban development in the county, but it attempts, by looking at a number of estates, to answer two questions. Firstly, for what reasons did landowners in the county exploit the mineral resources on their estates and turn to advantage the proximity of expanding towns, particularly from the middle of the century, which altered the character of their income from agricultural rents to a varying dependence on industrial and urban revenues? Secondly, how did they view and use the large industrial receipts which set them apart from their predecessors of fifty years before and from their neighbours in southern counties?

The importance of industrial revenues for Staffordshire landlords was widely observed, and the possession of income from outside of agriculture was considered to set the county landed interest on a better footing during the fluctuations in agricultural fortunes over the third quarter of the century, than southern and western landowners who depended almost entirely on their farm rents. John Bateman's survey of landownership in the 1870s may be used to give a rough indication of the distribution of industrial income among the larger landowners in the county.[1] Two pounds an acre was a high agricultural rent on large estates in the county in the seventies, and incomes per acre in excess of this may be assumed to have an industrial or urban element. Nine land-owners out of the twenty-two with more than 3,000 acres whose main seat was in the county had incomes from estates in Stafford-shire exceeding £2 an acre. In addition, twelve landowners with their main family seats in the county had incomes from estates outside the county exceeding £2 an acre, whilst estates of more than £2 an acre provided incomes for twenty-six landowners with their family seats elsewhere.

For individual landlords revenue from coal and iron mines, blast-furnaces and urban ground rents could be large and in-creased over the century. Lord Dudley's estate on the South Staffordshire coalfield yielded him a total of £68,000, whilst Lord Anglesey's on the Cannock Chase field yielded him £91,000 a year in the seventies.[2] Lord Dartmouth's coalmines on the Sandwell estate on the edge of West Bromwich increased their share of total estate revenues from 14 per cent in the 1850s to 56 per cent in the eighties.[3] Non-agricultural income on Lord Hatherton's estate on the Cannock Chase coalfield rose from a negligible proportion of total income in the thirties to 22 per cent in the seventies,[4] whilst coalmines and blast-furnaces and the development and sale of urban land increased non-agricultural revenue on the Keele estate of the Sneyd family on the western edge of the Potteries from 1 per cent of total revenue in the thirties to 37 per cent in the fifties and to a peak of 60 per cent in the seventies.

Enthusiasm for these new forms of income was slow to grow, however, because of the destruction of the rural and private character of the estate that they frequently entailed. For resident landowners in the early nineteenth century buildings in sight of the Hall were distasteful. In 1806 one of Lord Dartmouth's agents bid successfully, although expensively, against prospective building developers for some land near Sandwell Hall on the edge of West Bromwich. The agent would have recommended paying more if necessary, 'a Sacrifice I should have advised your Lordship to have made rather than to have submitted to the Nuisance in giving the opportunity of having Buildings there'.[5] This attitude was in contrast to the forceful policy of urban development pursued by the Earl's successors from the middle of the century, in which even the park was converted to urban housing land after the family seat was moved to a more rural setting a few miles away. Although Colonel Walter Sneyd participated vigorously in partnerships in order to develop the coal and iron under his estate at Keele in the 1790s, his son Ralph viewed the increasingly industrial and urban character of his estate with distaste and accepted it with resignation. Industrial development was pushed forward by his agent. In 1829 he complained of 'the unfeeling decision of my Steward that I am to live like a beggar for several years in order to buy some of the ugliest land I have ever beheld and the filthy coalpit it contains'.[6] His interest lay in landscaping Keele; and the nearby expanding ground rents of Newcastle-under-Lyme were viewed not as an attractive source of additional income but as a landscaping blemish. In 1836 he negotiated to buy some land and planned to build a road from Trentham Hall and village to Keele Hall 'which will avoid that foul smithy Newcastle and bring me 2 miles nearer to the South —and which will be moreover the prettiest approach imaginable'.[7] The increased revenues from the mines, blast-furnaces and ground rents which his agents reported from the mid-century and the remorseless expansion of mining and urban development in the Potteries by other owners forced him to swallow his distaste.

Entail similarly limited the development of land for building. Under the will of the second Earl of Dartmouth at the beginning of the century, land on his estate at Sandwell near West Bromwich could not be let on building leases for more than sixty years and the agent admitted that 'on [these] terms no person will be found to take the Land'.[8] No urban building occurred on the estate in the first half of the century and a policy was introduced in the mid-fifties only after the fourth Earl gave permission by will in 1853 to his son to let land for any period and to sell any part of the estate, so long as the proceeds were invested in the funds and the interest used to pay off the estate debt. On the Keele estate, Ralph Sneyd attempted to prevent the dispersal of the land he had so diligently and expensively bought and land-scaped by forbidding his successor to sell land in any parish un-less an equivalent amount was bought. This affected the sale of land for building in a developing part of Newcastle-under-Lyme in the seventies. The agent could only lament that because the will was made by solicitors whose 'local knowledge was nil, the sale of building land at Pool Dam Newcastle is entirely stopped and you are prevented getting rid of what is not of the slightest consequence to the Estate and would provide a large sum for re-investment'.[9] His successor removed this restriction in his own will, but sales in this area were delayed for seventeen years.

The prime source of income from outside of agriculture for Staffordshire landowners was coal, and the marked expansion of coal production in the county occurred in the first two-thirds of the century. From an estimated 750,000 tons in 1816, production rose to 7,500,000 tons in the mid-fifties and to 14,500,000 tons in the mid-seventies, but did not thereafter exceed 15,000,000 tons to the end of the century. But the output curve of the county as a whole concealed variations between the three coalfields. The rapid growth of county production in the first half of the century was largely caused by expansion of mining of the easily worked Ten Yard Coal of the South Staffordshire coalfield, whilst the stagnation of county production after the early seventies masked an expansion of working on the deeper and more-difficult-to-work North Staffordshire and Cannock Chase fields.

The ebb and flow of the fortunes of the Staffordshire coal-fields were closely linked to the development of local industries. In 1880 only one-third of Staffordshire production was exported outside the county. Earlier, in 1871, 40 per cent of coal from the Northern field was consumed in local ironworks and 14 per cent in the Potteries, and 31 per cent of Southern production was con-sumed in Black Country ironworks.[10] But the Potteries iron in-dustry had a significant advantage over that of the Black Country through the presence of local ironstone supplies. In 1880 these were considered 'no less remarkable than the seams of coal'.[11] But by that year the black band iron ores of the south were effectively worked out. Between 1860 and 1880 production of ironstone in the north of the county almost doubled itself from 750,000 to 1,300,000 tons, whilst southern production fell by a half from 750,000 tons. In order to understand how the industrial income of landowners changed on the different coalfields, some explanation of the rise and fall of the exploitation of the coalfields is necessary.

The territorial expansion of workings on the South Staffordshire coalfield, in which the Earl of Dudley and the third and fourth Earls of Dartmouth played a part, occurred in the first three decades of the nineteenth century. In the first decade of the century the easily worked Ten Yard Seam could be mined at 150ft in the shallow south-west corner of the field around Dudley. Because of the ease of extraction, mining was marked by extravagance over the first half of the century. The bord and pillar method was employed, whereby large pillars of coal were left in the shaft to support the roof, and by 1859 one observer could remark, 'it is not too much to assert that from one third to one half of the coal is thus left useless . . . an amount of squandered natural resources almost without parallel'.[12] By the seventies working had moved to the deeper north-east of the field and problems of drainage were encountered. These problems, which caused an increase in costs, thus occurred at a time of falling coal prices. In 1870 the Thick Coal was only estimated to last for forty years at the present rate of production and by 1900 only three collieries were employing more than 250 men underground.

The expansion of the North Staffordshire coalfield in the first half of the century was limited by technical problems. The main seams lay from 780 to 950ft below the surface whilst the dip of the seams could amount to 2–4in a foot. Problems of drainage were slowly overcome over the first half of the century, and between 1856 and 1861 the coalfield's share of county production rose from 21 to 31 per cent. In 1875, its reserves were considered sufficient to last for more than 1,000 years at the rate of production of the 1870s, it being considered that 'its resources of coal

M

and ironstone greatly exceed that of the South Staffordshire coalfield though smaller in extent'.[13] From the mid-eighties to the late nineties its production of county production rose sharply from 31 to 70 per cent.

Because of the depth of the seams and the unsuitability of the coal for coking purposes, the development of the Cannock Chase field was confined to the second half of the century. Coal was mined at 300ft in the sixties and working afterwards moved to the deeper north-east. From a very small proportion of the combined production of the Cannock Chase and South Staffordshire coalfields in the fifties, the Cannock Chase field was responsible for more than one-third of production in 1880. Thus, as a source of revenue, the working of coal in the county was more important for landowners in the south than those in the north before the middle of the century and for those in the north and on Cannock Chase than for those on the southern field in the second half of the century.

As had been suggested by Professor Thompson for the country as a whole,[14] landowners in the county progressively put the working of their minerals into the hands of professional coal- and iron-masters over the first fifty years of the century. This had important implications for the attractiveness of owning a colliery on the northern field in this period of continuing technical problems of deep mining, if the large development charges of opening a mine had to be borne by the landowner in his capacity as coalmaster. By the forties Lords Hatherton, Dartmouth, Dudley and Crewe and F. E. Heathcote were amongst the band of owners who had leased their collieries, although Ralph Sneyd only did this in 1850, and Lord Granville continued as a coal- and iron-master into the nineties. The responsibility of ensuring that lessees worked their mines both judiciously and profitably was generally given to a professional mine agent, and in 1851 William White could list twenty-seven mine agencies in the Potteries and Black Country.[15]

Whether as coalmasters or as receivers of royalties, landowners played an important part in pressing the exploitation of their mineral property. As coalmasters working their own seams at the beginning of the century owners were in the van of development and, although they progressively shed this role for that of lessor over the first half of the century, they still retained a vigorous interest in ensuring that their coal tenants exploited their royalty-earning mines to the full. The association of the family of the Earl of Dudley and Ward with the mining of Thick Coal on the shallow south-western corner of the South Staffordshire coalfield went back at least to the mid-seventeenth century.[16] In 1800 the working of the coalfield was confined to a small area between Stourbridge and Bilston. Eight miles to the north-east on the, as yet, undeveloped part of the field, four years later, the new agent to the Earl of Dartmouth 'took the Opportunity yesterday of viewing the surrounding Country adjacent to Friars Park and the Estates near Wednesbury and I think in the latter there is every possibility of meeting with valuable minerals'.[17] After a larger survey he considered that the coal and iron deposits 'are certainly very valuable, and I am pretty certain the Ten Yard Mine exists under a considerable Tract of the Estate which will prove a considerable source of Income if properly drawn forth'.[18] This was twenty years before the working of this deeper section of the coalfield and in view of the assiduity with which it was worked from the late twenties, it can only be surmised that technical difficulties were the cause of delay. On the Teddesley estate lying over Cannock Chase coalfield, in the middle of the eighteenth century, Sir Edward Littleton bored two shafts to 117ft 'and no signs of coal in either place'.[19] Exploitation of the deep Cannock coal on the Teddesley estate occurred first in the 1830s. The first colliery to be opened on the estate was in operation in 1832 but had closed with pits 210ft deep in the fifties. In 1847 the first Lord Hatherton, Sir Edward's successor, paid for a boring to be made on one of his farms and in the next year the working was leased.[20] This coincided with the beginning of the extensive working of the coalfield.[21] At the turn of the century mines on the Keele estate lying on the western edge of the North Staffordshire coalfield were operated by partnerships and Colonel Walter Sneyd held only a fifth share in the control of the enterprise on his estate. But by 1816 he was running one of the two collieries himself and, after the partnership controlling the other and its associated iron furnaces had fallen upon bad times and one of the partners had died, the other partners transferred their interest to him at his request.[22]

The influence of landowners in mining matters did not wane after their mines were leased. When Frederick Thynne assumed the Sandwell agency in 1853 he was critical of the scale of mining operations on the estate. He ordered a new survey of mineral deposits on the estate by the existing mine agent and rejected its cautious findings when it was presented, ordering another survey by an independent agent. The low level of activity at one of the collieries offended him and he informed Lord Dartmouth 'when you release me from Mr Davis and his Colliery lease I will set to work in a different way and with a different Spirit'.[23] Two years later he took the mines agency into his own hands. The estate remained financially involved in mining operations. Over the seventies Lord Dartmouth lent the Sandwell Park Colliery Company £2,000 towards its development charges after the reaching of the Thick Seam,[24] and in 1859 he made a small grant of £50 to the ironstone lessee to sink a trial shaft near the old ironstone mine at Friars Park.[25]

Although the curve of revenue received by individual landowners was directly related to the nature of the coalfield over which their estate lay and the extent to which they worked their mines themselves, the golden years of coal receipts on the three coalfields of the county extended only from the twenties to the seventies. On the Teddesley estate of Lord Hatherton, in the van of development on the Cannock Chase field, the peak occurred in the seventies. Accounts only exist from 1861 to 1882,[26] but as the expansion of mining on the estate only dated from the late twenties, whilst all the mines lay idle in the six years after 1839,[27] the first half century of mining on the estate appears to have been one of acutely fluctuating revenues. From the early eighties to the early years of the twentieth century mining on the estate was severely depressed. One of the collieries was closed down after its tenant went into liquidation in 1880, and the larger of the two remaining mines was plagued with flooding over the eighties, during which time no royalties were paid. Royalties amounted only to £800 a year in the mid-eighties and early 1900s. The extent of distress caused by flooding on Cannock Chase might, however, have been particularly great on this estate. On the neighbouring mineral property of the Marquess of Anglesey all the mines were leased in 1890 and Anglesey received £30,000 in royalties.[28] The years of available accounts on Teddesley estate appear therefore to coincide with mining prosperity. Coal royalties averaged £2,400 a year between 1861 and 1880 and reached a peak of £3,827 in 1876.

On the shallow south-western part of the Southern field where activity was great, although restricted in area, in the first half of the century the Earl of Dudley hoped to receive £15,000 from the lease and working of his coal, limestone and ironstone mines and from furnaces on his estate in 1799. But as the receiver of large mineral revenues on the Southern field at the turn of the century Lord Dudley's experience was exceptional. Before the thirties operations were confined to an area of 28 to 30sq miles from Stourbridge to the north-west of Dudley. In the boom years of the mid-forties, Lord Dudley's coal and ironstone mines produced more than a million tons annually[29] which, at the royalty level of the early 1880s, would have yielded at least £50,000.

On the Sandwell estate of the Earl of Dartmouth, lying on the deeper north-east of the field near West Bromwich, by contrast, the profitable working of the Ten Yard Seam was concentrated into two periods, the 1820s and 1830s, and the last quarter of the century. The intensive exploitation of the coalfield around West Bromwich occurred from the early twenties, but when a new agent, Frederick Thynne, assumed the Sandwell agency in 1853 he was critical of what he considered to be the backwardness of working and the level of revenues paid by one of the colliery tenants.[30] Over the sixties mining activity on the estate contracted. One colliery was almost exhausted by the mid-sixties and ten years later operations were 'confined entirely to the pickings of the Thick Coal',[31] while the ironstone mine was closed in 1873, the agent feeling 'in consequence of the high rate of wages and reduction of hours of work, with the increased cost of all materials, that it has rendered Ironstone Measures in South Staffordshire incapable of being worked at a profit'.[32] In 1876 however, Thick Coal was struck again at a depth of 1,260ft by Sandwell Park colliery and from the mid-seventies a new era of buoyant revenues appeared as mining on the estate became concentrated on the Park colliery. From an average £2,237 a year in 1858–67 royalties fell to an average of £1,463 in 1868–78 but rose to £4,742 from 1879 to 1889 when the accounts end.[33] The prosperity of the mine during the nineties appears to have continued, because in 1893 'the company are laying out the new underground roads on an extensive scale. The Directors are encouraged by the present state of affairs. The recent selling prices have enabled them with the increased output to raise funds to carry out these new works.'[34] In the prosperity of mining in the last quarter of the century however, the estate was exceptional. Sandwell Park was one of the few surviving large collieries on the Southern field, being one of the three employing more than 250 men below ground in 1900.[35]

On the Northern field the Sneyd family retained the working of the two collieries and four furnaces they owned and one colliery they had leased in their own hands until 1850, and therefore had to bear the cost of solving the technical problems of drainage encountered before the middle of the century. Hulton colliery was a drain on estate finances throughout these years. Over the first twelve years of Ralph Sneyd's inheritance from 1829 to 1840 the colliery earned an average annual working profit of only £301; in 1841–3 it made an average annual loss of £452.[36] The total excess of receipts over working costs in these fifteen years was £2,253 or an average of only £150. In December 1840 the Hulton overdraft amounted to £11,167 and at the minimum rate of interest paid on Sneyd's other debts of 4 per cent it would have been paying £446 in 1840. The colliery clearly could not pay the interest on a debt accumulated probably from 1816. On the combined Silverdale colliery and iron smelting enterprises an overdraft of £13,535 was outstanding in 1838.[37] It is unfortunately not possible to separate the Silverdale revenues from aggregate mines income. Also, as the financial relationship of the Silverdale colliery to the Silverdale furnaces is not known, it is not possible to establish how far the profit from the combined Silverdale enterprises were earned on the iron, and the probability of the Silverdale coalmine being run at a notional loss cannot be excluded. But, as the Hulton mine, which sold predominantly to the pottery industry and to a lesser extent to the Cheshire salt industry,[38] was accounted separately, as was the leased Leysett mine, which supplemented the Silverdale colliery's coal in the Silverdale furnaces, claims by the agent of the 'profits' of the combined mines may be accepted. In 1837 working profits on the two collieries amounted to £1,752 which was a slight advance on those, including profits from the leased mine, of £1,555 in 1829.[39] Neither years were ones of low prices and the larger one can be taken as indicative of annual working profits in the years 1829–40 during which time a combined debt of £20–24,000 was accumulated. Thus, even before the bad years of the early forties, the mines income, after paying interest on its debt, could not have exceeded £1,250 a year, with an indeterminate contribution from the furnaces. Only the persisting confidence of the agent in the mines sustained their working, and this in turn was only made possible by Ralph Sneyd's indifference to mining matters. In 1850, Sneyd leased his collieries and furnaces and thereafter received an annual income unburdened by large capital outlays. Royalties rose from £7,000 in the first year of leasing to £26,000 in 1870. From a peak of £29,000 in the following year they fluctuated downwards to £15,000 in the mid-nineties.[40] In spite of falling royalties the last quarter of the century was one of expansion, two new collieries being opened near Silverdale in the mid-eighties. As one of the largest coal-and iron-masters on the North Staffordshire coalfield, Ralph Sneyd's fortunes may be taken as typical of such landowners as Lord Granville and the Williamson, Clive and Kinnersley families who did not begin to lease their enterprises until the middle of the century.

As a considerable source of landed income, therefore, coal-mining appears to have been a feature of estates on the Southern field in the first half of the century and of the Northern and Cannock Chase fields in the second half. For individual owners on the Northern field the timing of the leasing of their mineral property would affect the claims upon their other income at the beginning of the century and, despite an extension of working, royalties fell from the seventies. The spread of mining beyond the south-west corner of the Southern field occurred in the 1820s and the demise of operations in all but a few large collieries occurred in the sixties. The period therefore when revenues were buoyant and increasing on the coalfields of the county as a whole was confined to the middle fifty years of the century.

The second activity in which landowners were in the forefront and from which they reaped financial rewards was urban development. The pressure for house building came from population growth in the expanding coal, iron and pottery industries of the two conurbations, and not until these pressures had made themselves felt could the search of agents for additional income find direction and plans for the creation of ground rents be introduced. In common with all the industrial northern and midland counties, Staffordshire experienced a rate of population growth above the national average in the first two-thirds of the century, caused largely by the attraction of people into the expanding industries of the Potteries and Black Country from outside the county.[41] County population increased three-and-a-half times from 1801 to 1871, slower only than that in Durham and Lancashire. The increase of population and housing remained at a high level over these years in both of the conurbations. But whereas growth was maintained in the Potteries from the seventies, it fell drastically in the Black Country, mirroring the relative decline of mining and the iron industry on the Southern field.[42]

Despite this background of rapidly expanding population and housing in the first half of the century, planned housing development by large estates appears to have occurred only from the middle of the century. Although piecemeal sales of land in the Potteries were made by the Sneyd family in the early years of the nineteenth century to pay for such specific items as the furnishing of Colonel Sneyd's London house,[43] a policy of the planned sale of ground rents was not introduced until the appointment of a new agent in the early 1850s. But this policy was slow to get underway. In 1859 the agent informed a prospective purchaser, 'If we had a little more encouragement—more Applicants for building sites—we should be happy to extend the Roads and lay out more building land.'[44] By the early seventies, however, the agent could inform Sneyd, 'the sale of land for building purposes has gone on for twenty years at least and is a perfect matter of routine in the administration of the Estate'.[45] In 1847 the Earl of Dartmouth bought a new family seat a few miles away from his old home at Sandwell Hall on the edge of an expanding West Bromwich, and a new agent was appointed with the express duty of exploiting all the resources of the now absentee Sandwell estate. Sentiment was eschewed in his schemes, and the Park, which skirted West Bromwich, was allocated for building development.

The form of this development posed a problem, however. The new agent advised against an immediate sale of land to building developers considering that, despite the proximity to West Bromwich, conditions were not suitable for the most profitable sale, and that a few years hence, after the land had been let on long building leases, it could command a higher price as ground rent land instead of, in its existing form, as accommodation land.[46] In the mid-fifties he was discouraging prospective purchasers.[47] The ordered and progressive selling of ground rents did not begin until 1862. On Lord Hatherton's estate in Walsall only forty-three building leases were let by the mid-forties, and before the early thirties no policy of development seems to have been evolved. Because he was so pessimistic about the prospect of increasing the revenues from the estate he considered selling it in 1832.[48] Although he did not carry this out he gave his successor the power to sell the whole estate despite its settlement.[49] But by the mid-fifties the letting of building leases was established policy, and he could congratulate himself on the increased value of the estate to which this had contributed.[50] Against the forty-three leases which had been let in the seventeen years after the granting of the first lease in 1828, 113 were granted between 1845 and 1855, and on his death in 1863 291 leases had been created.[51] New building leases granted on the Earl of Bradford's estate in Walsall amounted only to fifty-one in the thirties and twelve in the forties. In the fifties, however, they jumped to 132.[52]

The coincidence either of the adoption of building schemes or of expansion in leasing or selling plots under existing schemes after the middle of the century on the estates examined requires an explanation, although one can only tentatively be offered here. Such an explanation is important because, if these estates are typical of all those in the county with property in or near to expanding towns, this coincidence would suggest that large landowners contributed to urban growth in an organised and forceful way only from the mid-century.

The flimsiness of evidence for other estates makes it impossible to establish how typical these few estates were of the many ground rent landlords in the county. William White mentions twenty-three different owners of land in the towns of the Potteries and eighteen owners in the Black Country towns in 1851. But because of the importance of the subject and the existence of evidence for at least these four estates a more detailed look is justifiable, if not to permit generalisations about the growth of towns in the county at least to establish more accurately the forces influencing these substantial house developers. Only more research from the viewpoint of the towns and not, as here, from that of the landowner can fill this large gap in urban history.

The timing of the decision of the Sneyd and Dartmouth families to develop land for building was determined by the sudden awakening to the size of the family debt in one case and a large addition to this debt in the other. But, despite Sneyd's decision, his agent found difficulty in selling urban land in the fifties, although sales increased in the next fifteen years. The rate of population growth in the Potteries during the fifties was almost the same as that of the four previous decades. Despite this, however, population grew by 20 per cent over the decade and the explanation for the failure to put the plans into operation in the ten years after the decision to build was taken must lie in the local situation in the areas in which Sneyd's scattered estates lay or in some inadequacy in the operation of the plans, neither of which can be determined.

Lord Dartmouth's agent began to develop Sandwell Park for building purposes in 1861. West Bromwich experienced its lowest decennial rate of population increase of the period 1801–71 in the sixties. But the urban development of the Park can be explained in terms of the character of the Sandwell houses. They were specifically of the villa type and this development appears to have been concerned with providing for the middle class of West Bromwich who were fleeing the developed parts of the town. On these two estates then the absence of a demand for houses, probably combined on the Sneyd estate with the lack of a forceful policy, seems to have limited earlier activity.

The attaining of a peak in the granting of leases on the Hatherton and Bradford estates in Walsall in the fifties, on estates where leases had been granted from at least the early thirties, can be explained in some degree by the fact that population growth reached its highest decennial rate in the fifties of almost 50 per cent. In the tens, twenties, forties and sixties, the increase was less than 20 per cent. But in the thirties it reached 40 per cent and the failure of both Hatherton and Bradford to accelerate building on their land when both were already granting leases in this decade must either have been because the land of the two estates was not in the expanding part of the town or because a policy of development had not yet been adopted. In view of the size of the Hatherton property in Walsall and the fact that it was formally held by his mother until 1841, the latter was probably the case on this estate. Nothing is known about building policy on the Bradford estate.

The limited point can only be made here that four of the substantial landowners of the county who owned property in or near to expanding areas in the north-west Potteries, Walsall and West Bromwich participated in urban development only from the middle of the century. These central decades were ones of rapid population growth, but the scattered nature of estate property in towns renders parish figures of population increase inadequate as an indication of the rate of growth in those particular areas where the estate was located. More important, house building on these estates did not accurately reflect bursts in population increase of the parishes or conurbations either in the fifties or before.

In the case of Sneyd and Dartmouth, family debt was the goad directing thoughts to urban development but their building plans met with little demand for land for almost a decade. On the Hatherton estate a caprice of inheritance might have influenced the timing of the addition of comprehensive plans despite the fact that piecemeal development was long observed. All that can be concluded is that no common factor lay behind the burst in house building in the fifties on these four estates.

On whose land then and on whose initiative were houses built for the great expansion of population of the first half of the century? The period of most rapid growth in the Potteries occurred in the first decade of the century and thereafter growth stayed constant at a lower level to the middle of the century. Between 1801 and 1851 population increased more than three fold from 27,596 to 87,957. In the Black Country towns the peak was reached in the thirties in Wolverhampton and West Bromwich and in the fifties in Wednesbury and Walsall, and the population of the four towns rose from 44,878 to 167,981 over the half century. Was urban development in these years carried out by small traders, mineowners and industrialists (sometimes landowners in these latter two capacities) on land belonging to urban owners such as burgesses, industrialists and the Church, or on common land near to expanding towns? And what part did landowners other than those studied here play in this development, such as the Duke of Sutherland in the Potteries? With the exception of one study,[53] Staffordshire towns still await their social historian.

On two of those estates for which evidence exists, the policy of creating and selling ground rents was provoked by the need to reduce family debt. In 1847 the Earl of Dartmouth bought Patshull Hall and estate for £297,000 and moved his family from Sandwell Hall. [54] The purchase price raised no problems. Mortgages could be raised on the London and Kent properties and on railway shares, and part of the Yorkshire estate could be sold. But this posed the question of the future use to which Sandwell was to be put. Frederick Thynne, agent to Lord Dartmouth for his other property, put the choice of outright sale, or the retention and development by piecemeal sale as occasion arose of the mineral and surface resources of the estate. Thynne argued persuasively for the latter. He gave as an example a plot of land which, if sold immediately, would have realised £2,944. 'Supposing this to have gone towards paying off the mortgage of Patshull, you would have reduced your payment of interest about £103 a year. But by letting you have increased your rental £122 14s which enables you to pay your interest of £103 a year and £19 14s a year in addition. Thus we have the measure of the value of the proceeding.'[55] This decision determined the building development on the estate in the second half of the century.

After the death of his agent in 1848, Ralph Sneyd was forced to take stock of the estate finances to which he had shown such indifference in the first twenty years of his inheritance. An audit revealed a debt of £189,195, and this financial crisis in his affairs introduced four years of distasteful but effective activity on

Sneyd's part. He frankly admitted the blame: 'My own indolence, negligence and easy submission to whatever saved me trouble has been the Chief Cause of this disaster.'[56] Taking a consultant's advice, he leased the coal and iron enterprises, and raised a mortgage of £130,000 with the Equitable Assurance Company on the fee simple of the estate, in order to consolidate his debts.[57] A comprehensive scheme of drainage and building of farmsteads was carried out on the estate in the early fifties in order to permit tenants to pay their rents punctually and so enable Sneyd to meet his commitments. In 1849 Sneyd appointed a Scotsman, Andrew Thompson, as his new agent, and under him a policy of selling urban land in the Potteries was introduced.

On the estates examined policies concentrated either on raising the value of land by letting builders erect houses and subsequently selling the valuable ground rents or on retaining the developed ground rents and receiving an increasing yearly rent-roll. As discussed earlier, the new agent to Lord Dartmouth followed a policy of allowing builders to develop plots for the first eight years after the introduction of the plan and then began to sell the developed ground rents. By contrast, the scheme of the new agent to Ralph Sneyd in the fifties concentrated from the beginning on sales. It is unfortunately not possible to establish whether these sales were merely of accommodation land or of developed building land. Over the fifties and sixties sales became an established part of estate policy and even in the bad years between 1870 and 1888 yielded £4,806.[58] On Lord Hatherton's estate in Walsall a policy both of retention and sale of leases was followed. Thus despite a decline by 18 per cent in the acreage of the Walsall estate changing from agricultural and accommodation to urban land, surface rents rose slightly from an average £3,560 a year in the late sixties to £3,860 in the late nineties.[59]

Where land was retained and developed under the auspices of the estate considerable control was asserted over its development. Frederick Thynne, agent to Lord Dartmouth, paid regard to amenities in his schemes. In 1854 he informed the Lord Mayor of Birmingham, 'I am now planning the Sandwell Estate for building purposes—and it strikes me that if the Corporation of Birmingham are desirous of obtaining public Parks, an opportunity is presented here which may not occur again.'[60] On Lord

Hatherton's Walsall estate the number of houses per plot leased, their cost and the date of completion were stipulated.[61]

This discussion poses the question how landowners in the county viewed their industrial revenues and to what use they put these revenues which set them apart from southern landowners. Did this addition to their income mean that in times of falling agricultural rents they were able to maintain the level of personal spending and at the same time to carry the burden of settlements and to reduce debts on their estates as contemporaries hoped? At the onset of agricultural slump on his estate in 1879 Lord Hatherton had an:[62]

> Animated Triangular discussion with Northumberland—and Percy about Agricultural prospects—in which we eventually agreed that there were gloomy times ahead for landed proprietors —especially those whose Estates are heavily charged (as is my Case—tho' My house property at Walsall and Mining property put me in a better position than those who have only farm rents to depend on).

As the Teddesley estate was heavily indebted with both a mortgage and provision for dependants and attempts were being made to reduce the mortgage, this better position that Lord Hatherton hoped to find himself in must have referred to his style of living which consumed an average £5,500 a year in the seventies.

Although much more research will have to be carried out before generalisations can be made, it is considered that evidence exists for two of the three estates discussed here sufficient to cast doubt on this view. On these estates it appears landowners found that, far from being able to maintain existing patterns of living free from the anxiety of growing indebtedness, the decline of revenues from all sources except urban land, at a time when claims of interest on earlier debts were high and constant and when expenditure on rapidly changing physical equipment of farming estates was undertaken as a matter of course, they were forced to retrench in the nineties. Attempts to relive earlier glories of the estates were accompanied by an increase of debt to or above the level of the mid-century.

Over the century landowners retained a continuing optimism in the industrial side of their estates as the only dynamic element in their income which could release them from their persisting problems of debt and incumbrances. After a period of large investment in his two collieries in 1800 Colonel Walter Sneyd observed that 'if things go on at all (which with me is now always a doubt) I am in hopes that the produce of my Mines will enable me annually to diminish my Incumbrances'.[63] At the other end of the century Sneyd's grandson, ignoring his agent's restraining hand, increased the family debt by indulging in horse-breeding and racing and by renovating the Hall. Faced with this debt and falling industrial and agricultural revenues his agent was forced to advise him in 1901:[64]

> The best way to make all the money out of the place for you that we can is to knock everything of that sort (horseracing) on the head here, and turn all our attention to developing the estate for minerals, building etc.; if we can secure a good increase of these, and I think we can, you could always start a better stud again.

In the early thirties the first Lord Hatherton advised his mother to put aside the surplus above the cost of the mines on the Walsall estate to the repayment of debts on the estate. On viewing a depressing showing of his accounts in 1841 he admitted the dependence of his precarious finances on his mining income. 'This is a frightful state of things—and the remedy is exceedingly difficult. A good state of Trade would do much for me by enabling me to let mines—But still nothing but retrenchment will meet the case.'[65] After the last Baron's death in 1863 a peculiar administrative device was introduced to allocate surplus revenue from the industrial Walsall estate to debt redemption. The debts on the combined estates were placed on the agricultural Teddesley property and the expanding revenues of the Walsall mines and ground rents were 'given' to the Teddesley estate in order to reduce the debt. Between 1865 and 1882 £40,223 was thus allocated to debt reduction.[66] The exploitation of the Sandwell estate with its dominating mining and urban character in the 1850s was specifically for the purpose of paying off the mortgage raised by Lord Dartmouth to permit him to move his seat to the more rural Patshull Hall.

But in the first half of the century industrial revenue did not always fulfil the optimism of owners who, as operators of their own mines, had to accept the financial burden of meeting lengthy and expensive technical problems. On the Keele estate on the Northern field, where drainage problems were being met, no returns were earned for the first four years of the development of the Hulton colliery during which time a £2,000 overdraft was accumulated.[67] Under Ralph Sneyd an average of £150 a year was earned above working costs between 1829 and 1844. Interest on the colliery debt at the lowest rate paid by Sneyd amounted to £446 in 1840, and at least in the early forties the return was insufficient even to cover the charge on borrowed capital. Even on the easily worked shallow seams of the Southern field the Netherton colliery of Lord Dudley was still not paying its way four years after its opening in 1799.[68]

The heavy development charges of mines could put an acute strain on estate finances. On the Keele estate mining had preference over all other claims on the overstretched financial resources. In 1798 the agent informed Sneyd, 'If I can hear of any money that is to be borrowed for the purchasing of Land Tax I will inform you, at present all that can be procured is wanted for the Colliery afore mentioned (Hulton).'[69] The large expense of opening collieries at Walsall on the Southern field limited the Earl of Bradford's attempts to expand mining on his estate and this was made possible only by the sale of other property. To open the mines £3,320 would have to be spent including £1,500 on a second-hand steam-engine, and his agent advised him:[70]

> If Mr Bowman is to pay that Sum, his remittances here, to answer current expenses, will be less by that amount and the deficiency in your Income to answer your Expenses will be much less than I have ever had occasion to state it. The deficiency, as I have said before, can only be supplied by . . . the actual Sale of Estates, of which your Creditors require for the Interest more than the Income.

In the 1840s it was reckoned in the Black Country that the establishment of two blast-furnaces and the mines to supply them would require an outlay of £20,000, and two of Lord Dartmouth's pits together cost £28,000 to open because borings encountered running sand and water.[71] The Marquess of Anglesey, who owned mines in Cannock Chase as well as being involved in the mining of copper on Anglesey, found the latter a burden on his other strained income. Between 1785 and 1788 nearly £62,000 was invested in the Mona mine on Anglesey, most of which Lord Anglesey as the larger partner had to find.[72] The making of large capital outlays, however, was a feature of the early part of the century and declined thereafter as working was increasingly transferred to coal and ironmasters. These outlays, which were to become remunerative by the twenties or the fifties, would not have placed a strain more exceptional than any other investment requiring a large lump-sum but for the otherwise cramped budgets of many landowners. Because of the demands of interest on debt and incumbrances which changed from year to year and because of the casual form of accounting, calls upon income were met as they arose, and, as on the Keele and Teddesley estates before the middle of the century, accounting was on a crisis-to-crisis basis as clashes occurred over the allocation of an only slowly changing income.

In the years of buoyant industrial revenues on the Teddesley estate from the early fifties to the mid-seventies mine royalties and urban income were devoted strictly to the repayment of debts accumulated because of the personal extravagance of the first Lord Hatherton in the first half of the century. When he died in 1863 he left a combined mortgage and settlement on the Teddesley estate of £147,666.[73] The annual mortgage repayment charge was just under £5,000 and the settlement raised this to £7,879 a year. The second Baron calculated that when all his outgoings were paid he would have £8,000 left from an income of £17,000 a year.[74] The cause of this debt on an estate which, when the first Baron inherited it in 1812, was indebted only to the extent of £720 a year in settlements, was predominantly land purchase aggravated by political expenses as the member for South Staffordshire and by maintaining a large house in which all the leading political figures were guests at one time or another in the 1820s and 1830s. Hatherton admitted, 'My living has been attempted on a scale to which my Means have never been quite

N

adequate.'[75] Between 1812 and 1863 he added 2,500 acres to the 8,500 acres of the estate on his inheritance, and this was financed almost completely by borrowing on personal bonds. The size of the debt on the estate forced the second Baron to make economies. The Teddesley household suffered an immediate reduction, the number of employees on the estate falling from 200 under his father to 78 in 1873,[76] and he evolved a plan for the gradual redemption of the debt. All future income from the industrial and building development of the Walsall estate was to be applied rigidly to reduction of the debt and the farm rents of Teddesley were to meet interest charges on this debt and personal expenditure after the payment of estate repairs. Thus the fall in farm rents after 1878 severely eroded his disposable income. In only three years between 1871 and 1882 was there a positive balance on the Teddesley account after payment of interest on the debt and estate repairs, and even to meet his reduced personal spending Hatherton had to 'borrow' from the Walsall account. After 1871 personal expenditure stayed between £4,900 and £6,300 a year,[77] in contrast to the spending of his father who had lived to the hilt of his estate income of upwards of £10,000 a year after paying estate expenditure whilst accumulating a debt of £117,000.

On the Keele estate Ralph Sneyd discovered in 1848 that in the first twenty years of his inheritance his estate debt had risen from £2,400 to £189,195.[78] This debt was paying an annual interest of £6,239 on a rental, net of settlements, of £11,693. As in the case of Lord Hatherton, an important cause was land purchase. Between 1829 and 1850 Sneyd added 2,000 acres to the estate of 4,867 acres, in addition to making considerable alterations to the Hall. At the same time, his costly if unwilling participation in mining and iron smelting left him with an overdraft of £12,000 on the colliery account in 1848. In the second twenty years of his inheritance a large degree of retrenchment could not be escaped, and his agent constantly reminded Sneyd to give priority to payment of interest on the consolidated debt and to estate outgoings instead of to personal spending. The size of this interest payment, however, stayed almost constant over these years and, with provision for his dependants, rose to £7,863 at his death in 1869. As both agricultural and mines income, even at their 1850 level, exceeded debt interest and a high level of estate expenditure in the fifties by some £11,000 a year, and as this was supplemented by receipts from urban land sales from the mid-fifties, no attempt would appear to have been made by Ralph Sneyd to reduce the debt principal. But, as a large expenditure was made on the drainage of the estate in the fifties and at the same time the Hall was almost completely rebuilt, attention appears to have been concentrated on improving the physical condition of the estate and maintaining personal spending whilst merely servicing the debt. In his will, however, Sneyd made provision for a sinking-fund to reduce the debt, and under his successor annual interest charges fell from £7,863 in 1871 to £2,913 in 1887.[79]

Thus, although both the second Lord Hatherton and Ralph Sneyd made provision for reduction of their debts, both were able to live on a level befitting a large disposable income buoyed by rising industrial and farm revenues over the fifties and sixties. Hatherton could do this by drawing upon his Walsall account and Sneyd by merely servicing his debt. The burden of owning a heavily indebted estate with a severely pinched personal expenditure, as industrial and farm receipts fell from the seventies, was to be borne by the generation which inherited in these years, following their extravagant predecessors of the first half of the century.

As mine and farm receipts fell from their peak of the seventies, with mine royalties falling the faster, room to manoeuvre disappeared and priority for claims on total income had to be established. On the Keele estate mine royalties, wayleaves and railway rents fell from 60 per cent of total income in 1874–8 to 50 per cent in 1891–5. The estate lay on a mixed although generally heavy soil which was largely under grass and its farmers provided milk, poultry, pigmeat and beef for the nearby Potteries. Rents on these dairy and stock farms were buoyant over the eighties and nineties and in the mid-nineties were at the same level as in 1870 and only 9 per cent below their peak of 1878.[80] Receipts from the sale of ground rents are not known for the whole of this period and are therefore not included. But at their level of the eighties they would not have compensated for the fall in mine royalties.

The Rev Walter Sneyd inherited the estate in 1869 and, despite a high level of receipts, immediately asked his agent to complete the programme of estate farm investment, which his predecessor had put underway in the fifties, as speedily as possible. In 1874 the agent recommended the expenditure of a further £6,330 and thereafter expenditure could fall to a maintenance level. Average annual expenditure on farm building and repairs fell from £5,316 in the first five years of his inheritance from 1870 to 1874 to an annual average of £3,632 in the last fourteen years of his inheritance to 1888. As mentioned earlier, his predecessor, Ralph, made provision in his will for reduction of debt by establishing a fund from estate income. In the first part of his inheritance, therefore, despite rising revenue from all sources, the Rev Walter Sneyd found two pressing claims on his augmented income, agricultural improvements and debt repayment. One economy was open to him in order to release money for private expenditure, and that was to reduce the gratuities to dependants of the estate. In his capacity as retrenching landlord he found this easy to do and between 1871 and 1887 gratuities fell from £2,686 to £581. This left room for an increase of personal spending and in the first six years of his inheritance extensive alterations to the Hall were made, amounting to £10,373 in the three available years of accounts in 1871–2, 1875. Thereafter economy was observed, and spending on the Hall, gardens, park, stables, game and woods fell from £6,108 in 1871 to £3,230 in the last year of his inheritance.[81]

His son Ralph, however was of a different bent. His great interest was in horseracing and breeding, and in reviving some of the estate's former glory. No stipulation appears to have been made by his father that he should continue the policy of debt reduction, and he himself had no belief in austerity. Because of the strong representations of his agent, the provision of money for the farming estate was respected and the yearly average equalled that under his father. Despite the fact that he inherited at a time of declining mine royalties and increased farm arrears in the late eighties and the nineties, his oblivion of the state of his finances matched that of his namesake fifty years before. In the early years of his inheritance he built a stud farm and racecourse on the estate, and in the first fourteen years of his inheritance spent

£15,000 on renovating the Hall, £7,000 on the stud farm, and £3,000 on the racecourse.[82] In 1896 he bought a yacht, and his harassed agent admitted, 'The difficulty seems to me to find in what direction you can reduce your present expenditure anything like sufficient to meet the considerable increase which this yacht must neccessitate.'[83] Against expenditure of £3,230 in 1888 by his father, Ralph Sneyd was spending between £4,300 and £18,695 a year before the end of the century. In the years 1893–6, 1898–1900, for which accounts are available, interest paid on debt averaged £4,000. The fact that this fluctuated wildly from £1,872 in 1893 to £6,134 in 1900 can only be explained by a hidden accounting device or by the fact that a number of sources were being manipulated in order to maintain the debt. By the late nineties Sneyd's agent advised retrenchment: in 1897 Keele Hall was leased to a Russian grand duke for seven years;[84] and the agent recommended, in addition, the closing of the stud farm and the more intensive exploitation of the mineral property. The success of these measures in rescuing the Sneyd family fortune from embarrassment for the second time in the century is not known, although Ralph Sneyd did return to the Hall after its temporary leasing.

Because mine and urban revenues were strictly allocated to reduction of debt principal and the decision was implemented to use agricultural rents for interest payment and personal spending on the Teddesley estate, movements in farm rents became of vital importance in determining the size of the household. As farm receipts fell from the seventies household expenditure suffered. The Teddesley estate lay on light sandy soils on which the 'turnip husbandry' was in decline over the last quarter of the century as two of its main sources of revenue, corn and wool, suffered falls in price. Lord Hatherton strove vainly to persuade the London & North-Western Railway to stop its trains at nearby Cannock on Sundays, so that a milk trade with neighbouring towns could be built up.[85] Farming changed slowly to the provision of beef, lamb, hay, straw and milk for Black Country towns over these years. This was inadequate, however, and failed to prevent a large fall of 23 per cent in farm rents from the late seventies to the mid-nineties.[86] Teddesley household expenditure was tied to these movements. Expenditure on the household was

now accepted to be the residue of total revenue after more pressing claims had been met. A spending sufficient to keep the estate
in good repair was made as a matter of course. At the end of 1874
the second Lord calculated that 'the cost per cent of keeping the
Estate in repair' in the previous year amounted to 14 per cent of
received rents.[87] In 1879 he reckoned this cost at 12½ per cent.[88]
In 1883 he calculated the financial position his successor might
expect to inherit. Although he anticipated a further fall in farm
rents, he expected that estate expenditure would stay near its 1882
level.[89] His son observed this policy and in the nineties spending
on the estate rose above that of the high level of the seventies.

    All other avenues of economy were explored. Hatherton bar-
gained hard with his new agent, appointed in 1864, over the
latter's salary. Hatherton fixed on an unspecified percentage of
the Teddesley rents and £50 a year for the Walsall agency.[90] In
1871 the agent, Foden, asked for an increase on the basis of the
rising Walsall revenues, and Hatherton appealed to his solicitor
for advice. The latter considered that Foden was a superior agent
who could greatly increase his salary if he did not confine himself
to an agency, adding rather pointedly, that 'the salary of an Agent
is very frequently determined as much by the fact whether or not
the Estate is encumbered as by the real value of his services'.[91]
By 1880 Hatherton was paying Foden 1⅜ per cent of Teddesley
rents as well as his fixed Walsall salary and he believed that Foden
would amply reap the benefit of the more prosperous condition
of the estate over the seventies.[92]

    Under the second Lord spending on personal matters re-
mained at a constant level considerably below that of his father.
But even this was only made possible by drawing on his industrial
revenues from 1880. Teddesley received rents fell 10 per cent in
the last nine years of his inheritance below the level of the first
fourteen years. His private spending averaged £5,124 a year from
1865. This compared with some £12,000 a year, before estate
outgoings were deducted, which the first Lord spent during his
last years whilst at the same time accumulating a large debt. But
following the granting of a 10 per cent reduction on Teddesley
farm rents in 1881, Hatherton began drawing upon his Walsall
account. This had begun in the previous year, Hatherton admitted apologetically, 'for the first time'.[93]

Two luxuries which were dispensed with under the second Lord were participation in politics and land purchase. Although his feelings were strongly in favour of the moderate element in the Liberal Party, falling farm rents limited his ability to participate. When the Liberal agent requested Hatherton's support for his son's candidature for East Staffordshire in 1880 he admitted that:[94]

> If times had been good I might have endeavoured to overcome Edward's indifference to it—but considering that my reduction of rents will not leave me with a penny to spare this year with a prospect of next year being the same . . . we settled without giving reasons that he would decline the honours.

Land purchase was only a fraction of that of the first half of the century. Between 1865 and 1888 only 26 acres were added to the estate by purchase, and 310 acres by enclosure.

The third Lord inherited in austere times. He had married in 1867, and had four sons and five daughters when he succeeded to the estate in 1881. This large family placed a heavy burden on the estate during the nineties, when received rents fell by 19 per cent below their level of 1865–78. Provision was made, presumably on the Teddesley estate, of £200 a year for each younger son and £100 for each daughter. If a further £200 is allowed for his eldest son, the annual burden on the Teddesley estate would have increased by £1,300 in the nineties. Under his father's will the Walsall estate had to bear provision for his four brothers and the Walsall debt rose again in 1888 to £54,000. This diminished the ability of the Walsall account to continue reducing the combined debt and meeting the periodic calls on it for personal spending which the second Lord had made. The third Lord, like his father, was forced to direct all surplus Walsall revenue to debt repayment and rely on the Teddesley rents for his own purposes. Estate expenditure continued to be made as a matter of course, all claims by farmers for repairs being left in the hands of his agent; and the building of hay barns on all the farms of the estate raised annual expenditure in the mid-nineties above the level of the seventies.

Hatherton's dependence on Teddesley farm rents led to a financially precarious existence. In the late eighties he could complain that, after paying £13,000 on charges and after estate expenses at Teddesley, he was left with 'but £1,000 for payment of Household expenses'.[95] Because of provision for his sisters and mother under his father's will the consolidated Teddesley debt had grown to £159,000. He moved into the Hall on his inheritance from a sense of obligation to the family tradition, despite the financial burden of the gesture. Only the continued generosity of his mother in refusing to take her £2,000 jointure each year permitted a balance for the upkeep of Teddesley. In 1889 this balance on the Teddesley rental amounted to 'in round figures £300—that margin however is too small for safety, as one farm thrown on my hands would swallow up the margin at once'.[96]

At first he had high hopes of a steady move towards solvency. Following an increase in the letting of urban leases and a temporary improvement in the payment of agricultural rents he made a new will in 1890. 'I made the former one immediately after succeeding and circumstances have now altered. If I am spared another five or six years and my sons [not] unusually Extravagant I hope to be in a better position than I found myself pecuniarily on my succession.'[97] But in the following year increased estate expenditure and an expensive harvest destroyed this hope and he realised that further retrenchment was the only answer. 'I am sadly afraid that I am living somewhat beyond my income—I must leave a larger margin for contingencies and possible reductions in income. Oh! What a dreadful thing it is to inherit a debt.'[98] Accounts are unfortunately not available over the last years of the century to chart more accurately movements in the family fortune and to give quantitative expression to the third Lord's fears.

This section has been concerned only to show that on these two estates the possession of mine and urban revenues over the last quarter of the century did not permit these landowners to maintain the lavish standards of living of the first half of the century or even the moderately reduced levels of the fifties and sixties without further resort to retrenchment. Because they were jolted into an awareness of their indebted financial position by the falling revenues of the period 1888–1900, pressing claims of debt reduction and large estate expenditure to increase the ability of their tenants to pay punctual rents had priority over personal spending. Mining royalties fell steeply with farm rents from the seventies and to the generation inheriting in the next two decades the financial picture from the moment of their inheritance was one of large and persisting claims on a shrinking income. The fact that some third or half of their income came from coal or houses held no exciting prospect for them and if, by attempting to relive earlier glories of the estate they exceeded the bounds of their cramped budgets, they had once again, like their predecessors, to resort to retrenchment.

Although Staffordshire was distinguished from southern counties by the presence of coal and iron under her soil, the working of these minerals became a feature of the county only in the nineteenth century. As a source of landed revenue, mineral working varied according to which of the three coalfields of the county an estate lay over, but the period of buoyant revenues for most landowners was the middle fifty years of the century. Coinciding with this, the larger estates which have been examined introduced schemes of urban building from the fifties (in two cases provoked by their indebted position) and this permitted large landed households to be maintained, despite overriding claims of interest on debt and of estate expenditure. The next generation found this level of living difficult to maintain without further increasing the family debt. Thus, even in a county as richly endowed with coal deposits as Staffordshire, the greatest contribution of receipts from coal working to the finances of the larger landowners seems to have been to permit them to maintain their personal spending at a higher level than it would otherwise have been over the fifties, sixties and early seventies, at a time of pressing claims of debt repayment and large investment in the equipment of their farms. This spending had to bear the brunt of a declining total revenue from the seventies, as high expenditure on debt repayment and farm investment pressed up against failing coal and agricultural income. Even for landowners in Staffordshire who drew a large part of their income from coal or ground rents the financial support of their splendid landed way of life was becoming more and more hollow after the 1880s.

NOTES

1   J. Bateman *The Great Landowners of Great Britain and Ireland* (1883 edn). I am grateful to the late Mr T. W. Fletcher of Edinburgh University for suggesting this general technique to me.
2   Bateman, *Great Landowners*, passim.
3   Dartmouth collection, rentals 1853–89 (StRO), D564/5/4.
4   Hatherton Collection, rentals and accounts (StRO), D260/M/E, 188–9.
5   W. James to Lord Dartmouth, 2 May 1806 (StRO), D564/12/18.
6   R. Sneyd to H. Vincent, 10 Sept 1829, Sneyd Papers (ULK), S3.
7   R. Sneyd to H. Vincent, 26 May 1836.
8   W. James to Lord Dartmouth, 2 Sept 1805 (WSL), D1778/V1290.
9   H. W. Hollis to W. Sneyd, 2 Nov 1872 (Sneyd Papers), S174.
10 R. Meade, *The Iron and Steel Industry of the UK* (1882), 140.
11 Ibid, 140.
12 J. B. Jukes, *Memoirs of the Geological Survey* (1859), 221.
13 Meade, *Iron and Steel Industry*, 140.
14 F. L. M. Thompson, *English Landed Society in the Nineteenth Century* (1963), 265–6.
15 W. White, *History, Directory and Gazetteer of Staffordshire* (1851), passim.
16 W. H. B. Court, *The Rise of the Midland Industries* (1938), 151.
17 W. James to Lord Dartmouth, 13 Dec 1804 (WSL), D1778/V1790.
18 W. James to Lord Dartmouth, 18 Feb 1805 (StRO), D564/12/18
19 Annotation to Teddesley Rental, Hatherton Collection (StRO), D260/M/E12.
20 Expenditure Accounts, 1847, Hatherton Collection (StRO), D260/M/E156.
21 PP, 36 (1890), Q2261.
22 S. Peake to W. Sneyd, 30 April 1816 (Sneyd Papers), S78.
23 F. Thynne to Lord Dartmouth, 20 May 1854 (StRO), D564/7/1.
24 Report of S. & J. Bailey, 26 April 1878 (StRO), D564/8/1.
25 Sandwell Rentals and Accounts, 1859 (StRO), D564/5/4.
26 Walsall Mine Accounts (StRO), D260/M/E188–9.
27 Hatherton Diaries, 3 April 1845 (StRO), D260/M/F/5/26.
28 PP, 41 (1890–1), Q13716.
29 Report of Board of Trade on London, Worcester & Wolverhampton Railway, 39 (1845).
30 F. Thynne to Lord Dartmouth, 20 May 1854 (StRO), D564/7/1.
31 Reports of S. & J. Bailey, Sandwell Memoranda, 24 Nov 1876.
32 Ibid, 1 Nov 1873.

33 Sandwell Rentals and Accounts, 1856–89 (StRO), D564/5/4.
34 S. & J. Bailey to E. L. Thynne, 9 Dec 1893 (StRO), D564/7/4/41.
35 W. J. Wise (ed), *Birmingham in its Regional Setting* (1950), 242.
36 Observations on Sneyd Green Colliery, 17 May 1844 (Sneyd Papers), S128.
37 S. Peake to R. Sneyd, 19 March 1839 (Sneyd Papers), S78.
38 T. Breck to W. Sneyd, 9 May 1798 (Sneyd Papers), S71.
39 Rentals 1829 and 1837 (Sneyd Papers), OS5.
40 Thompson's Accounts, OS4; OS5. Abstract of Accounts, S82.
41 R. Lawton, 'Population Migration into and out of Staffordshire and Warwickshire 1841–1901', Liverpool University MA thesis, 1951, vol 2, 147–8.
42 Census Returns, Enumeration Abstracts, 1801–1901.
43 W. Sneyd to T. Breck, 13 Nov 1806 (Sneyd Papers), S71.
44 A. Thompson to E. Wedgewood, 12 Jan 1859, S172.
45 H. W. Hollis to W. Sneyd, 2 Nov 1872, S174.
46 F. Thynne to Lord Dartmouth, 8 July 1854 (StRO), D564/7/1.
47 F. Thynne to J. Stubbs, 18 March 1854.
48 Hatherton Diaries, 15 Jan 1832 (StRO), D260/M/F/5/26.
49 Settlement of Lord Hatherton, 2 May 1837 (StRO), D260/M/T/6/112.
50 Hatherton Diaries, 8 May 1859.
51 Walsall Lease Book (StRO), D260/M/E183.
52 Bradford MSS, vols 1/31–33 Muniment Room, Weston Hall, Shifnall.
53 J. Huffer, 'The Economic Development of Wolverhampton 1750–1850', London University MA thesis, 1958. Much anecdotal evidence is given in the works of F. W. Hackwood and others on the Black Country towns, but a systematic study of Staffordshire towns in this period comparable with R. Church's on Nottingham and J. D. Marshall's on Barrow-on-Furness is sadly lacking.
54 F. Thynne to Lord Dartmouth, 30 Dec 1847 (WSL), D1778 Y1311.
55 F. Thynne to Lord Dartmouth, 8 July 1854 (StRO), D564/7/1.
56 R. Sneyd to H. Vincent, undated 1848 or 1849 (Sneyd Papers), S3.
57 R. Sneyd to Equitable Insurance Company, undated [1849], S73.
58 Conveyances signed by Rev Walter Sneyd, S77.
59 Walsall Rental, 1863–1900 (StRO), D260/M/E156.
60 F. Thynne to Lord Mayor of Birmingham, 18 March 1854 (StRO), D564/7/1.
61 Walsall Rental and Lease Book (StRO), D260/M/E173.
62 Hatherton Diaries, 9 March 1879.
63 W. Sneyd to T. Breck, 17 Nov 1800 (Sneyd Papers), S71.
64 H. V. Boothby, 25 Jan 1901, S87.
65 Hatherton Diaries, 4 Dec 1841.

66 Teddesley Rentals and Accounts, 1865–1900 (StRO), D260/M/E156.
67 T. Breck to W. Sneyd, 17 Nov 1801 (Sneyd Papers), S71.
68 C. Roberts to W. Shirley, 3 May 1804 (Dudley Papers, Leicester Borough Record Office), 25D53/2005.
69 W. Sneyd to T. Breck, 17 Nov 1800 (Sneyd Papers), S71.
70 J. Heaton to Lord Bradford, 23 July 1813 (Bradford Muniment Room, Weston Hall, Shifnall), 18, 25.
71 PP, 13 (1843), 101, 104.
72 J. R. Harris, *The Copper King* (1964), 143.
73 Teddesley Rentals, 1864 (StRO), D260/M/E/56. Memorandum by 2nd Lord, June 1862, D260/M/E338.
74 Hatherton Diaries, 16 April 1862.
75 Ibid, 11 Feb 1843.
76 Memorandum, 1872, in Teddesley Rentals, and the pension lists (StRO), D260/M/E156 and D260/M/E218.
77 Teddesley Rentals and Accounts, 1865–1900 (StRO), D260/M/E156.
78 Thompson's Accounts, 1849–50 (Sneyd Papers), S4.
79 Rentals and Accounts, 1870–1900, OS8, OS20.
80 Rentals and Accounts, 1870. 1874–1900, OS8, OS20.
81 Ibid. This section is based on these accounts.
82 Memorandum, 13 April 1903, S87.
83 H. V. Boothby to R. Sneyd, 16 Aug 1896, S87.
84 Indenture to Lease, 1897, S86.
85 *Staffordshire Advertiser*, 25 Dec 1897.
86 Teddesley Rentals and Accounts (StRO), D260/M/E171 and D260/M/319.
87 Calculation, 1874 (StRO), D260/M/E156.
88 Calculation, 1879, ibid.
89 'Estimated Ways and Means of my Successor, April 1883' (StRO), D260/M/E156.
90 Lord Hatherton to A. E. Foden, 18 Aug 1864 (StRO), D260/M/E334.
91 Mr Hand to Lord Hatherton, 4 Aug 1871, ibid.
92 Lord Hatherton to A. E. Foden, 13 March 1880, ibid.
93 Annotation to Rental, 1880 (StRO), D260/M/E156.
94 Hatherton Diaries, 10 March 1880.
95 Ibid, 18 April 1888.
96 Ibid, 28 May 1889.
97 Ibid, 13 Sept 1890.
98 Ibid, 10 Nov 1891.

6

Glasgow Colonial Merchants and Land, 1770-1815

T. M. DEVINE

Any analysis of the influence and impact of profits from colonial trade on the Scottish economy of the late eighteenth century must lay considerable weight on the place of mercantile fortunes in the gathering momentum of the Scottish 'agricultural revolution'. It is an axiom of Scottish economic history that widespread 'improvement' (as distinct from the dramatic but atypical efforts of the classic improvers of the 1730s-50s) was a feature of the 1770s and especially of the 1780s.[1] The steep upward swing in prices galvanised landowners into the introduction of the artificial grasses, root crops, improved implements, plantations and enclosures which were the hallmarks of the new agricultural orthodoxy. The part played by colonial merchant-landowners in this essential base for general economic progress was continually commented on by percipient contemporaries. From his chair of Moral Philosophy in the University of Glasgow, Adam Smith sung the praises of such men:[2]

> Merchants are commonly ambitious of becoming country gentlemen, and, when they do, they are generally the best of all improvers. A merchant is accustomed to employ his money chiefly in profitable projects; whereas a mere country gentleman is accustomed to employ it chiefly in expense. The one often sees his money go from him and return to him again with profit; the other, when once he parts with it, very seldom expects to see any more of it. Those different habits naturally affect their temper and disposition in every sort of business. The merchant is commonly a bold, a country gentleman a timid undertaker. The one is not afraid to lay out at once a large capital upon the improvement of

his land, when he has a profitable prospect of raising the value of
it in proportion to the expense . . .

Sir John Sinclair, renowned 'improver' and arguably the most
knowledgeable man on agricultural matters in late eighteenth-
century Scotland, pointed out the impact of mercantile capital on
land: 'the opulent merchant and manufacturer, employing part of
their capital in the purchase of land and improvement of the soil,
became most spirited cultivators'.[3] More specifically, the activities of such tobacco and West Indian merchants as John Glassford, Alexander Houston, Archibald Smith, the McDowalls, the
Spiers and William Cunninghame in their respective estates,
encouraged much comment at the time.[4]

It would be wholly crude to present a picture of mercantile
profits and vigour disturbing the stagnation of the agriculture of
west-central Scotland in the latter half of the eighteenth century,
yet there seems little doubt that the flow of wealth from commerce into land which took place in this period (as it had done at
least over a century) was a contribution of the first order to the
complex of factors which made up the Scottish 'agricultural revolution'. This paper does not attempt to evaluate or gauge that
contribution; its aims are more modest. It is intended to investigate the extent of landholding among the colonial merchant
community of Glasgow in the period 1770–1815 and to ascertain
the methods of estate acquisition, whether through purchase,
inheritance or through the more romantic means of marrying an
eligible heiress. Some attempt will also be made to note the
favourite areas for land buying and finally to analyse in some
depth the series of socio-economic motives which pulled merchants to the land.

For the purpose of this study, it was calculated from customs
records, co-partnership agreements, memberships of bodies such
as the Glasgow Chamber of Commerce and the Glasgow West
India Association and lists examined in the various Glasgow
directories of the time, that there were roughly 140 Glasgow
merchants involved in either the pre-1776 tobacco trade to the
North American colonies or in the growing commerce with the
British West Indian islands between 1770 and 1815 (see Appendix

3). Given the inevitable gaps in the material consulted, this figure must be taken as very much a minimum, but since any merchants omitted were likely to be of small account and since several of those included had been operating only for a few years when death or bankruptcy interrupted their career, the total number is not likely to be substantially incorrect. The gross figure of 140 includes only those colonial merchants operating in the period 1770–1815 and excludes those deceased by the first date and those who did not reach partnership level until after 1815.

Intensive examination of the Register of Sasines revealed that 78 of the total of 140 (55 per cent) owned land at some period during their lifetime. A full breakdown of the information and sources on which this conclusion is based is given in Appendix 2, but certain observations can be made here about this figure.

It should be emphasised that seventy-eight is again a minimum figure. Several of those enumerated as 'landless' could well have acquired an estate after 1815. The criticism that the figure quoted considerably underestimates mercantile landholding could be especially levelled at the situation of those Glasgow West Indian merchants who evolved to partnership level at or after the turn of the century. Of those sixty-three merchants who subscribed to the Glasgow West India Association between 1807 and 1810, no less than forty-two did not own land according to the sources consulted.[5] This is not surprising as most of these were in the early stages of their commercial careers and could have obtained the coveted estate later, and this outwith the provenance of the sources examined. Indeed a rise in landownership among them would be likely since it will be one of the major themes of this essay that ownership of land was generally an essential feature of the career of the *successful* colonial merchant.[6] A second difficulty arises out of the implications of the word 'land': for the purposes of this essay 'land' will be used in the sense of 'landed acres' of estates of at least 500 acres, rather than of the small 'tenements' of land in Glasgow itself, which changed hands with astonishing rapidity throughout the period, which were used for the erection of counting-houses, dwelling houses and small industrial units, and which neither in extent or function were 'landed estates' in the classic sense.

A clear correlation can now be constructed between success in trade and the owning of an estate. Among the colonial merchants examined there is evidence of an élite core who were very wealthy, whose families tended to intermarry, had interests in several co-partnerships (both in trade and domestic industry) and whose names persistently occur in the lists of provosts, deans of guild and town councillors. It was these men whose names are commemorated in the modern street names of Buchanan Street, Glassford Street, Ingram Street, Oswald Street and Gordon Street.[7] Of this group, of which just over ninety merchants were designated as members in the period, 1770–1815, only eighteen (20 per cent) did not own an estate at some time in their career. Subsequent research may cut this figure down even further.

A proportion of those who did own estates were scions of well-established merchant families who in time succeeded to the paternal acres. Thus Robert Dunmore inherited Kelvinside from his father, Thomas, a pioneer in the early eighteenth-century Virginia–Glasgow tobacco trade.[8] Significantly the estate had been in merchant hands throughout most of the century, having been conveyed to Dunmore *père* in 1749 by a daughter of James Peadie, a name as famous in the Glasgow of the later seventeenth century as Buchanan and Dunlop were in the eighteenth.[9] The sons of men who had made their fortunes earlier in the century came to a similar inheritance. The estate of Jordanhill purchased by the rising colonial merchant, Alexander Houston between 1750 and 1752, was acquired by his son Andrew in 1773.[10] Robert Bogle the elder, had obtained the lands of Daldowie in March 1731 from the University of Glasgow to add to his first purchase —Whiteinch—acquired in 1720.[11] From that point on they continued in the family: Robert's elder son, George, had the lands made over to him the following year (1732); at his death in 1782, his eldest son, Robert, succeeded to the estate, by this time under trust;[12] only in 1825 did the family seat leave Bogle hands in a symbolic sale: the property of one of the wealthiest and most powerful colonial merchant families passed to a member of the emerging industrialist class, John Dixon of Calder Ironworks.[13]

The McDowalls of Castlesemple and Garthland were other examples of colonial merchants with a secure hereditary base in the land. William McDowall II and William III were the beneficiaries of the founder of the 'dynasty', Colonel William McDowall.

With the benefit of a lucrative marriage settlement and profits from the West Indian firm of James Milliken & Company behind him, the Colonel, a younger son of McDowall of Garthland in Wigtonshire, had purchased in 1727 the ancient barony of Castlesemple, Renfrewshire, from Hugh, eleventh Lord Semple, in whose family it had previously been for several hundred years.[14] Andrew Buchanan fell heir in 1762 to his father George's estate of Windeyedge in Old Monkland renaming it Mount Vernon in honour of George Washington.[15] His uncle James was as fortunate, succeeding to Drumpellier on the death of his father Andrew in 1759.[16]

This continuity of ownership in a single family could generate an obvious loyalty to a particular estate. At the sequestration of Buchanan, Hastie and James and George Buchanan and Company in 1777, both Mount Vernon and Drumpellier were sold. At the time of the crash, David Buchanan, Andrew's younger brother, was only seventeen; he seemed to have determined to recover the family lands and proceeded to Virginia where by 1802 he had made a considerable fortune. Returning home, he purchased Mount Vernon from his brother's trustee.[17] Not content with this he went on to recover one of Andrew's subsidiary properties, Boghead in the Barony of Glasgow, and in 1808 to purchase Drumpellier.[18]

The strongly established and wealthy tobacco aristocracy were always likely to leave an estate to their eldest sons. Depending on the landed resources available, younger sons and daughters generally received a cash gift. Robert Bogle II inherited the family patrimony of Daldowie, his younger brothers John and George being contented with the not inconsiderable sum of £1,000 each. The cash gift hardly compares with Robert's inheritance, however, which was valued in 1808 (certainly during a period of inflated land prices) at little less than £24,000.[19] Where possible, even more generous provision could be made. Alexander Spiers, possibly one of the three richest men in Glasgow in the late eighteenth century, settled his major interest, the Barony of Elderslie, on his eldest son Archibald, but by another deed of entail of 1780 conveyed his estate of Culcreuch in Stirlingshire to his younger son, Peter. In addition, he instructed his trustees 'to lay out and expend the sum of £8,000 in the purchase of lands

o

for behoof of the said Peter'. By a life-rent disposition subscribed by him in 1777 his wife Martha was to succeed to his lands of Yoker and Blauarthill in Renfrewshire.[20]

Spiers's vast wealth was very rare and the general principle of keeping the estate in the family, in a viable condition, could probably best be obtained through single settlement on the eldest son. Extensive and scattered estates could lead to individual settlement among male offspring, yet action would depend very much on the policy adopted by a particular merchant: William McDowall II owned separate estates in Renfrewshire, Lanarkshire and Wigtonshire yet they all devolved on his eldest son William III.[21] Wives and unmarried daughters could also succeed, though more commonly an enticing dowry would attract suitors for the latter, and even when the estate changed hands the use of the life-rent ensured the surviving spouse and spinster daughters an adequate income until their death.[22]

Yet of the seventy-eight merchants designated as landowners, only eighteen (23 per cent) acquired at least part of their estates through direct inheritance from a father. That inheritance played a fairly minimal part in mercantile landowning in late eighteenth-century Glasgow can be further illustrated by the fact that several of those who did inherit went on to acquire still more property through purchase. Here the inherited land could provide an essential basis for continued purchase. James Ritchie succeeded his father John, 'merchant burgess' of Glasgow, in the estate of Craigton, Lanarkshire, bought by the latter in 1746. In 1783 James added to this by obtaining Busby in Ayrshire. The progressive acquisition of landed power can be nowhere better illustrated than in the case of the McDowalls. Colonel William's purchase of Castlesemple in 1727 had acted not as a climax but as a stimulus and a base from which to buy up more land. William II obtained the family estate of Garthland in Wigtonshire and by the 1790s William III's properties included these in addition to lands in the parish of Dalry in Ayrshire, in the Barony parish of Glasgow and the estates of Auchingray and Caldercruix in the parish of New Monkland, Lanarkshire.[24] Robert Dunmore, owner of Kelvinside by his father's bequest, in 1785 commenced a series of land purchases in Stirlingshire, beginning with Auchinreoch in the barony of Cumbernauld. Through marriage and purchases he had, in 1793, acquired the barony of Ballin-dalloch and several adjoining areas in Stirlingshire.[25] This would appear to be a planned transfer of landed interests: in 1785 Dun-more had sold Kelvinside to Dr Thomas Litham of the East India Company.[26] Having realised a substantial capital gain from this sale to a wealthy 'nabob', Dunmore was able to purchase the barony of Ballindalloch from Captain William Cunninghame of the 58th Regiment of Foot for £8,000 of which Dunmore paid £6,500, the remainder to be used to supply an annuity for Cun-ninghame's widowed mother.[27] James Dunlop, later to involve himself in landholding on an enormous scale, especially in the coalbearing Monklands in Lanarkshire, was heir to his father Colin in the estate of Carmyle. There was no sign of this acting as a hindrance to further land acquisition.

In fact, of the eighteen merchant-landowners investigated who had inherited the paternal acres, at least nine had added signifi-cant tracts to their existing possessions.[28] That this was an im-pressively high proportion is made clear when it is remembered that the estates of James and Andrew Buchanan were seque-strated early in the period under consideration and those of George and Robert Bogle were under trust by 1772.[29] Extension of landed assets on the part of these four was therefore unlikely.

One could not only inherit from the father, however, and there is evidence of younger sons succeeding through other close rela-tives. A desirable spouse from the point of view of the rising or successful merchant would be an heiress with the prospect of inheritance to land. The sons of such a marriage often benefitted —the elder succeeding to the father's estate and the younger (under the benevolent eye of a landed grandfather) to the mother's present or future inheritance. Thus Robert Dunlop obtained Drumhead from his mother, the daughter of Archibald Buchanan of Auchintorlie.[30] Dunlop's good fortune was still not complete. His eldest half-brother, James, died without male heirs and Robert acquired his lands of Househill.[31] Much the same division can be seen in the inheritances of the sons of Alexander Houston, Andrew and Robert. Alexander had married Elizabeth, sister of Colin Rae of Little Govan: Andrew, being the eldest son, suc-ceeded to the Houston patrimony of Jordanhill but Robert, his younger brother, obtained Little Govan through the settlement of his unmarried uncle.[32] John Coats Campbell, son of Archibald Coats, inherited Clathic through his mother, Jean Campbell, heiress to the lands.[33]

Careful matrimonial strategy could also guarantee possession of the coveted estate. By the latter half of the eighteenth century it was even unnecessary to marry into the gentry or nobility to obtain a dowry of land, so widespread had mercantile penetration into the counties around Glasgow become by the 1750s.[34] Robert Dunmore wed the only daughter of his partner, John Napier of Ballikinrain. In 1787, Dunmore was able to add the latter estate to his adjacent barony of Ballindalloch, when Napier, in settling Ballikinrain on Dunmore's eldest son, appointed his former partner procurator and attorney of the land until his grandson had attained the age of maturity.[35] John Dunlop, younger brother of James of Garnkirk was unlikely to succeed his father unless his brother died. John, however, married into the wealthy and influential Murdoch family.[36] Through this matrimonial bond, the estate of Rosebank, purchased by Provost George Murdoch in the early 1700s devolved on Dunlop in 1791.[37] Thomas Buchanan, already possessor of Ardoch through inheritance from his father, obtained Dalmarnock in 1784 from his father-in-law, John Gray.[38] The marriage contract between William Cross and Ann Buchanan, daughter of Neil Buchanan of Auchintoshan specified that the Buchanan lands would be settled on the future husband.[39]

Out of the total of seventy-eight merchants who owned land in the period 1770–1815, twenty-five (33 per cent) succeeded to at least part of their estates through marriage or inheritance. Of these a minimum figure of fourteen added significantly to their existing landed resources by purchasing further tracts, sometimes to round off their inheritance, but also to take in estates in quite distinct and separate geographical areas.[40] An important conclusion from this first section is therefore that the bulk of the landed property held by Glasgow colonial merchants in the late eighteenth and early nineteenth centuries was acquired through purchase. Another interesting point also emerges: a traditional method of obtaining landed status was—as has been pointed out above—through marriage to a rich heiress. There is little evidence of this being common in eighteenth-century Glasgow. In fact, only those merchants mentioned in the text above obtained land in this way of the seventy-eight men examined: two of these, Robert Dunmore and Thomas Buchanan had already inherited estates from their fathers. Of the other two, John Dunlop and William Cross, only the latter could be categorised as an 'arriviste' in the sense of being a newcomer to mercantile wealth.

The reasons for the disproportionate role of purchase in relation to inheritance are not far to seek. The upward social mobility conferred by success in trade often meant that a merchant-landowner would prefer to have his son follow a more prestigious occupation than that of commerce—the law, the armed forces and the Church all found recruits from the offspring of the merchant élite.[41] Again the prospect of succession to land with all its many-sided 'social' rewards tended to steer the eldest son away from a commercial career. James Dennistoun, son of one of the most famous tobacco merchants in eighteenth-century Glasgow, devoted himself entirely to the land on his succession, typically raising a troop of Yeomanry in Dunbartonshire in 1796.[42] Archibald and Peter, the two elder sons of Alexander Spiers, withdrew from their father's trading concerns at his death, simply keeping an interest in one or two of the small 'manufactories' in Glasgow.[43] Likewise Henry Glassford gave up, in 1790, his father's shares in John Glassford & Company, Glassford, Gordon & Company, James Gordon & Company, Arch Henderson & Company, and Henderson, McCall & Company.[44] There was no inevitability behind this leakage of the second generation away from trade: examples could be quoted to show the opposite occurring and the choice of career depended on the many variables implicit in upbringing or the wishes of the father.[45] Yet there can be no doubt that such movement away from trade was a persistent phenomenon throughout this period and one which goes far to explain the imbalance between acquisition of estates through purchase and through inheritance. Many of the sons of merchant landowners who did inherit could no longer be classified as 'merchants' and had therefore to be excluded from the sample. Similarly, those of gentry families who contributed much to the pool of talent among the colonial merchants of Glasgow were unlikely to inherit land. In almost every case they were younger sons, a position which excluded them in the main from succession to the family estate and thus gave them the motive in the first place to enter trade.[46]

Given the fact that most of the land held by Glasgow colonial merchants in this period was purchased during the lifetime of the respective owner, some explanation is needed to account for the consequent availability of such land. It has become very much the established convention of English agrarian history, that the post-1750 period saw a recognisable decline in the inflow of new-comers (lawyers, bankers, merchants) into the ranks of the landed classes. The principal explanation for this trend was that the late eighteenth-century land market was narrowing almost to the point of stagnation.[47] This view clearly has limited relevance for the west of Scotland in the period 1770–1815. There, sixty-two colonial merchants were able to obtain estates with very little difficulty. During their lifetimes twenty of these owned at least two estates in different counties and purchase was by and large restricted to counties adjacent to the town of Glasgow.[48] There is little evidence (at least in the period 1770–1815) that merchants eager to purchase land were forced into looking to distant areas. Of the seventy-eight who owned estates both through purchase and inheritance only six (7 per cent) held at least some of their land in counties outside Lanarkshire, Renfrewshire, Dumbarton-shire, Stirlingshire and Ayrshire: the McDowalls with the family property of Garthland in Wigtonshire, Alexander Campbell with Kingledoons and Hallyards in Peebleshire, Thomas Buchanan with Ardoch in Perthshire, Mungo Nutter Campbell with Balli-more in Argyll, John Stirling and John Coats Campbell with Kippendavie and Clathic respectively in Perthshire.[49] Apart from these exceptions the table on page 215 affords an insight into the location of the respective estates.

As would be expected the number of holdings tended to fall as distance from the town increased: there were no insurmountable obstacles in the way of the possession of an estate relatively close to Glasgow.

Various factors can be held to account for the availability of land in the west of Scotland at this time. Two coincident events in the 1770s—the failures of the Ayr Bank (Douglas, Heron &

Company) and of the ill-fated York Building Company—brought considerable areas of land on to the market within a short period:[50] George Bogle's trustees noted in 1779,[51]

> The immense losses that have been incurred by the partners in the bank of Douglas Heron and Company and the sale of the extensive property of the York Building Company will bring a much greater proportion of land into the market for many years to come.

By August 1775, 114 out of the 226 partners in the Ayr Bank, many of them notable landowners, were insolvent and the determination to repay creditors meant the sale of several estates. One estimate is that £750,000 of landed property changed hands as a result of the collapse.[52]

Area	No of merchants owning land	No of estates
Barony of		
Glasgow	27	33
Lanarkshire	27	34
Renfrewshire	16	22
Dunbartonshire	9	9
Stirlingshire	7	11
Ayrshire	7	8

Source: Information contained in Appendix 2

The beginning of the American War of Independence in 1776 further lowered land prices. Traditionally, wartime brought a slump in the land market as potential buyers preferred to invest in the Funds; to this weakening of demand was added the factor of increased supply as wartime taxes and high interest rates produced bankruptcies among landholders, especially towards the end of hostilities.[53] By 1780 the establishment of a £20 million loan resulted in subscribers receiving an annuity of £4 to continue for eight years for every £100 paid in and two years later the real permanent interest rate had risen to $5\frac{1}{2}$ per cent.[54] With such returns the incentive to buy land was reduced and a group of lawyers and bankers commented in 1779 with only some exaggeration: 'the vast demands of government and the high terms they are obliged to offer to procure money occupy all the extensive capital'.[55]

For any Glasgow merchant eager to purchase land and with the available financial resources, conditions were clearly attractive. William Cunninghame, enriched with the profits of two decades in the Virginia trade and having made a fortune in the selling of tobacco at wartime boom prices, purchased the estate of Lainshaw in Ayrshire in 1778 for £20,200.[56] Rich pickings from trade and the perilous conditions of colonial commerce during the war would both encourage land purchase as the stringency of credit in the Scotland of 1778 forced bankrupt estates on to the market. By 1775, 'the debts affecting the estate of Lainshaw appeared so considerable, that a sale was unavoidable'.[57] The owner, J. M. Beaumont, was himself approaching bankruptcy.[58] Even after the sale of the estate he had to dispose of the annuity from the lands which he had retained 'because his affairs were in bad order'.[59]

The situation could not have been more attractive for both parties in 1778. The great magnet of mercantile liquid funds would entice any prospective seller, especially one in such straits as Beaumont. Merchants involved in colonial trade, because of the minimum of fixed capital required and high profits made, were likely to pay a considerable part of the purchase price immediately in cash form.[60] Cunninghame promptly paid down the £20,200 for Lainshaw, quite obviously gaining from the sluggishness of the land market and the eagerness of the owner to sell—the estate having been valued at £24,300 in 1774.[61]

It would be unwise, however, to overstress the influence of war in mercantile landbuying. The American War was to some extent atypical because windfall profits in the early years were available for investment, but even here one has to search carefully for positive evidence to justify the theoretical point which has been made. Most of the prominent tobacco merchants had acquired estates by 1776. 'The mercantile god of Glasgow', Alexander Spiers, purchased Inch in 1760 and Elderslie in 1769: Neilstonside and Arthurlie, both followed in 1775.[62] Possibly the only property obtained by him during the period of hostilities was Culcreuch in Stirlingshire, advertised for sale in December 1775 and in Spiers's hands by 1782, a year before his death.[63] The Oswald family had completed the bulk of their pre-1783 purchases of land by 1770.[64] John Glassford had obtained his major estate of Dougalston in Dunbartonshire in 1707.[65] Thomas and Robert Donald, members of an old-established family of tobacco importers held Mount-blow and Geilston long before the outbreak of the American War.[66] Of the sixty-seven merchants who bought at least part of their land between 1770 and 1815, only three have been identified by the author as having made significant estate purchases during the period of the American War. These were Cunninghame, Spiers (and he only marginally) and James Somervell, who obtained Hamilton Farm in 1781.[67] Significantly they were among the very wealthiest of the élite tobacco aristocracy.

On the other hand, there was an interesting cluster of purchases in the last few months of war and first few years of peace. Credit conditions were easier in 1782–3 and as Professor Mingay has pointed out it was during the final stages of war that bankrupt estates began to flow on to the market, the varied credit and tax pressures of wartime tending only to bite after a considerable period. James Hopkirk, Robert Dunmore, Robert Findlay, Alexander Houston, James Dunlop, William Cunninghame, George Crawford and John Alston jnr, were just some of the names involved in estate purchase between 1782 and 1785.[68] Potential landbuyers clearly felt the necessity to curtail spending during hostilities. Land's position as the best type of financial security was axiomatic in the eighteenth century and at first glance this would appear to make it an attractive mercantile investment during times of financial instability. Yet there was an ambiguity here. Although the safest, it was also one of the most illiquid methods of holding existing wealth. It was precisely the difficulty of resolving it into hard cash (especially during a period of war) which led the greatest West India houses in eighteenth-century Glasgow, Alexander Houston & Company, to bankruptcy during the Napoleonic Wars, although landed assets alone between the partners almost equalled ascertainable debts.[69] The broader credit base required by colonial merchants during wartime—caused by increased time of voyages as a result of the convoy system, the upward climb of the wages of seamen, increased cost of ships' equipment and the necessity for arming vessels, together with the falling off of credit from banks— probably stimulated a wary approach to land acquisition during the period 1776–83, except, of course, for the very wealthy who could afford to pay less heed to changing financial conditions.

Any analysis of the factors behind the availability of land in the areas around Glasgow in the late eighteenth century must take account of what Dr T. C. Smout has called the 'Revolution in Manners'.[70] The desire for an increased standard of living among the aristocracy and landed gentry led several of them to live above their means. More varied leisure activities, more elaborate clothing, 'improvement' of estates, more exotic diets all required an increased income. Such were the pressures of social competition and convention that often desires were fulfilled on very narrow financial margins. Contemporary commentators emphasised how this led to estates changing hands through the extravagances of the 'old' occupier. Colonel William Fullarton noted how in Ayrshire, 'a great proportion of the landed estates have changed their owners in consequence of individual extravagance, expensive engagements'.[71] Later he returned to the same point, denouncing families of 'very ancient standing' for their 'reigning spirit of conviviality and speculation' which obliged them to sell their property. He blamed 'the natural tendency of counting upon imaginary rentals long before they became real ones, including too, the prevailing course of entertaining, drinking, electioneering, show, equipage and the concomitant attacks upon the purse'.[72]

Ten years before, John Knox had pointed out how, although rents had 'mostly trebled' since 1750, the gentry were not wealthier than their forefathers:[73]

On the contrary, the increase of income, though incredibly rapid, hath not amongst the generality of families, corresponded with their taste for the elegancies and luxuries of a more opulent people: insomuch that estates are constantly upon sale, the old families gradually disappear and the landed property falls into new hands, especially in the neighbourhood of Glasgow.

The historic penetration of merchant families into the counties around Glasgow also tended to forestall any stagnation in the land market. The extraordinary vulnerability of merchants involved in foreign trade—always more at the mercy of the fortuitous hazard than those engaged in the domestic section—meant a disproportionately high bankruptcy rate among them. This meant a continual flow of land to the market. This tendency was accelerated by the habit of raising credit on land. James Buchanan mortgaged Drumpellier in its entirety before the crash of Buchanan, Hastie & Company.[74] Robert Dunmore and William McDowall both gained further time and credit by mortgaging their estates.[75] Examples could be multiplied of this happening[76] and several merchants gained land as a result of the misfortune of their fellows. The bankruptcy of Alexander Houston & Company left Andrew Houston's son Hugh with his father's debts: the family estate of Jordanhill was thus offered for sale and bought by Archibald Smith, successful West India merchant and partner in Stirling, Gordon & Company and Leitch & Smith.[77] Moses Steven, leading partner in Buchanan, Steven & Company gained also from the collapse of Houstons; he obtained Polmadie, one of Robert Houston Rae's estates.[78] James Hopkirk of Dalbeth further added to his property on the bankruptcy of Archibald Smellie by obtaining parts of Easter Dalbeth in 1783.[79] Thomas Buchanan of Ardoch purchased areas in Dalmarnock on the sequestration of John Gray's estate.[80]

The availability of suitable land for mercantile purchase does not appear to have presented many problems. It is now proposed to consider the situation from the demand side and examine the motives for land acquisition by the merchants concerned.

There was a whole amalgam of interrelated factors encouraging a merchant to acquire land, and any attempt to erect these into a hierarchical order of importance is doomed to failure. It is intended, however, for the sake of analysis to simplify the motivations involved by attempting to isolate each of them for separate consideration.

As has often been said, Scotland, at least until well into the nineteenth century, was dominated by landowners.[81] The prospect of joining this select band, their estates the symbol of their social prestige and power, must have had considerable attractions for the ambitious colonial merchant. In their position as heritors, from the Patronage Act of 1712, landowners chose the parish minister. Political power, both at national and local levels, was very much their prerogative and as Commissioners of Supply, Lords Lieutenant and Justices of the Peace their authority extended everywhere. Even the twelve members of Parliament who represented the Glasgow Burghs, the very centre of Scottish commercial life, were, with two exceptions, landed gentlemen. [82] John Millar noted how 'Property was the great source of distinction among individuals' and the most respected and tangible type of property was land. [83] William Marshall, writing in 1804, put the landowners' power in a nutshell: 'Landed property is the basis on which every other species of material property rests; on it alone mankind can be said to live, to move and to have its being.'[84]

The immense social prestige that could be attained by the simple expedient of investing one's profits in the purchase of an estate proved irresistible for most merchants, particularly as the financial drawbacks to landownership were less obvious in Scotland than in England. Charity rather than regulated subscription controlled the maintenance of the poor and the incidence of the tithe was lower in Scotland than south of the Cheviots as was the ubiquitous land tax, a reflection probably of the generally accepted differences in standards of living between the two countries. [85]

There is much evidence that merchants took to the landowner's way of life with gusto. Thus William Cunninghame showed an almost aristocratic solicitude for the retention of the family name in the subsequent ownership of his estates, his testament specifying that[86]

> All heirs whomsoever succeeding to the said lands and estates shall be obliged to use, bear and constantly retain at all times after their succession the surname of Cunninghame and the title and designation of Cunninghame of Duchrae as their proper title and designating their arms from the Lord Lyon's office bearing the proper mark as evidence of the family of Lainshaw.

He went even further, insisting that in the case of a female succession, the young lady would be required to marry a gentleman of the surname of Cunninghame—or at least a husband who would assume the name of Cunninghame immediately after the succession took place.[87] Once ensconced among the landed élite every effort would be made to retain the prestige which the family name had acquired.

The merchant-landowner would attempt to obtain a coat of arms to accompany his arrival to landed power. Archibald Smith of Jordanhill's arms consisted of 'Gules, a Chevron Ermine, between two crescents, in chief and a Garb in base, within a Bordure Engrailed, Or; crest on Eagle's Head erased proper, gorged with a Ducal Coronet'.[88] Andrew Thomson of Faskine in Lanarkshire obtained a coat of arms in 1760, the figuration being an interesting combination of pride in commercial success and an accompanying desire for the conventions of the landowning classes. The crest encompassed a hand holding a bunch of lint flowers in bloom, with the motto 'Industriae Munus'.[89]

Successful merchants wished to attain the marks of landed respectability but there is little sign of a simple antithesis between the superiority of the landed estate and the inferiority of the counting-house. One gets an impression of a justifiable pride in mercantile achievement which is hinted at in the legend included in Thomson's coat of arms. It will be pointed out below how entry into county society was valued by the merchant group but equally how there was a co-existing and vital urban culture. The Literary Society of Glasgow, the Anderston Club, the Buchanan Society, the Sacred Music Society and the Humane Society were all manifestations of this and were well supported by the colonial merchant community.[90] In 'Hints to those who are destined for a mercantile life', a sort of primer for budding merchants, the anonymous commentator spoke glowingly of 'that honourable character, a British merchant, who has acquired opulence with mistaken integrity and who is able to enjoy and adorn it with a noble liberality'. He went on to contrast the drawbacks of the life of 'a fine gentleman and . . . a man of pleasure', who is 'always adorning his person and frequenting theatres, assemblies and public gardens . . .', with the solid virtues of the hard working man of business.[91] Likewise the contemporary Glasgow statistician, James Cleland, became fulsomely lyrical over the achievements of commerce:[92]

These are thy blessings, Industry! rough power!
Nurse of Art, by thee, the City rear'd in beauteous
pride her tower encircled head; and commerce brought
into the public walk; the busy market, the big
warehouse built; rais'd the strong crane;
choak'd up the loaded street.
With foreign plenty
All is the gift of industry.

Commerce, and especially colonial trade had a prestige and a validity of its own yet the merchant élite were also keen to embrace the conventional pursuits of the gentry. There is little to be wondered at here because several of them were the scions of landowning families. They showed considerable interest in that growing obsession of the late eighteenth and early nineteenth centuries, the preservation of game for sport. Members of the Rutherglen Association to preserve the game and fences on their estates included in the early 1790s, Robert Houston Rae, William McDowall III and James Somervell along with such illustrious 'county' figures as the Duke of Hamilton, Sir John Stuart of Castlemilk and Sir William Maxwell of Calderwood.[93] James Dunlop, Andrew Buchanan, Robert Bogle and John Buchanan of Ardoch were all members of a 'Game Association' established for the same purposes of preservation.[94] A contemporary print of 'a Meet of the Lanarkshire and Renfrewshire Foxhounds at Crookston Castle, Renfrewshire' shows a whole array of mercantile gentry: James Oswald, William Cunninghame, Robert Dunmore, Charles Stirling, Alexander Dennistoun and Archibald Bogle.[95] Again the legal and administrative posts which formed the cornerstone of the landowner's authority were infiltrated by merchants. Among those Lanarkshire JPs who subscribed on oath of loyalty to the King in 1793, were Andrew Buchanan, William McDowall III, James Hopkirk of Dalbeth, John Campbell of Clathick, James Dunlop of Garnkirk and Lawrence Dinwiddie of Germiston.[96] Six years earlier Robert Bogle, James Ritchie, James Corbett, John Wallace, Andrew Houston, John Alston and Robert Dinwiddie were also designated JPs in the same county.[97] The creation of Deputy Lieutenancies in the 1790s, found colonial merchants among those selected: John McCall of Braehead and Robert Bogle of Daldowie were Deputy Lieutenants for Lanarkshire;[98] William McDowall III was appointed Lord Lieutenant of Renfrewshire in 1793;[99] James Dennistoun of Colgrain, John Buchanan of Ardoch and Archibald Buchanan of Auchintorlie were Deputy Lieutenants of Dunbartonshire during the Napoleonic War period.[100] Likewise, George Oswald, James Dennistoun, Archibald Smith, Robert Findlay, John Gordon, Cunninghame Corbett and John Alston had been created land and income commissioners for the counties around Glasgow by the wartime government—probably as much for their accounting experience as for their 'respectability'.[101]

There is, however, an obvious danger in overemphasising the degree of mercantile penetration into positions of social and political power. Close examination of the names cited above immediately dispels any notion of wholesale 'bourgeois' conquest of the landed interest's traditional preserves. The merchants quoted represented the very highest echelons of the Glasgow colonial merchant community. Few could equal the income of a McDowall, who owned lands to the value of £287,000 in three counties, or a James Dunlop, whose estates were sold for £88,000, an Oswald or a Ritchie.[102] Almost by definition they were atypical of their fellow merchants. A second point is that the great majority of those who attained office through possession of a landed estate were themselves related to the gentry around Glasgow or were the sons or grandsons of men who had obtained estates long before the period under consideration: that is, they were as much members of the landowning classes as were the traditional landholders. James Dunlop of Garnkirk could trace his ancestors back to the Dunlops of that Ilk in Ayrshire;[103] Archibald Smith was the younger son of a Stirlingshire laird, James Smith of Craigend;[104] John Wallace and Robert Dunmore were the sons of merchant lairds.[105] James Dennistoun was the direct descendant of one of the first Norman knights to settle in Scotland and whose family's 'proud boast',[106] according to a nineteenth-century Dumbartonshire historian was 'not that they had come of kings, but that kings had come of them . . .'. Archibald Buchanan's family had held land for generations[107] and he himself had inherited Auchintorlie from his uncle George.[108] The McDowalls were of ancient lineage in Wigtonshire.[109] Cunninghame Corbett was from a family of lesser lairds in the neighbourhood of Glasgow and had fallen heir to Tollcross on the death of his father.[110] In fact, of the merchants who had been appointed to the type of office discussed, only John McCall and Robert Findlay could be classified as first generation newcomers to landed wealth.[111]

The conclusion would indirectly substantiate Professor Campbell's point that merchants could purchase their way[112]

> into a social position with . . . speed and completeness . . . because assimilation was easy in the eighteenth century, when many of the successful lawyers, merchants and bankers were themselves scions of ancient landed families and so were returning to their heritage.

Yet the premise on which his view is based must be modified to some extent. Only a section of the Glasgow colonial merchants under discussion were 'scions of ancient landed families'. An analysis of the biographical background of those merchants owning land revealed that forty out of the total of seventy-eight were obviously not born of landed families. Even then an exaggerated impression is obtained of the degree of flow of younger sons of the gentry into land via trade, since, of the remaining thirty-eight merchants who were classified as born of landed families, no less than eighteen came from the four great merchant dynasties of Bogle, Dunlop, Campbell and Houston. The conclusion is therefore irresistible that colonial commerce was drawing more and more of its recruits, as the eighteenth century neared its end, from within itself, from domestic trade and from offspring of the professional families. Equally clearly the composition of landed society in the Glasgow area was constantly being refreshed with new blood.

The powerful force exerted by the factor of prestige in mercantile landbuying cannot be overestimated, but it is submitted that an explanation, solely in these terms, of the movement of merchants into land would be wholly inadequate. 'Rational' economic calculation also played a crucial role.

Colonial merchants commonly invested in mineral-bearing land. The twin factors of rising demand for coal in the town of Glasgow and the evolution of new transport developments such as the Monkland and Forth and Clyde canals, turnpikes and waggonways prompted a desire to invest in coal-producing

areas.[113] Advertisements for the sale of estates later acquired by
colonial merchants emphasised opportunities for coal exploitation. When Jordanhill was put up for sale in 1799, the Houston
family's lawyers pointed out that of the £500 rental per annum,
£80 was made up of coal royalties paid by William Dixon of the
Govan Coal Company.[114] On James McDowall's estate of Hag-
tonhill there were three seams of coal, 'Smiddie, Main and Soft',
and several posts of limestone.[115] The co-existence of these two
minerals could immensely enhance the productivity of an estate
even if neither was to be exploited for sale to the market. There
was an obvious connection between the rising coal prices of the
late 1780s and Robert Dunmore's land purchases in Stirlingshire.
He bought small areas in the parishes of Kilsyth, Baldernock and
Campsie and, as an advertisement noted in 1795, his mines were
'most advantageously placed for an extensive sale' of both coal
and lime.[116] James McCall had purchased Belvidere in 1798.
When advertised, it was pointed out that the estate was a mere
two miles from Glasgow and that 'the lands abound with coal,
which, from the vicinity of Glasgow, may become extremely
valuable'.[117] Lainshaw, William Cunninghame's large estate in
Ayrshire had 'plenty of coal and limestone in every part of it', and
both Thomas Hopkirk and Archibald Smellie had extensive
seams of coal on their lands.[118] James Dunlop's post-1783 property purchases all had three elements in common—proximity to
Glasgow, cheap transport there, and the availability of extensive
mineral resources (both of coal and iron ore) on the lands to be
acquired. Dunlop saw an estate's value not simply in its social
cachet but as an integral part of his commercial and industrial
interests. He had an existing background of colliery ownership—
his father Colin, together with another famous colonial merchant,
Alexander Houston, had worked the Gorbals–Govan coal
measures since 1768.[119] By 1772–3 when James joined the
partnership the 'principal objects' of the concern were the Govan
and Knightswood Coalworks.[120] In addition, Dunlop had been an
important figure in the Glasgow coal combination of 1776 and in
the more notorious attempt to create a coal monopoly with the
foundation of the Glasgow Coal Co in 1790.[121] Again, he had an
extensive interest in the Dunbarton Glasswork Co—in 1789
holding £10,400 (26/40) of the capital—which had a voracious

P

appetite for coal, and he had founded the Clyde Iron Works in 1786.[122]

Dunlop, by his leadership in the two Glasgow coal combines, was already trying to halt the infiltration of newcomers into the monopoly profits of the Glasgow coalmasters. The more positive side of his policy was to move into those virgin areas which, if exploited, threatened the Glasgow market with oversupply. Thus as the Monkland Canal neared completion, Dunlop began to buy up as much land as he could in the parishes of Old and New Monkland which were 'reckoned to be full of coal', culminating in the purchase of the immensely rich coal-bearing estate of Barrowfield from John Orr, one of the giants of the west of Scotland coal trade in the late eighteenth century.[123]

As Dunlop's banker and confidant, Sir William Forbes was in an excellent position to judge his client's motives for land purchases:[124]

> He had embarked deeply in two branches [of trade], which, had peace continued and money been plenty, must have made his fortune; having largely engaged in the working of coal mines, in which he was supposed to be uncommonly skilful, he had reduced these two branches of trade to a system of which he proposed every year to accumulate such a working fund as would enable him soon to pay off the great debt he was obliged to extract for them, and then leave him in possession of a clear, solid landed property.

Dunlop was the outstanding example of a merchant buying up mineral-bearing land but he was by no means unique. In the two decades between the ending of the American War of Independence and the turn of the century, Andrew Buchanan of Ardenconnal, William French, John Campbell of Clathick, George Coats and James Hopkirk were all buying small estates in the mineral-rich parishes of Old and New Monkland and, interestingly enough, purchasing was concentrated in the period after the opening of the Monkland Canal in 1793.[125] All of these were already substantial estate owners and were searching for smaller pieces of land, not for amenity or prestige, but as an economic asset. Archibald Spiers held his main estates in Renfrewshire yet he also purchased smaller, if extremely valuable, areas in Lanarkshire and so in 1804 was able to obtain the promise of lucrative royalties when he gave a subtack to the Shotts Iron Co 'of the coal, ironstone, lime-stone, fire clay and all other metals and minerals' in these lands.[126]

Another major 'economic' reason making for estate purchase was the rising land values and changing land uses (which put land at a higher premium) in the late eighteenth century. In such a period, the buying of an estate and later the selling of it could lead to substantial capital gains. The evidence for dramatic increases in land values in the areas around Glasgow at this time is quite conclusive. In 1791 an anonymous commentator noted how in Lanarkshire the prices of many estates had doubled in the previous decade. In Renfrewshire 'the real rent' was 'nearly double, if not more than it was forty years ago', and in the barony of Glasgow, 'the rents are everywhere rising'.[127] The Bogle estate of Whitehill, unsaleable in 1778 at £3,200 during a period of great credit stringency, was sold in 1809 for £15,000![128] To the age-old influx of 'new' landlords, their desire for estates bidding up the price of land, had been added the stimulus of an incipient Industrial Revolution boosting mineral rentals and mill site-values. Again, the 'improving movement' and its essential base, population growth, had encouraged the raising of rentals. This environment led to a fluidity in the land market as particular estates passed from one merchant to another, with capital gains as the end of the operation. James Mackenzie in 1798 purchased from his fellow West India merchant, John Gordon, a section of his estate of Cullochfould, renamed it Craigpark and built an elaborate mansion on it.[129] Alexander Oswald had obtained Langlands in the parish of Govan in 1782 and two years later sold it to James McCall.[130] Peter Murdoch acquired his estate in Renfrewshire by purchase from Archibald Spiers.[131] Lands adjacent to the main estate, outlying lands or marginal areas of the estate were particularly suitable for such transactions. Such land was simply one of a merchant's many assets to be used judicially for profit maximisation.

Again, anyone with lands in the immediate vicinity of Glasgow was likely to have a highly remunerative investment in the late eighteenth century: from 1783 onwards the town was in the throes of a virtually continuous building boom which resulted in steady movement outwards from the core of the old town, the area around the Gallowgate.[132] When the estate of Ibrox was advertised for sale in 1812, to the customary line of 'a desirable purchase as an estate' was added 'containing good situations for building' and it was pointed out that the area was in an excellent position as 'a speculation for letting out for villas'.[133] A similar advertisement for Whiteinch, Whitehill and Daldowie appeared when they were put up for sale in 1808-9.[134] In this period Alexander Oswald of Shieldhall emerged as a relatively new type of merchant-landowner—a speculator in land, holding particular areas for brief periods until a profitable sale was possible—and Archibald Smith of Jordanhill and George Oswald of Scotstoun, whose estates were strategically placed in relation to Glasgow's expansion were congratulating one another in 1800 as they realised that leasing land to farmers or mineowners was much less remunerative than dividing it up into plots.[135] The amenity value of an estate was ruthlessly subordinated to its function as an economic asset by those merchant-landowners fortunate enough to be in the path of urban expansion.

Possession of a viable area of land would also offer the colonial merchant attractive advantages within his own commercial regimen. Credit accommodation was more likely to be given to those who held the safest assets. It is a commonplace of eighteenth-century economic history that land represented the most solid and most enduring security and therefore traders had a quite powerful motive to acquire this valuable commodity.[136] The Bogles of Daldowie, the family who were among the outstanding pioneers of the Glasgow–Virginia tobacco trade in the late seventeenth century, would almost certainly have had their property sequestrated after the financial crisis of 1772 if credit had not been obtained from George Bogle's friends who were willing to advance loans only if the estates of Daldowie and Whiteinch were offered them in trust as security.[137] Examples could be multiplied of land being utilised in this way. A few must suffice. The partners of Alexander Houston & Co were able to borrow a total of £304,000 on the security of their landed estates in Scotland between 1794 and 1800.[138] As the spectre of financial collapse hovered over Buchanan, Hastie & Co in 1775, James Buchanan raised £2,000 on the security of Drumpellier.[139] James Dunlop snr in 1763 was trying to borrow £10,000 from four other merchants, but no cash was to be transferred until Dunlop's estate of Garnkirk was put up as security.[140]

There was, however, ambiguity in land's role as a desirable asset. Broad acres were safe from depreciation but they were also extremely illiquid as a financial asset. The results of this were not entirely detrimental to the merchant-landowner: debtors would be unwilling to bring a creditor's landed security to sale if they were going to experience difficulty in selling it at a price which would at least recoup them for a proportion of their loan. This may well have been a factor in the persistence with which Alexander Houston & Co survived for nearly ten years although besieged by creditors—the sale of the partners' land (valued in 1800 at over £390,000) would have been self-defeating. It is doubtful if the land market could have absorbed such quantities during wartime when liquidity was at a premium without show-ing a drastic decline in the price of the estates. Creditors thus restrained themselves: they would have been the losers.[141] Yet, using the same example, it is just as clear that Houstons would not have found themselves in such an extreme situation if their funds had been more liquid; funds outdistanced debts by over £223,000 at the time of their bankruptcy.[142] In periods of grow-ing credit restriction when liquid funds were essential to combat the drying up of bank loans, with creditors demanding payment and debtors unwilling or unable to pay and all in the context of a highly volatile and speculative trade, disproportionate investment in land could prove a considerable obstacle to a merchant's successful negotiation of a crisis.

Yet land's image of solid immobility must have attracted many, particularly given the enormous risks (if also huge profits) of colonial trade. As a contemporary lawyer noted, 'A thing felt by every man in trade is the uncertainty of his fortune', and this sentiment was echoed by a colleague in the legal profession: 'Everyone is acquainted with the precarious tenure of a West India property. It is liable to calamities which are unknown in this country; to the hazards of wars and of hurricanes; to the variable value of the produce etc.'[144]

The wealthiest were no more exempt from the threat of financial disaster than was the small trader operating on a shoestring: Robert Dunmore, Peter Murdoch, John Glassford, Andrew and

James Buchanan, George and Robert Bogle, William Bogle, Hugh Wylie, Andrew Houston, Robert Houston Rae, William McDowall III—the great names in Glasgow's colonial trades—all became insolvent.[145] One does get the impression that several of these merchants fell between two stools. There is little evidence to support the view that merchants cut off their interests in trade when they had acquired the coveted estate. Of the seventy-eight colonial merchants examined here it cannot be said with confidence that any of them severed their connection with commerce after buying their estate. The lucrative profits possible in the colonial trades proved too magnetic and ensured that a merchant-landowner would continue to retain his interests in commerce, even if only at the level of a sleeping partnership. In this context the landed estate could at times play a helpful part as a secure asset for credit expansion purposes, but equally at others could, by its illiquidity, ensure bankruptcy for a merchant desperate for cash resources.

One final likely motive for mercantile penetration into land can be considered here. Land's function as a secure asset made it an excellent method of safeguarding the incomes of wives, minors and spinster daughters on the decease of a merchant. Land rentals and the holding of government stock were the eighteenth-century version of pensions, endowments and insurance schemes. An examination of the surviving testaments of several of the merchants under discussion reveals only a very narrow and limited investment in government securities, which, in the pre-railway age was perhaps the only means to a 'rentier' income. Thus William Cunninghame had an income of a little over £400 from government securities and East India Company stock in 1800: a considerable sum, but one which fades a little in comparison with the annual rental from his several landed properties which approached the £3,600 mark.[146] Andrew Houston at his death had owing him £4,442—from the Greenock Banking Company, the Dumbarton Glasswork Co, Alexander Brown & Co—but there is no mention of income from government stock.[147] Thomas Hopkirk, had investments in concerns as diverse as the Gourock Ropework Company and the Glasgow Theatre Co but again there is no reference to government securities.[148] Examples such as these could be multiplied.[149] Return from investment in government stock played no significant part in the overall income of these merchants, something especially surprising given the high government interest rates of the Napoleonic War period.[150]

Other ways of obtaining a safe income for dependants quite obviously had to be utilised. Return on canal shares in the west of Scotland did offer an attractive investment. The Forth and Clyde canal was one of the most profitable of the man-made waterways which were now traversing central Scotland and at the date of his settlement in 1782, Alexander Spiers had twelve shares in the company valued at £1,200.[151] Laurence Dinwiddie had three shares valued at £325.[152] Alexander Spiers, James Buchanan of Drumpellier, John Glassford and James Ritchie of Craigton were early subscribers to the Monkland canal.[153] It is doubtful, however, if returns on such interests were sufficient to meet the needs of clusters of female relatives. In dire extremes, merchants could fall back on the benevolence of friends to ensure care for their widows and family. Hugh Wylie was insolvent at his death in 1780.[154] A petition was presented to the town council in 1780, informing them of the fact that most of Wylie's property was in America 'from which no remittances had been made since his death'. In the circumstances, the council decided that 'an interim supply of money should be given to his widow and children'.[155] Likewise Andrew Buchanan's wife obtained £40 per annum from the town after his bankruptcy.[156] These cases were unique, however. Both Wylie and Buchanan were men who had given long service to the town, Wylie having been elected baillie of Gorbals in 1770, baillie of the merchant rank in 1771, Dean of Guild from 1776 to 1778 and Lord Provost of the city 1780-2,[157] while Buchanan was a member of one of the most influential Glasgow merchant families. In any case, few of the proud and successful colonial merchant community would be willing to leave the livelihood of their closest relatives in the hands of friends or of town charity.

Almost universally life-rent provisions for wives were written into marriage contracts. When Archibald Ingram wed Rebecca Glassford he consented to pay a life-rent annuity of 2,000 marks 'Scots money' and in his settlement it was emphasised that he had to do with his funds as was set out in his marriage contract.[158] David Russel obtained a handsome dowry of £1,000 sterling on his marriage to Elizabeth McCall but he also had to promise to pay her a substantial life rent.[159] John Riddell was similarly bound before his betrothal to Elizabeth Campbell.[160] It is within this environment of few alternative secure investments and the necessity of providing for a family in the event of the death of the breadwinner that much mercantile landbuying must be seen. According to the convention of primogeniture James McCall's estates of Meikle Govan and Deanfield were disposed to Samuel, his eldest son, but only[161]

> under the burden of the payment to Sarah Reid my wife . . . of the sum of fifty pounds sterling money at two terms in the year by equal portions beginning the first term's payment at the first of these terms which shall happen after my death and so forth termly thereafter during her lifetime.

In addition, Samuel McCall had to lay aside £150 from annual rentals to provide three £50 annuities for his unmarried sisters, 'so long as they shall remain unmarried'. Mrs McCall's share was to cease in the event of her re-marrying.[162] John Alston inherited the estate of Westertoun in Dumbartonshire and Blythswood and Provanside in the barony of Glasgow from his grandfather, John Millar. In addition to being burdened with the expenses of Millar's 'sick bed', debts and funeral charges, Alston had to pay a yearly annuity of £125 to Christine Park, Millar's wife, and a smaller sum to his grandfather's spinster daughters from the income of the estate.[163] It was an assumption of the time that wives were unable to cope with the manifold pressures of business life; far better to leave them a steady secure revenue from land rather than a wildly fluctuating income from colonial trade. As the great seventeenth-century English merchant Josiah Child put it,[164]

> If a merchant . . . arrives at any considerable estate, he commonly withdraws his estate from trade before he comes near the confines of old age; reckoning that if God should call him out of the world while the main part of his estate is engaged in trade, he must lose one third of it, through the inexperience and ineptness of his wife to such affairs; and so it usually falls out.

The very wealthiest of the merchant community were able to

ensure the financial security and continued high status of their closest relatives by buying lands for them in addition to acquiring the family estate. James Dunlop of Garnkirk was disposing lands in Old and New Monkland throughout the 1780s to his wife: in the event of any financial disaster she, at least, would have a comfortable income.[165] In 1801, the trustees of Alexander Spiers were buying land in Bothwell for the tobacco merchant's two unmarried daughters.[166] Earlier Spiers had been able to make 'ample provision' for his family by purchasing estates for them throughout central Scotland. Through strict entail arrangements he could secure the movement of his sons into a higher rank of society. On Archibald, he settled the barony of Elderslie and to Peter, his second eldest son, he conveyed the estate of Culcreuch in Stirlingshire. His wife was to inherit Yoker and Blawarthill in Renfrewshire.[167] William Cunninghame stipulated that his main estate of Lainshaw was to fall to his eldest son but Duchrae and other lands in Kircudbrightshire (rental £523 10s 2d per annum in 1800 as compared with Lainshaw's £2,123 3s 3d) were to be subdivided to cater for the needs of subsequent children and grandchildren.[168]

The first base of financial security for the female dependant was, of course, marriage; and life-rents were usually cancelled if a widow re-married.[169] Again, if a husband died without having made due provision for his spouse, a close relative could intervene. In 1800, for example, James Hopkirk of Dalbeth bought land for his sister in the Old Monkland parish of Lanarkshire; her husband had died the year previously.[170] Even when estates owned by merchants were sold, care was often taken to preserve at least a proportion of the widow's income. In 1801 Archibald Smith purchased Jordanhill, an estate owned for almost half a century by the wealthy West India merchants, the Houstons. Smith had paid £16,500 for the lands but retained £3,000 of the purchase price to operate as funds for a life-rent annuity of £150 for Lillias Calder, wife of Alexander Houston and grandmother of the then heir to the estate, Hugh Houston.[171] The trustees of Alexander Campbell of Hallyards in 1817 considered that his widow 'should be secured in her jointure of Kingledoons' one of Campbell's lesser properties, but when his son Mungo attained majority and succeeded to this estate Mrs Campbell was to have 'either security or government stock or land which will yield a free revenue equal to her jointure'.[172] The Bogle family had never quite recovered from the financial crisis of 1772 and in 1809 it was decided to sell Whiteinch and Daldowie, but a transaction would only take place on the condition that Miss Bogle should remain in residence at Daldowie 'during her lifetime and have full possession of the house, furniture and garden on her paying the taxes only'.[173]

No suggestion is being made here that land was the only source of income for widows, spinster daughters and minors. In addition to the other methods mentioned above there is evidence that a lucrative if precarious livelihood could be obtained through widows lending liquid funds to merchant houses—at the failure of Buchanan, Hastie & Co, John Brown of Moore, Carrick & Co, Glasgow bankers, pointed out that the firm owed £50,000, 'mostly bonded money', in Glasgow and that 'much of the money they owe belongs to orphans and widows that cannot well afford it'.[174]

There are several similar examples of such lending throughout the entries of the Register of Deeds and occasionally an odd reference to a widow's full membership of a co-partnership agreement. Thus Neil Buchanan's widow in 1768 held £500 of the capital stock of the Pollockshaws Printfield Co.[175] Yet for the purposes of obtaining a secure long-term income for dependents in the later eighteenth century, Glasgow merchants were still looking to land. Its role in this area was virtually unchallenged before the railway era. For those who could afford to acquire them, estates conferred the benefits of a reliable income and social respectability and did not demand the constant supervision required in commerce.

Several general conclusions can be drawn from the detailed analysis which has been carried out. There was obviously a close correlation between success in trade and movement into land-ownership and the extent of estate buying discovered among the Glasgow colonial merchant community must have important implications for the debate on the place of profits from the colonial trades in Scottish economic change in the late eighteenth century. One is indeed led to doubt the view that Glasgow's commercial prosperity was largely isolated and insulated from the domestic economy of Scotland in this period.[176] Certainly evidence of widespread penetration of mercantile wealth into the agricultural sector of the Lowland economy has been presented in this paper and such infiltration could have important results on agricultural advance and indirectly on industrial development through the building and leasing of cotton mills and the exploitation of mineral resources on the estate. Again in the period 1770–1815 there was no clear-cut sign of a decline in the influx of 'new' landowners into estate ownership in the counties around Glasgow. Merchants were as eager as ever to buy land and there still appeared to be enough of it to satisfy those who had the necessary financial resources to acquire it. Quite clearly few commodities could provide, in quite the same way as an estate could, for the social, aesthetic and financial needs of the eighteenth-century businessman.

NOTES

1 J. A. Symon, *Scottish Farming Past and Present* (1959), 136–55; H. Hamilton, *An Economic History of Scotland in the Eighteenth Century* (Oxford 1963), 70–87; T. C. Smout, *A History of the Scottish People* (1969), 298.

2 [J. R. McCulloch (ed)], Adam Smith, *An Inquiry into the Nature and Causes of the Wealth of Nations* (Edinburgh 1863), Book 3, 181. Probably Smith is a little too extreme: for the first time 'improvement' became not a mildly eccentric and esoteric activity, but almost a nation-wide mania engaging the energies of most landlords. The supposed dichotomy between 'old' and 'new' landowners is to this extent invalid. The 'country gentlemen' were certainly not 'timid undertakers' in Ayrshire. See Col William Fullarton, *General View of the Agriculture of the County of Ayr* (1793), 104; William Aiton, *General View of the Agriculture of the County of Ayr* (Glasgow 1811), 115–18; J. T. Ward, 'Ayrshire Landed Estates in the 19th Century', *Ayrshire Collections*, ns, 8 (1967–9).

3 Sir John Sinclair, *General Report of the Agricultural State and Political Circumstances of Scotland* (Edinburgh 1814), vol 1, 27. For a similar comment from England see Henry Brougham, *An Enquiry into the Colonial Policy of the European Nations* (1803), vol 1, 80.

4   For Glassford see, Andrew Wight, *Present State of Husbandry in Scotland* (Edinburgh 1778–84), vol 3, 309; Houston—P. A. Ramsay, *Views in Renfrewshire with Historical and Descriptive Notices* (Edinburgh 1839), 90; Smith—[G]lasgow [C]ity [A]rchives, Smith of Jordanhill MSS, TD1/38/27, George Oswald to Archibald Smith, 18 Dec 1800; the McDowalls—[S]cottish [R]ecord [O]ffice, GD237/139, Notebook of work done on Castlesemple Estate, 1771–7; the Spiers—Alexander Martin, *General View of the Agriculture of the County of Renfrew* (1794), 8, 13; *The New Statistical Account of Scotland* (Edinburgh 1842), vol 8, 43; Cunninghame—SRO, GD247/140, William Cunninghame to William Dick, 25 May 1786.

5   [M]itchell [L]ibrary, Glasgow, Abstract of Minute Books of West India Association of Glasgow, 1807–15, vol 1, 7–8.

6   The new industrialists—Kirkman Finlay, David Dale, Henry Houldsworth, William Dunn—were no less conscious of an estate's many attractions. Finlay purchased Auchenwellan in Argyllshire in 1819 for £14,050 (James Finlay & Co, Glasgow, Finlay MSS, Journal of Kirkman Finlay, 9 Nov 1831); David Dale bought Rosebank in 1801 (SRO, [P]articular [R]egister of [S]asines 29/294); Houldsworth obtained Coltness in Lanarkshire (W. H. Macleod and H. H. Houldsworth, *The Beginning of the Houldsworths of Coltness* (1937)), and Dunn various areas in Dumbartonshire (Joseph Irving, *The History of Dumbartonshire* [Dumbarton 1857], 483).

7   See Appendix 3 for a list of the merchants included in this group.

8   Anon, *Old Country Houses of the Old Glasgow Gentry* (Glasgow 1884), sect LXII; A. Brown, *History of Glasgow* (1795–7), vol 2, 179.

9   Ibid, John McCure, *A View of the City of Glasgow* (Glasgow 1736), 170, 228, for information on Peadie.

10   GCA, Smith of Jordanhill MSS, TD1/2, Decreet of Sales of land and Estate of Jordanhill in favour of Alexander Houston & Co; SRO, PRS (Renfrew), 22/416.

11   ML, Bogle MSS, Bundle 54, Inventory of writs of Daldowie, 8 April 1825. This corrects the assertion made in *Old Country Houses*, 74, that Robert purchased the estate from one John Muirhead in 1724.

12   SRO, PRS (Lanarkshire), 446/14.

13   ML, Bogle MSS, Bundle 54, Sederunt Book of the Trust Disponees appointed by the Settlements of Robert Bogle of Daldowie, 42.

14   J. O. Mitchell, *Old Glasgow Essays* (Glasgow 1905), 377, n 10; G. Crawford and G. Robertson, *A General Description of the Shire of Renfrew* (Paisley 1818), 358; SRO, GD237/139.

15   SRO, Register of Deeds, 207/2/549 DAL, Disposition, George Buchanan to his eldest son, 8 June 1770.

16   MS Buchanan Family Geneology in Gartsherrie Parish Church. I am indebted to Mr R. D. Corrins for this reference.

17   Ibid, G. Stewart, *Curiosities of Citizenship in Old Glasgow* (Glasgow 1884), 20.

18   SRO, [G]eneral [R]egister of [S]asines, 639/184; *Old Country Houses*, 189–90.

19   ML, Bogle MSS, Sederunt Book of Trust Disponees, 27; Bundle 54, Bond of Provision by George Bogle of Daldowie in favour of his younger children, dated 1781, registered, 1784.

20   GCA, Register of Deeds, B.10.5/8435, Settlement, Alexander Spiers esq, 16 Dec 1782.

21   Sir Lewis Namier and John Brooke (eds), *The History of Parliament: the House of Commons, 1754–90* (1964), vol 3, 82.

22   This will be explored in greater detail below. See pp 230–4.

23   James Paterson, *History of the Counties of Ayr and Wigton* (Edinburgh 1866), vol 3, 462.

24   SRO, Reg of Deeds 280/735 DUR; GRS 517/50.

25   *Old Country Houses*, sect LXII.

26   SRO, PRS (Stirlingshire), 29/411.

27   ML, MS Notes on the Family of Dunlop of Garnkirk . . . , 63.

28   See Appendix 2 for a breakdown of these figures.

29   SRO, Currie Dal Sequestration B1/1, Buchanan, Hastie & Co (1777); ML, Bogle MSS, Bundle 54, Trustees of Daldowie to George Bogle, 3 March 1779.

30   Stewart, *Old Glasgow*, 202.

31   SRO, GRS 508/176.

32   GCA, Smith of Jordanhill MSS, TD1/15, Inventory of Title Deeds belonging to Mr Smith's heirs, SRO, Reg of Deeds, 251/1/615 DUR, Disposition, Colin Rae to Robert Houston; PRS 31/11 (Renfrewshire).

33   Anon, *Memorial Catalogue of the Old Glasgow Exhibition* (Glasgow 1894), 46.

34   This had been happening since the early seventeenth century. See T. C. Smout, 'The Glasgow merchant community in the seventeenth century', *Scottish Historical Review*, 47 (1968), 53–71. For the emergence of mercantile land buying even earlier in east coast Scottish burghs see S. G. E. Lythe, *The Economy of Scotland in its European Setting, 1550–1625* (Edinburgh 1960), 124–5; and for the middle decades of the seventeenth century, David Mathew, *Scotland under Charles I* (London 1955), 125–6.

35   SRO, PRS (Stirlingshire), 29/78.

36   SRO, GRS 489/125.

37   Ibid.

38   SRO, PRS (Barony of Glasgow), 24/411.

39   SRO, GRS 524/270.

40   See Appendix 2.

41   See generally, Stewart, *Old Glasgow*, passim.

42   *Memorial Catalogue, Old Glasgow Exhibition*, 98; Irving, *Dumbartonshire*, 451.

43   GCA, Reg of Deeds, B.10.5/8435, Settlement, Alexander Speirs esq, 10 Dec 1782.

44   *Glasgow Mercury*, 10 Jan 1790.

45   No better example of an education fitting a merchant's son to be a landowner and 'county' figure can be found than in National Library of Scotland, Spiers Papers, ACC3296, Educational expenses of Peter Spiers.

46   R. H. Campbell, *Scotland since 1707* (Oxford 1964).

47   See G. E. Mingay, *English Landed Society in the Eighteenth Century* (London & Toronto 1963), 27–8, 39; 'the inflow of new families into the ranks of landowners was much lower before the 1730s and the end of the eighteenth century than in the previous 200 years'. See also H. J. Habakkuk, 'The English Land Market in the Eighteenth Century' in J. S. Bromley and E. H. Kossmann (eds), *Britain and the Netherlands* (1960), 155–65.

48   See Appendix 2.

49   Baillie's Library Glasgow, 'A.H. and Co, Law Papers', Advertisement of Lands; Paterson, *Counties of Ayr and Wigton*, vol 3, 462; ML, Campbell of Hallyards MSS, Codicil to Settlement by Alex Campbell, 12 April 1817; Stewart, *Old Glasgow*, 184; *Old Country Houses*, 213–14; *Old Glasgow Exhibition Catalogue*, 117.

50   See H. Hamilton, 'The Failure of the Ayr Bank, 1772', *Econ Hist Rev*, 2S, 8 (1955–6); David Murray, *The York Buildings Company* (Glasgow 1883). The Company's lands were still being advertised in 1781, *Edinburgh Evening Courant*, 29 April 1781.

51   ML, Bogle MSS, Bundle 54, Trustees of Daldowie to George Bogle, 3 March 1779.

52   Hamilton 'The Failure of the Ayr Bank', 415; R. S. Rait, *History of the Union Bank of Scotland* (Edinburgh 1930), 105; A. W. Kerr, *History of Banking in Scotland* (Glasgow 1926), 93.

53   Mingay, *English Landed Society*, 38.

54   20 Geo III, c 16 (1780); David Macpherson, *Annals of Commerce, Manufactures, Fisheries and Navigation* (1805), vol 3, 685; *Edinburgh Evening Courant*, 21 Jan 1782.

55   ML, Bogle MSS, Bundle 54, Trustees of Daldowie to George Bogle, 3 March 1779. For credit restrictions see NLS, Alexander Houston & Co, Letter Book 'E', passim.

56   Stewart, *Old Glasgow*, 24, 190; [S]ignet [L]ibrary, Edinburgh, Court of Session Processes, 162/3, Information for the Misses Cunninghame against James Dougal . . .; SRO, GD247/141, accompt showing price of estate of Lainshaw.

57   SRO, GD247/140, Petition of H. R. Cunninghame and others . . ., 3 Dec 1784, 1.

58 Ibid, 3.

59 Ibid, Answers of W. Cunninghame to Petition of H. R. Cunninghame and others, 4 Jan 1785, 7.

60 See, for example, the case of Robert Dunmore and Ballindalloch, SRO, PRS (Stirlingshire), 29/411.

61 SRO, GD247/140, Answers for W. Cunninghame to the Petition of H. R. Cunninghame, 4 Jan 1785, 5.

62 Crawford and Robertson, *Shire of Renfrew*, 299; *NSA*, vol 7, 328; *Old Country Houses*, sect XL; GCA, Reg of Deeds, B.10.5/8435, Settlement Alex Spiers esq, 16 Dec 1782.

63 *Edinburgh Evening Courant*, 27 Dec 1775.

64 They owned Scotstoun and Balshagray; Crawford and Robertson, *Shire of Renfrew*, 341.

65 SRO, PRS (Dumbartonshire), 12/208; *NSA*, vol 8, 45.

66 Stewart, *Old Glasgow*, 198.

67 SRO, PRS (Lanarkshire), 21/216; GCA, Reg of Deeds, B.10.5/8293, Disposition, Trustees of Will Bogle. In addition to Lainshaw, Cunninghame also purchased the smaller estates of Duchrae, in the Stewartry of Kirkcudbright, and Kelluchs in Peebleshire during the war: see SRO, GD247/139, Memorial and queries for Lainshaw Trustees, 5.

68 See Appendix 2 for a full breakdown of details on these.

69 Total debts amounted to £554, 378 11s 7d; total funds to £978,115 3s 11d. Of this £503,834 18s 10d was in land. See PP, 55 (1800), Report of Select Committee on Mr McDowall's Petition, 428; S. G. Checkland, 'Two Scottish West India Liquidations after 1793', *Scottish Journal of Pol Economy*, 4 (1957).

70 Smout, *Scottish People*, 285–91. See also, H. G. Graham, *The Social Life of Scotland in the Eighteenth Century* (5th edn, 1969).

71 Fullarton, *Agriculture of County of Ayr*, 104.

72 Ibid, 137.

73 J. Knox, *A View of the British Empire more especially Scotland* (1785), vol 1, 97.

74 SRO, Reg of Deeds, 218/783 DAL.

75 SRO, Reg of Deeds, 280/735 DUR; GRS 604/69, 384/149.

76 See also, SRO, Reg of Deeds, 290/1/618 MACK: 212/13 DAL.

77 SRO, PRS (Renfrew), 40/15; GCA, Smith of Jordanhill MSS, TD1/15, Inventory of title deeds belonging to Mr Smith's heirs.

78 SRO, PRS (Renfrew), 61/24; Baillie's Inst, Library, 'A.H. and Co Law Papers', Advertisement for sale of lands . . ., 4.

79 GCA, Reg of Deeds, B.10.5/8341.

80 SRO, PRS (Barony of Glasgow), 24/411.

81 For a brief summary of this see, T. C. Smout, 'Scottish Landowners and Economic Growth, 1650–1850', *Scottish Journal of Pol Economy*, 11 (1964).

82 James Muir, *Glasgow Streets and Places* (Glasgow & Edinburgh

1899), 65, List of Members of Parliament for Glasgow Burghs.
83 Quoted in H. Perkin, *The Origins of Modern English Society, 1780–1880* (1969), 38.
84 Ibid, 41–2.
85 L. J. Saunders, *Scottish Democracy, 1815–40; the Social and Intellectual Background* (Edinburgh 1950), 198–9, 21–2. Although poor rate assessment was beginning to break through by 1800, only 92 parishes out of 878 had accepted it by that date. T. Ferguson, *The Dawn of Scottish Social Welfare* (1948), 5–6, 187.
86 SRO, GD247/139, Scroll of the Tailzie for the estate of Duchrae and others, 9.
87 Ibid.
88 Crawford and Robertson, *Shire of Renfrew*, 348.
89 C. G. Thomson, 'An Old Glasgow Family of Thomson', Paper read before members of the Old Glasgow Club, 19 Jan 1903.
90 R. Duncan, *Notices and Documents illustrative of the Literary History of Glasgow during the greater part of last Century* (Glasgow 1880), 132; *The Glasgow Almanack for 1792*, 175–7; *The Glasgow Almanack for 1798*, 234.
91 *Glasgow Courier*, 15 Sept 1791.
92 James Cleland, *The Annals of Glasgow* (Glasgow 1817), 344.
93 *Glasgow Mercury*, 14 Sept 1790.
94 *Glasgow Courier*, 1 Sept 1792.
95 *Old Glasgow Exhibition Catalogue*, 152.
96 *Glasgow Journal*, 22 Jan 1793.
97 *Reprint of James's Directory of Useful Pocket Companion for the 1787 with an introduction and notes of Old Glasgow Celebrities by 'the Rambling Reporter'* (Glasgow 1868).
98 H. B. McCall, *Memoirs of My Ancestors* (Birmingham 1884); ML, Bogle MSS, Bundle 66, Instructions by his Grace the Duke of Hamilton.
99 Crawford and Robertson, *Shire of Renfrew*, 358.
100 SRO, Buchanan of Auchintorlie Papers, GD1/512/33, Minutes of the General Meeting of the Lord Lieutenant and his Deputies for the County of Dumbarton, 27 July 1802.
101 *Glasgow Courier*, 17 Nov, 8 Dec 1798, 8 & 10 Aug 1799.
102 PP, 55 (1800), Report on Mr McDowall's Petition, 428.
103 ML, MS Notes on the Family of Dunlop of Garnkirk, 68.
104 Ibid, 3–4.
105 *Old Glasgow Exhibition Catalogue*, 75.
106 Anon, *View of the Merchants' House of Glasgow* (Glasgow 1866), 531; Brown, *History of Glasgow*, bk 2, 179.
107 *History of Dumbartonshire*, 494.
108 SRO, GD1/512/21, Life-rent disposition of the estate of Auchintorlie and others by George Buchanan.
109 Mitchell, *Old Glasgow Essays*, 377, n 10.

110 Stewart, *Old Glasgow*, 191.
111 For a full breakdown of those concerned see Appendix 2.
112 Campbell, *Scotland since 1707*, 5.
113 B. F. Duckham, *A History of the Scottish Coal Industry*, vol 1 (Newton Abbot 1970), 217–18.
114 *Glasgow Courier*, 12 Nov 1799; GCA, Smith of Jordanhill MSS, TD1/38/27, George Oswald to Arch Smith, 23 Dec 1800.
115 *Glasgow Mercury*, 30 Oct 1792.
116 *OSA*, vol 18, 239, vol 15, 331; *Glasgow Mercury*, 19 Jan 1796.
117 *Glasgow Courier*, 28 Nov 1797.
118 *Edinburgh Evening Courant*, 9 Aug 1775; *Old Country Houses*, sect XXXII & XXXVII.
119 SRO, Reg of Deeds, 259/869 DUR, Bond of Copartnery betwixt Dunlop and Houston.
120 SRO, Bill Chamber Process, I, 29,063, Bill of Advocation for Colin Dunlop & Sons, 1.
121 Duckham, *Scottish Coal Industry*, 235–8; H. Hamilton, 'Combination in the West of Scotland Coal Trade, 1790–1817', *Economic History*, 2, no 5 (1930); SL, CSP 225/24, Extract registered contract and agreement between James Dunlop and others . . ., 4 Aug 1790.
122 SRO, Unextracted Process, 1 Currie Mack, D/5/14, Memorial for the partners of the Dumbarton Glasswork Co . . ., 1; *Regality Club of Glasgow*, 2S (1893), 148.
123 *Glasgow Mercury*, 20 May 1794; SRO, PRS (Barony of Glasgow), 29/387; 31/117; 29/92; 28/80; GRS 484/157.
124 Sir W. Forbes of Pitsligo, *Memoirs of a Banking House* (London & Edinburgh 1860), 77.
125 For Buchanan, see SRO, PRS (Lanarkshire), 25/128; French—SRO, GRS 415/35; Campbell—PRS (Lanarks), 25/164–6; Coates—PRS (Lanarks), 27/87; Hopkirk—PRS (Lanarks), 29/189.
126 SRO, PRS (Lanarks), 32/171.
127 *Scots Magazine*, 53 (1791), 562–3; *OSA*, vol 1, 324; vol 15, 498; vol 7, 379; vol 13, 117; John Naismith, *General View of the Agriculture of the County of Clydesdale* (Glasgow 1798), 80.
128 ML, Bogle MSS, Bundles 54, 59, Missive Letter upon the sale of Whiteinch, 12 Oct 1809.
129 *View of Merchants' House of Glasgow*, 535.
130 SRO, GRS 412/223.
131 SRO, PRS (Refrewshire), 33/232. See also a similar transfer of outlying lands between James Dunlop and John Mackenzie, SRO, PRS (Glasgow), 22/412.
132 For this, see Hamilton, *Economic History of Scotland*, 20–1; J. R. Kellet, 'Property Speculators and the Building of Glasgow, 1783–1830', *Scott Journ of Pol Econ*, 8 (1961); *Scots Magazine*, 56 (1799), 856.

133   *Glasgow Courier*, 17 March 1812.
134   *Glasgow Herald*, 10 June 1808; 14 & 28 Aug 1809.
135   R. Reid, *Old Glasgow and its Environs* (Glasgow 1864), 28; GCA, Smith of Jordanhill MSS, TD1/38/27, George Oswald to Archibald Smith, 23 Dec 1800.
136   B. F. Duckham (*Scottish Coal Industry*, 194) has pointed out how landed coalmasters 'stood a better chance of cash-credits than many tradesmen'.
137   ML, Bogle MSS, Bundle 54, Memorandum for Mr Bogle of Daldowie, 2.
138   SRO, BCP, I, 58, 514, Answers for William Cunninghame of Craigie . . ., 21–2.
139   SRO, Reg of Deeds, 218/783 DAL, Bond, Buchanan and Naismith to Wm Clavil, 13 Sept 1775.
140   SRO, Reg of Deeds, 234–699 DUR, Heritable Bond, Dunlop to Dunlop.
141   PP, 55 (1800), Report on Mr McDowall's Petition, 428.
142   Ibid.
143   SL, CSP 162/23, Information for Elizabeth and Barbara Cunninghame, 14–15.
144   SL, CSP 413/27, Petition of James Allan and Alex Young, 16.
145   For Dunmore, see SL, CSP 368/21, Answers for Arch Newbigging . . ., 20; Murdoch—G. Thompson, 'The Dalnottar Iron Co', *Scottish Historical Review*, 35 (1956), 19; Glassford's debts as an individual at his death in 1783 amounted to £93,130, his assets only amounting to £40,000. See [James Gourlay], *A Glasgow Miscellany; The Tobacco period in Glasgow* (privately printed, nd), 48; for the Buchanans, see SRO, Currie Dal Seq B1/1, Buchanan, Hastie & Co (1777); the Bogles—ML, Bogle MSS, Bundle 54, Trustees of Daldowie to George Bogle, 3 March 1779; William Bogle—GCA, Reg of Deeds, B.10.5/9250; Hugh Wylie—GCA Council Minute Book, C1/1/37, 420; Andrew Houston, R. H. Rae, William McDowall III—PP, 55 (1800), Report on Mr McDowall's Petition.
146   SRO, GD247/141, Jotting of income, 2 Oct 1800.
147   SRO, Commissariat of Glasgow Testaments, 1801–23, CC9/7/78/181.
148   Ibid, CC9/7/80/514.
149   See ibid, CC9/7/79/344 (George Kippen); CC9/7/650 (John McCall); CC9/7/84/253 (John Riddell).
150   Macpherson, *Annals of Commerce*, vol 4, 407.
151   Lindsay, *Canals of Scotland*, 34–7, 220; GCA, Reg of Deeds, B.10.5/8435, Settlement, Alex Spiers esq, 16 Dec 1782.
152   SRO, Glasgow Testaments, CC9/7/79/623.
153   Lindsay, *Canals of Scotland*, 54.
154   GCA, Reg of Deeds, B.10.5/8440, Settlement, Hugh Wylie, 30 Dec 1782.

155   GCA, Council Minute Book, C1/1/37, Minute of 28 Nov 1782.
156   Ibid, Minute of 24 June 1784.
157   Ibid, CC1/1/36, Minute of 16 Oct 1780; *Glasgow Mercury*, 21 Feb 1782.
158   Baillie's Inst, Library, Sederunt Book of the Trustees of Provost Arch Ingram, 4; GCA, Reg of Deeds, B.10.5/7332, Bond of Provision, Archibald Ingram to Rebecca Glassford, 27 July 1770.
159   GCA, Reg of Deeds, B.10.5/9671, Contract of marriage between David Russel and Elizabeth McCall, 29 April 1803.
160   Ibid, B.10.5/9715, Contract of marriage between John Riddell and Elizabeth Campbell, 27 Dec 1803.
161   GCA, Reg of Deeds, B.10.15/7587, Settlement of James McCall.
162   Ibid.
163   GCA, Reg of Deeds, B.10.5/8814, Disposition and settlement by John Millar of Westertoun in favour of John Alston, 12 May 1788.
164   Quoted in P. Mathias, *The First Industrial Nation* (1969), 54.
165   SRO, GRS 411/64; PRS (Barony of Glasgow), 24/404; GRS 411/64.
166   SRO, GRS 680/238.
167   GCA, Reg of Deeds, B.10.15/8435, Settlement, Alex Spiers esq, 16 Dec 1782; SL, CSP, 180/7, Answers for Arch Spiers of Elderslie to the petition of the Misses Spiers, 2.
168   SRO, GD247/139, Scroll of the Tailzie for the estate of Duchrae and others; GD247/141, Jotting of income, 2 Oct 1800.
169   See, for example, GCA, Reg of Deeds, B.10.15/7587, Settlement of James McCall.
170   SRO, PRS (Lanark), 29/189.
171   SRO, PRS (Renfrew), 46/15; GCA, Smith of Jordanhill MSS, TD1/15, Inventory of the Title Deeds belonging to Mr Smith's heirs.
172   ML, Campbell of Hallyards Papers, Minute of meeting of trustees of Alex Campbell of Hallyards, 27 Aug 1817.
173   ML, Bogle MSS, Sederunt Book of the Trust disponees appointed by the settlements of Robert Bogle esq of Daldowie, 1808,35.
174   Ibid, Box XCI, Old John Brown's Recollections, vol 2, 54. For a list of their creditors see SRO, Currie Dal Seq, B1/1, Buchanan, Hastie & Co (1777).
175   SRO, Buchanan of Auchintorlie Papers, GD1/512/14, Memorial submitted to the trustees appointed by the deceast Mrs Neil Buchanan.
176   See Professor R. H. Campbell's review of Professor Henry Hamilton's book, *An Economic History of Scotland in the Eighteenth Century* (Oxford 1963) in *Scottish Journal of Political Economy*, 11 (1964), 19, where he considers the eighteenth-

century Scottish economy to consist of 'two distinct sectors' and R. H. Campbell, *Scotland since 1707* (Oxford 1964), 46. Cf also M. W. Flinn, *The Origins of the Industrial Revolution* (1966), 57, and W. E. Minchinton (ed), *The Growth of English Overseas Trade in the 17th and 18th Centuries* (1969), 44, n 1.

177 I am much indebted to my colleagues Dr John Butt and Dr J. H. Treble for their helpful comments on an earlier draft of this study.

Appendix 1

PRINCIPAL MANUSCRIPT COLLECTIONS
AND THEIR ABBREVIATIONS

These abbreviations are also used in chapter notes

APL: Armagh Public Library
BLO: Bodleian Library, Oxford
CCRO: Cornwall County Record Office
CRO: Cumberland, Westmorland and Carlisle Record Office
ERRO: East Riding Record Office
HRO: Hertfordshire Record Office
KRO: Kent Record Office
LAO: Lincolnshire Archives Office
LCA: Leeds City Archives
LCL: Leeds City Library
LRO: Lancashire Record Office
MRO: Middlesex Record Office
NRO: Northamptonshire Record Office
NRRO: North Riding Record Office
PRO: Public Record Office
PRONI: Public Record Office of Northern Ireland
SCL: Sheffield City Library
SRO: Scottish Record Office
StRO: Staffordshire Record Office
ULK: University Library, Keele
UNL: University of Nottingham Library
YAS: Yorkshire Archaeological Society Library

LIST OF MANUSCRIPT COLLECTIONS

Abercorn MSS (PRONI and at Baronscourt, Co Tyrone)
Adair MSS (PRONI)
Alnwick Castle MSS (Alnwick Castle, Northumberland)
Arundel Castle MSS (SCL)
Bedford MSS (Bedford Estate Office, Bloomsbury, London)
Blair of Blair Muniments (SRO)

Bogle MSS (Mitchell Library, Glasgow)
Bolton Abbey Estate MSS (Bolton Abbey, Yorkshire)
Bradford MSS (Weston Hall, Shropshire)
Breadalbane Muniments (SRO)
Bretton Hall MSS (Bretton Hall, Yorkshire)
British Museum Additional MSS
Broughton and Cally Muniments (SRO)
Brownlow MSS (PRONI and in the custody of Messrs Watson and
    Neill, Lurgan, Co Armagh)
Buchanan of Auchintorlie Papers (SRO)
Burnett and Reid Papers (SRO)
Campbell of Hallyards MSS (Mitchell Library, Glasgow)
Cary-Elwes MSS (LAO)
Chaloner MSS (NRRO)
Chatsworth MSS (Chatsworth House, Derbyshire)
Clerk of Penicuik Muniments (SRO)
Clifton MSS (LRO)
Court of Session Records (SRO and Signet Library, Edinburgh)
Crewe-Milnes Muniments (SCL)
Cunninghame MSS (SRO)
Curwen MSS (CRO)
Darley MSS (ERRO)
Dartmouth Collection (StRO)
Denison MSS (UNL)
Derby MSS (LRO)
Donegall MSS (PRONI)
Downshire MSS (PRONI)
Draycott Hall MSS (NRRO)
Dudley Papers (Leicester Borough Record Office)
Eastern Counties Railway minutes (British Transport Commission
    Archives)
Ellesmere Brackley MSS (NRO)
Ferrand MSS (YAS and Cartwright Memorial Museum, Bradford)
Finlay MSS (Messrs James Finlay & Co Ltd, Glasgow)
Frickley Hall MSS (Frickley Hall, Yorkshire)
Furness Railway minutes (British Transport Commission Archives)
General Register of Sasines (SRO)
Glasgow Register of Deeds (Glasgow City Archives)
Gosford MSS (PRONI)
Greer MSS (PRONI)
Hamilton Bruce Muniments (SRO)
Hastings MSS (Huntington Library, California)
Hatherton Collection (StRO)
Holkham MSS (Holkham Hall, Norfolk)
Jersey MSS (MRO)
Lambton MSS (Lambton Estate Office, Co Durham)
Lane-Fox MSS (LCL)

Lawson MSS (CRO)
Leconfield MSS (Cockermouth Castle, Cumberland)
Leeds City Archives
Leeds MSS (YAS)
Leven and Melville Muniments (SRO)
Lodge MSS (APL)
London & Birmingham Railway MSS and minutes (British Transport Commission Archives and the Goldsmiths' Library, University of London)
Londonderry Estate MSS (PRONI)
Lowther MSS (CRO)
McDowall MSS (SRO)
Maryport & Carlisle Railway minutes (British Transport Commission Archives)
Massereene MSS (PRONI)
Netherby MSS (Netherby Hall, Cumberland; microfilmed copies in the Johns Hopkins University Library and Cambridge University Library)
Nostell MSS (Nostell Priory, Yorkshire)
Panshanger MSS (HRO)
Particular Register of Sasines (SRO)
Pennington MSS (ERRO)
Radnor MSS (KRO)
Rawlinson MSS (BLO; transcript in PRONI)
Register of Deeds (SRO)
Rudding Park MSS (Rudding Park, Yorkshire)
Seaforth Muniments (SRO)
Sefton MSS (LRO)
Senhouse MSS (CRO)
Smith of Jordanhill MSS (Glasgow City Archives)
Sneyd MSS (ULK)
Spencer-Stanhope Muniments (SCL)
Spiers Papers (NLS)
Tennyson d'Eyncourt MSS (LAO)
Vernon-Wentworth Muniments (SCL)
Waring MSS (PRONI)
Wentworth Woodhouse Muniments (SCL)
West India Association of Glasgow Papers (Mitchell Library Glasgow)
Wharncliffe Muniments (SCL)

Appendix 2

LANDHOLDING BY GLASGOW COLONIAL MERCHANTS, 1770–1815

Merchant	Estates	Purchase or Inheritance	County
GEORGE ALSTON	Muirburn	P	Lanark
JOHN ALSTON (Jnr)	Westertown	I	Dumbarton
	Blythswood, Provanside	I	Barony of Glasgow (henceforth shortened to 'Glasgow')
	Ralston	P	Renfrew
JAMES BLACK	Craigmaddie	P	Stirling
JOHN BLACKBURN	Killearn	P	Stirling
GEORGE BOGLE II	Daldowie and Whiteinch	I	Lanark
ROBERT BOGLE (Snr)	Daldowie and Whiteinch	I	Lanark
ROBERT BOGLE IV	Shettleston	I	Glasgow
JOHN BOWMAN	Ashgrove		Ayr
ANDREW BUCHANAN	Mount Vernon, Boghead, Sandyhills, Chryston, Over Bargeddie, Langlone	I	Glasgow, Lanark

Date of Acquisition *(if known)*	*Sources*
	W. J. Addison (ed), *The Matriculation of the University of Glasgow* (1728–1858) (Glasgow 1913), Matric no 4744
1788 1788	GCA, Reg of Deeds, B/10/15/8814, Disposition and Settlement by John Miller. SRO, PR (Renfrew), 25/37
1785	
1798	G. Stewart, *Curiosities of Glasgow Citizenship* (Glasgow 1881), 176; J. Gourlay (ed), *The Provosts of Glasgow* (Glasgow 1942), 116
	Memorial Catalogue of the Old Glasgow Exhibition (Glasgow 1894), 144
First purchased by family, 1731 and 1720	ML, Bogle MSS, Bundle 54, Inventory of Writs of Daldowie, 8 April 1825, 1–3
1787	ML, Bogle MSS, Bundle 54, Bond of Provision by G. Bogle in favour of his younger children; SRO, PRS (Lanark), 446/14
	Old Country Houses, 76–7
	Stewart, *Curiosities of Glasgow*, 178
Inherited, 1770	SRO, GRS, 639/184; SRO, Currie Dal Seq, B1/1, Buchanan, Hastie and Co (1777); *Old Country Houses*, sec LXXVI; SRO, Reg of Deeds, 207/2 DAL/549, Disposition George Buchanan to his eldest son, 8 June 1770

Merchant	Estates	Purchase or Inheritance	County
ANDREW BUCHANAN	Ardenconnal	P	Dumbarton
	Langridge	P	Lanark
	Lochend, Auchingray	P	Lanark
ROBERT BOGLE	Gilmorehill	P	Glasgow
	Donaldshill	P	Glasgow
JAMES BUCHANAN	Drumpellier, Langloan	P	Lanark
JOHN CROSS BUCHANAN	Moss and Auchintoshan	I	Stirling
THOMAS BUCHANAN	Ardoch, parts of	I	Perthshire
	Dalmarnock	P	Glasgow
ALEXANDER CAMPBELL	Hallyards	P	Peebles
	Kingledoons	P	Peebles
	Cadenmuir	P	Peebles
	Ballenbridge	P	
	Hagtonhill	P	Lanark
COLIN CAMPBELL	Park	P	Renfrew
JOHN CAMPBELL (Snr)	Morriston	P	Lanark
MUNGO NUTTER CAMPBELL	Belvidere	P	Glasgow
	Ballimore	P	Argyll
JOHN COATS CAMPBELL	Clathic, Killermont	I	Perth, Dumbarton
	Ryden and Gartmillan	P	Lanark
ANDREW COCHRANE	Brighouse		Ayr
PATRICK COLQUOHOUN	Woodcroft	P	Glasgow
	Berriedykes	P	Glasgow
CUNNINGHAME CORBETT	Tollcross	I	Glasgow
	Uddingston	I	Lanark

Date of Acquisition (if known)	Sources
1783	SRO, GRS, 405/30
1791	SRO, PRS, 25/242
1793	SRO, PRS, 25/133; PR, 25/164, 166
1802	SRO, PRS (Glasgow), 49/41
1804	SRO, PRS (Glasgow), 50/116
1735	SRO, Reg of Deeds, 231 MACK/516, Agreement and Submission between trustees and creditors of J. Buchanan; SRO, GRS, 389/253; PRS (Lanark), 21/334; *Old Country Houses*, sect LXXVI
	Old Glasgow Exhibition, Notes and Indexes, 167
1784	Stewart, 184; SRO, PRS (Glasgow), 24/411
1816	ML, Campbell of Hallyards MSS, Alexander Campbell's estate, Revenue, August 1817; Instrument of Sasine in favour of the trustees of the late John Anderson esq over Hallyards, 27 June 1834; J. Hill to Andrew Clason, 12 May 1817
	Old Country Houses, 212
1796	SRO, PRS (Lanark), 27/28
	Old Country Houses, 213–14
1796	Matriculation Albums, Matric no 440; Jones's Directory (1789), 88; SRO, GRS, 562/41
	The Cochrane Correspondence regarding the affairs of Glasgow (Glasgow 1886), ix–xi
1782	SRO, PRS (Glasgow), 24/34
1783	SRO, PRS (Glasgow), 24/373
	Stewart, 191 SRO, PRS (Lanark), 22/27

Merchant	Estates	Purchase or Inheritance	County
ARTHUR CONNELL	Enoch Bank	P	Glasgow
GEORGE CRAWFORD	Midglen, parts of	P	Renfrew
	Barony of Houston	P	Renfrew
WILLIAM CUNNINGHAME	Lainshaw	P	Ayr
	Kirkwood	P	
	Bridgehouse	P	
	Duchrae	P	Stewartry of
	Kilbucho	P	Kirkcudbrig
	Temple Riccarton	I	,,
	Clerkland, Canaan	P	,,
JAMES DENNISTOUN	Colgrain	I	Dumbarton
RICHARD DENNISTOUN	Ferrylands of Cardross	P	Dumbarton
	Kelvingrove	P	Glasgow
LAWRENCE DINWIDDIE	Germiston	I	Barony of Glasgow
ROBERT DINWIDDIE	Whistle Berry	P	Lanark
THOMAS DONALD	Geilston		
JAMES DUNLOP	Garnkirk	P	Glasgow
————————	Carmyle (including Sandyhills)	I	Lanark
	Kipps	P	Lanark
	Auchinloch	P	Glasgow
	Gartcosh	P	Glasgow
	Fullarton	P	Glasgow
	Parts of Tollcross Glenhead, Shanks, Blackland, Gunny, Ryding,	P	Glasgow
	Gartmillan	P	Lanark

Date of Acquisition (if known)	Sources
	Ibid, 32; *Scots Magazine*, vol 54, 363
1784	SRO, PRS (Renfrew), 25/43
1785	SRO, PRS (Renfrew), 25/265
1778	SRO, GD, 247/140, Answers for W. Cunninghame to Petition of Henry Drumanerig–Cunninghame and others, 5
	SRO, GD, 247/139, Scroll of the Tailzie for estate of Duchrae and others
1782	SRO, PRS (Ayr), 28/54
1784	SRO, PRS (Ayr), 28/436
	SRO, PRS (Ayr), 30/72; PRS (Ayr), 30/15
1756	SRO, PRS (Dumbarton), 15/70, 1; Joseph Irving, *The History of Dumbartonshire* (Dumbarton 1857), 450
1803	SRO, PRS (Dumbarton), 16/69
	SRO, GD1/512/6, Andrew Buchanan to Arch Buchanan, 10 July 1813
	SRO, PRS, 58/152 (Glasgow); Reg of Deeds 220MACK/601
	Old Country Houses, sect XLIV; Stewart, *Curiosities of Glasgow*, 197–8
	Glasgow Mercury, 15 Aug 1787
1783	ML, MS Notes on Family of Dunlop of Garnkirk, 1–14; SRO, PRS (Glasgow), 24/202
1778	SRO, Reg of Deeds, 223–1 MACK/939, Disposition, Colin Dunlop to James Dunlop, 26 March 1778; *Glasgow Mercury*, 15 July 1794
1790	SRO, GRS, 484/157
1783	SRO, PRS (Glasgow), 24/201; 24/210
1789	SRO, PRS 29/92
1790	SRO, PRS, 29/387
1792	SRO, PRS (Glasgow), 32/264
1790	SRO, PRS, 557/147 (Lanark); *Glasgow Mercury*, 20 May 1794; 25 Oct 1793

Merchant	Estates	Purchase or Inheritance	County
JOHN DUNLOP	Rosebank	P	Lanark
	Parts of Coates	P	Lanark
	Carmylehill	P	Glasgow
ROBERT DUNLOP	Househill	P	Renfrew
ROBERT DUNMORE	Kelvinside	I	Glasgow
	Auchinreoch	P	Stirling
	Barony of Ballindalloch	P	Stirling
	Wester Ballat	P	Stirling
	Wester Mill of Cashlie	P	Stirling
	Drumship	P	Stirling
	Bankier Easter	P	Stirling
	Easter Blairkaith	P	Stirling
THOMAS DUNMORE	Kelvinside	P	Glasgow
JAMES EWING MACLAE	Strathleven	P	Dumbarton
ROBERT FINDLAY	Easterhouse, parts of	P	Glasgow
	Easter Dalbeth	P	Glasgow
WILLIAM FRENCH	Parts of Carmyle and Clydesmill	P	Glasgow
	Baillieston	P	Lanark
	Blackyards	P	Glasgow
ALEXANDER GARDEN	Croy	P	Dumbarton
HENRY GLASSFORD	Estates owned by his father John (see below)	I	Dumbarton
JOHN GLASSFORD	Dougalston	P	Dumbarton
	Netherwood	P	Stirling
	Kilmanar	P	Stirling
	Whitehall (sold 1759)	P	Glasgow

Date of Acquisition (if known)	Sources
1791	SRO, GRS, 489/125
1791	SRO, GRS, 489/121
1782	SRO, PRS (Lanark), 23/235
	SRO, GRS, 508/176
	Andrew Brown, *History of Glasgow* (Glasgow 1795–7), Bk 2, 179
1785	SRO, GRS, 426/206
1787	SRO, PRS (Stirling), 29/411
1789	SRO, PRS (Stirling), 30/361
1789	SRO, PRS (Stirling), 30/361
1792	SRO, PRS (Stirling), 32/78
1792	SRO, GRS, 504/226
1792	SRO, GRS, 517/50
1749	*Old Country Houses*, sect LXII; Brown, *History of Glasgow*, Bk 1, 179
	Old Country Houses, sect XXI; Stewart, *Curiosities of Glasgow*, 204
1784	Stewart, *Curiosities of Glasgow*, 205–6
1784	SRO, PRS (Glasgow), 25/126
	Ibid
1784	SRO, PRS (Glasgow), 25/86
	SRO, PRS (Glasgow), 26/14
1810	*Provosts of Glasgow*, 131
1783–4	SRO, PRS (Dumbarton), 12/208
1767	[J. C. Gourlay], *A Glasgow Miscellany* (privately published), 45
	SRO, PRS (Dumbarton), 12/208
	Glasgow Mercury, 16 Dec 1784; 10 March 1787
	SRO, GRS, 416/1
	Anon, *View of the Merchants' House of Glasgow* (Glasgow 1860), 530

Merchant	Estates	Purchase or Inheritance	County
JOHN GORDON	Aikenhead	P	Lanark
	Whitehill	P	Glasgow
JOHN HAMILTON	Northpark	P	Glasgow
ARCHIBALD HENDERSON	Nether and Over Middleton	P	Renfrew
JAMES HOPKIRK	Dalbeth	I	Glasgow
	Easter Dalbeth	P	Glasgow
THOMAS HOPKIRK	Dalbeth	P	Glasgow
ALEXANDER HOUSTON	Jordanhill	P	Renfrew
ANDREW HOUSTON	Jordanhill	I	Renfrew
JOHN LEITCH	Kilmardinny	P	Dumbarton
JAMES MCCALL	Belvidere	P	
JOHN MCCALL	Braehead	P	Lanark
JAMES MCDOWALL	Hagtonhill	P	Lanarkshire
	Blair, Milltown etc	I	
WILLIAM MCDOWALL III	Castlesemple	I	Renfrew
	Garthland	I	Wigton
	Provan, Gartsheugh	I	Glasgow
	Fergushill	P	Ayr
	Auchingray, Caldercruix	P	Lanark
JAMES MACKENZIE	Craigpark	P	Glasgow
WILLIAM MCNEIL	Murdistown	P	Lanark

Date of Acquisition (if known)	Sources
	Old Glasgow Exhibition, 135 GCA, Reg of Deeds, B/10/5/9232, Submission between James Corbett and Arch Marshall, 8 June 1795
1799	Provosts of Glasgow, 112
	SRO, Reg of Deeds, 213 MACK/74
1781 1783	Old Country Houses, sect XXXII; SRO, PRS (Glasgow), 24/209
1754	Old Country Houses, sect XXXII
1750, 1752	GCA, Smith of Jordanhill MSS, TD1/2. Decree of sale of the Land and Estate of Jordanhill in favour of Alex Houston and Co
1781	SRO, PRS (Renfrew), 22/416
1801	SRO, PRS (Dumbarton), 15/374
	Old Country Houses, sect XXXVII; C. G. Thomson, An Old Glasgow Family of Thomson (Glasgow 1903), 4
	Stewart, Curiosities of Glasgow, 228
1770	Glasgow Mercury, 30 Oct 1792
	SRO, GD, 237/139, Disposition in Security of Wm McDowall, 3 Nov 1798 Baillie's Lib, Glasgow A. H. and Co Law Papers, Advertisement of Lands
1787 1782	SRO, GRS, 596/57; SRO, PR (Glasgow), 27/101 SRO, GRS, 398/75 SRO, GRS, 004/69
1798	Provosts of Glasgow, 114
1801	SRO, PRS (Lanark), 29/388

Merchant	Estates	Purchase or Inheritance	County
NEIL MALCOLM	Poltalloch	P	
JOHN SPENS MUNRO	Garthwat and others; landed property in Scotland = £7,000	P	Lanark
JOHN MURDOCH	Rosebank	P	Lanark
PETER MURDOCH	Pirrotholm 'Lands in town and country' belonging to his uncle, George Murdoch	P I	Renfrew
ALEXANDER OSWALD	Shieldhall	P	Lanark
GEORGE OSWALD	Scotstoun	I	Renfrew
	Langside	P	Renfrew
	Auchencruive	I	Ayr
	Parts of W. McDowall's estates (valued at £33,180)	P	Renfrew, Ayr Lanark
JAMES RITCHIE	Craigton	I	Lanark
	Busbie	I	Lanarkshire
JOHN ROBERTSON	Plantation (Craigiehall)	P	Glasgow
WILLIAM ROBERTSON	Broomielaw	P	Glasgow
DAVID RUSSELL	Woodside	P	Glasgow
	Part of the barony of	P	Stirling
	Torwoodhead, Hamilton Farm	P	Stirling

Date of Acquisition (if known)	Sources
	Old Glasgow Exhibition, Notes and Indexes, 91; *Old Country Houses*, sect XLIII
1792	SRO, GRS, 513/286 SRO, GD, 237/151/5, Abstract of the estates of the private fortunes of some of the partners of Muirkirk Iron Co
	Old Country Houses, sect LXXXII; GRS, 583/187
1776	SRO, PRS (Renfrew), 33/232 SRO, Reg of Deeds, 220 MACK/232, Band of Obligation by Provost Murdoch to Peter Murdoch, 11 July 1776
1783	SRO, GRS, 407/44
1792	Crawford and Robertson, *Shire of Renfrew*, 347; ML, Bogle MSS, Bundle 59, Missive SRO, PRS (Renfrew), 33/85; Letter upon the sale of Whiteinch, 12 Oct 1809 James Kirkwood, 'Auchencruive House', *Ayrshire Collections*, 3 (1950–5)
1803	J. T. Ward, 'Ayrshire Landed Estates, 19th Century', ibid, vol 8 (1967–9), 133. Baillie's Lib, A. H. and Co Law Papers, Sale of Lands, 12
1783	James Robertson, *History of the Counties of Ayr and Wigton* (Edinburgh 1866), vol 3, 462 Ibid
1783	Stewart, *Curiosities of Glasgow*, 145–9
	SRO, GD, 237/151/3, Abstract of the states of the private fortunes of some of the partners of the Companies (Dalnottar, Smithfield, Muirkirk)
1801 1801	SRO, PRS (Glasgow), 51/101 SRO, GRS, 646/187 SRO, PRS (Stirling), 37/90

Merchant	Estates	Purchase or Inheritance	County
ROBERT HOUSTON RAE	Little Govan	I	Renfrew
	Shawfield-Polmadie	I	Renfrew
ARCHIBALD SMELLIE	Easterhill, Easter Dalbeth	P	Glasgow
ARCHIBALD SMITH	Jordanhill	P	Renfrew
JOHN SMITH	Craighead	P	Lanark
JAMES SOMERVELL	Hamilton Farm	P	Lanark
	Parts of Scotstoun	P	Lanark
	Sorn	P	Ayr
ALEXANDER SPIERS	Elderslie	P	Renfrew
	Inch	P	Renfrew
	Neilstonside	P	Renfrew
	Arthurlie	P	Renfrew
	Culcreuch	P	Stirling
	Lands in Lanarkshire	P	Lanark
MOSES STEVEN	Polmadie	P	Renfrew
CHARLES STIRLING	Cadder	I	Lanark
	Gargunnock	P	
	Kenmuir	P	
JOHN STIRLING	Tilliechewan	P	Dumbarton
	Kippenross	P	
	Kippendavie	I	Perthshire
ANDREW THOMSON	Faskine	P	Lanark

Date of Acquisition (if known)	Sources
1791	SRO, PRS (Renfrew), 31/11
1791	SRO, GD 237/134 Memorial for Arch Grahame, 2; Baillie's Lib Glasgow, A. H. and Co Law Papers, Advertisement and Sale of Lands
1750	SRO, PRS (Glasgow), 24/210; 25/126; *Old Country Houses*, sect XXXVII
1801	SRO, PRS (Renfrew), 46/14; GCA, Smith of Jordanhill MSS, TD1/15; Inventory of Title Deeds belonging to Mr Smith's heirs
'early 1800s'	*Old Country Houses*, sect XXVII
1781	SRO, PRS, 21/216; GCA, Reg of Deeds, B/10/5/8293, Disp Trustees of J. Robertson
1787	SRO, PRS, 22/442
1795	Helen J. Steven, *Sorn Parish: Its History and Associations* (Kilmarnock 1808), 34–5
1769	GCA, Reg of Deeds, B/10/5/8435, Settlement Alex Speirs esq, 16 Dec
1760	1782; *Old Country Houses*, sec XL; Mitchell, *Old Glasgow Essays*, 198
1775	
1775	Crawford and Robertson, *Shire of Renfrew*, 299; NSA, vol 7, 328
1776	*Edinburgh Evening Courant*, 27 Dec 1775; GCA, Reg of Deeds, B/10/5/8435 SL, CSP, 180/7, Answers for Arch Speirs of Elderslie and others to the petition of the Misses Spiers, 6 Dec 1799, 2
1805	SRO, PRS (Renfrew), 61/24
1816	*Old Country Houses*, sect XIV *Old Glasgow Exhibition*, 117
1806	*Old Country Houses*, sect LXIII
1792	Joseph Irving, *The History of Dumbartonshire*, 358 *Old Glasgow Exhibition*, 117
1775	Ibid
1763	C. G. Thomson, *Glasgow Family of Thomson*, 5

Merchant	Estates	Purchase or Inheritance	County
JOHN WALLACE	Cessnock	P	Ayrshire
	Kelly	P	Renfrew
	Neilstonside	P	Renfrew
	Whitehill	P	Glasgow
JAMES WARDROP	Springbank	I	Glasgow
HUGH WYLIE	Broomfield	P	Glasgow
	Ballornock	P	Glasgow

Date of Acquisition (*if known*)	*Sources*
	Crawford and Robertson, *Shire of Renfrew*, 429
1759	*View of the Merchants' House*, 531, 533
1783	SRO, GRS, 405/55
	GCA, Reg of Deeds, B/10/5/8440, Settlement, Hugh Wylie, 30 Dec 1782

Appendix 3

GLASGOW COLONIAL MERCHANTS, 1770–1815

George Alston
John Alston jnr
James Black
John Blackburn
George Bogle II (Daldowie)
Robert Bogle (Daldowie)
Robert Bogle (Shettleston)
Robert Bogle jnr (Gilmorehill)
William Bogle
John Bowman
Walter Brock
James Brown
Andrew Buchanan (Mount Vernon)
Andrew Buchanan (Ardenconnal)
James Buchanan
John Cross Buchanan
Thomas Buchanan
William Buchanan
Alexander Campbell
Colin Campbell
John Campbell snr
John Coats Campbell
Mungo Campbell
Mungo Nutter Campbell
William Coats
Andrew Cochrane
Patrick Colquohoun
Arthur Connell
James Connell
Thomas Connell
Cunninghame Corbett
George Crawford

Thomas Crawford
Adam Crooke
John Cross
William Cross
William Cunninghame
James Dennistoun
Richard Dennistoun
Robert Dennistoun
Robert Dewar
Laurence Dinwiddie
Robert Dinwiddie
Robert Donald
Thomas Donald
Archibald Douglas
Thomas R. Douglas
James Dunlop
John Dunlop
Robert Dunlop
Robert Dunmore
Thomas Dunmore
James Eccles
Thomas Eccles
David Elliot
John Ferguson
Robert Findlay
William French
James Fyffe
Alexander Garden
Francis Garden
John Glassford
Alexander Gordon
James Gordon
John Gordon
David Graham

Alexander Grindlay
John Guthrie
Robert Haddow
Robert Hagart
Thomas C. Hagart
A. W. Hamilton
Hugh Hamilton
John Hamilton
William Hamilton
Robert Hastie
Archibald Henderson
James Hopkirk
Thomas Hopkirk
Alexander Houston
Andrew Houston
James Jamieson
George Kippen
James Lamb
David Laird
John Leitch
Jasper Lyon
Aeneas Macbean
Alexander McCall
James McCall
John McCall
Robert McCall
James McDowall
William McDowall III
Alexander McGriger
Colin McLachlan
William McNeil
Robert Mackay
James Mackenzie
James Ewing Maclae
Neil Malcolm
Richard Marshall
Alexander Muirhead
Michael Muirhead

Alexander Munro
John Spens Munro
George Murdoch
James Murdoch jnr
Peter Murdoch
Alexander Oswald
George Oswald
James Oswald
Patrick Playfair
Robert Houston Rae
Henry Riddell
James Ritchie
James Robertson
John Robertson
William Robertson
David Russell
William Shortridge
Archibald Smellie
Archibald Smith
William Snodgrass
James Somervell
Alexander Spiers
Moses Steven
Alexander Stewart
Colin Stewart
Charles Stirling
John Stirling
Andrew Thomson
James Ure
John Ure jnr
James Murdoch Wallace
John Wallace
David Wardrop
James Wardrop
John Wardrop
Alexander Wighton
Hugh Wylie

S

Authors' Index

References are given to the first mention of each publication

General Index

Abercorn, James, 8th Earl of (d 1789), 125, 127, 128, 131; John, 1st Marquess of (1756–1818), 128; James, 1st Duke of (1811–85), 80

Aberdeenshire, 70, 91

Abingdon, Montagu, 6th Earl of (1808–84), 96

Acheson, Sir Archibald: see Gosford, Viscount

Adair, Sir Robert (1659–1745), 122

Ailesbury, Charles, 1st Marquess of (1773–1856), 30, 42

Aldam, William (1813–90), 77

Alexander, Claud (d 1809), 87–8

Allendale, Wentworth, 1st Lord (1829–1907), 29, 84–5, 90–1

Allison, George, 67

Alston family, 217, 223, 232

Alum, 17, 92

Anderson, Alexander, 82

Anglesey, Henry, 1st Marquess of (1768–1854), 78, 193; Henry, 3rd Marquess (1821–80), 174, 181

Anti-Corn Law League, 7–10.

Antrim, 121, 135, 137

Arch, Joseph (1826–1919), 10

Ardrossan, 11, 80

Arkwright, Sir Richard (1732–92), 158

Armagh, 119, 122, 128–30, 132, 135–6, 138

Armytage, Sir George, 5th bt (1819–99); Sir George John, 6th bt (1842–1918), 99

Arthington, Robert, 156

Ashley, Viscount: see Shaftesbury, 7th Earl of

Austen, Jane (1775–1817), 7

Ayrshire, 10–11, 68, 80, 85, 87, 214–16, 218, 223, 225, 235

Bagehot, Walter (1826–77), 53

Bailey, T. H., 71

Baird, James (1802–76), 11, 68, 87, 101–2

Balcarres, Alexander, 6th Earl of (1752–1825), 70; James, 7th Earl (1783–1869), 26, 32, 97

Bald, Alexander (d 1823) 72–4; Robert (1776–1861), 72–3, 83

Baldwin family, 101

Balfour, Charles (1823–72), 79; Charles Barrington (b 1862), 71; James (d 1845), 83; James (1820–56), 79; family, 80, 83

Balfour of Burleigh, Alexander, 6th Lord (1849–1921), 74

Bankes family, 97

Banks and bankers, 8, 10, 11, 90, 230, 234

Barker family, 101

Barrowman, James, 79

Barrow, 26, 45–8, 88, 96

Bathurst, Charles, 89

Beaufort, Henry, 7th Duke of (1792–1853), 78

Beaumont, Wentworth Blackett: see Allendale, 1st Lord; family, 29, 90–1, 99

Bedford, Francis, 7th Duke of (1788–1861), 25, 27–8, 39–42, 52, 92; William, 8th Duke (1809–72), 41–2, 101

Belfast, 47, 124–5, 128, 133, 135–6, 138

Belhaven and Stenton, Robert, 8th Lord (1793–1868), 79; James, 9th Lord (1822–93), 80

Beresford, G. R., 79

Berkeley, Frederick, 5th Earl of (1745–1810), 39

Biram, Benjamin (1804–57), 72; Joshua (c 1765–1835), 72, 84

Birkenhead, 39

Birmingham, 21, 42, 189

Blackett family, 90, 97, 98, 160 (and see Beaumont)

Blackpool, 39, 43

Blair, William Fordyce (1805–88), 87–8

Blake family, 97

Blenkinsop, John (1781–1831), 97–8

Blount, Sir Edward, 8th bt (1795–1881), 76

Blundell, Nicholas (d 1737), 12; family, 32

Blythe, 34, 42